P9-CCV-662

Responsibility for Child Care

The Changing Role
of Family and State
in Child Development

Bernard Greenblatt

Responsibility for Child Care

Jossey-Bass Publishers
San Francisco • Washington • London • 1977

RESPONSIBILITY FOR CHILD CARE
The Changing Role of Family and State in Child Development
by Bernard Greenblatt

Library of Congress Catalogue Card Number LC 76-50699

International Standard Book Number ISBN 0-87589-315-5

Manufactured in the United States of America

JACKET DESIGN BY WILLI BAUM

FIRST EDITION

Code 7714

The Jossey-Bass
Behavioral Science Series

To
Hans H. Gerth and Joseph Bensman
whose ideas and work made this book possible

Preface

Responsibility for Child Care attempts to explain a shift that has occurred in national policy. Before the 1960s, federal policy bearing on the family was generally based on the ideal of full-time maternal rearing of very young children in the home. Then, from 1962 to 1965, three laws were enacted that provided federal support for day care and nursery schools. These laws represented a departure in public policy from the familial ideal toward social parenthood, that is, participation by institutions other than the immediate family as parent surrogates in early child care.

The laws clearly departed from statutory precedent. The shift in policy also indicated an alteration in the relationships among several types of authority: parents, government, and other surrogate agencies, including the church. Moreover, public funds for day care (which traditionally was considered appropriate only for children of poor or working mothers), and for nursery schools (which convention defined as catering to middle-class children), connected national policy to the structure of social classes. Furthermore, the new laws embraced other social structures: The programs were enacted by the executive and legislative branches, administered by federal, state, and local agencies, and conducted by professionals of various disciplines.

From this conception of social policy—as the outcome of social structures and historical influences at work in the policy arena—several critical issues were singled out for attention:

1. Identification of the significant social, political, and legal obstacles that confronted advocates of preschool legislation and of the ways by which they were circumvented or overcome.

2. Dynamics of the tension between familial and social parenthood of very young children; that is, under what conditions did intervention into early child care by federal as well as nonfederal surrogates take place?

3. The interplay of social class, bureaucratic, and professional perspectives; specifically, their effects on the form, content, and repute of preschool programs and, eventually, on preschool policy.

4. The distinctive parts played by key groups of policy makers and the dynamics of the policy-making process by which preschool legislation was enacted.

Identifying these issues required research into preschool programs (for "normal" children in this country) from their inception and development through the mid-1960s when the pertinent laws were passed. *Responsibility for Child Care* tries primarily to account for passage of the legislation and touches on the practices and standards adopted by the federally aided programs.

The sources of information for this work include a wide range of historical material, professional literature, newspaper accounts, and legislative documents, as well as interviews with many of those who helped shape federal policy. The reader has to judge whether the pitfalls to accuracy and objectivity were avoided in dealing with such types of information, especially on policy issues involving conflict of values. This points to another dimension of the book. The aims were to describe and gain insight, not to prescribe or incite. Making recommendations leads to confusion by seeming to extend the policy analyst's claim of objectivity to subjective preferences.

I am grateful to the State University of New York at Buffalo for the sabbatical leave that provided time for writing the manuscript. Boston University helped greatly by providing access to the library consortium in Boston. A special debt of gratitude must be acknowledged to Senator and Mrs. William Proxmire for facilitating access to respondents. Paul Barkla gave invaluable assistance in making arrangements for many of the interviews. For the receptivity shown and information provided by the respondents, I am very appreciative.

For reviews, helpful comments on earlier drafts, and encouragement in preparing this book, I express gratitude to Joseph Bensman, Gail Bruder, David Gil, Arnold Gurin, Leonard Hausman, Alfred Kadushin, Morris Schwartz, and Arthur Vidich.

For careful typing and for assistance with the several drafts, thanks are due to Lois Doebler and Ina Moses.

Buffalo, New York   Bernard Greenblatt
February 1977

Contents

xiii

The Author

Bernard Greenblatt, an associate professor of social work at the State University of New York at Buffalo, works on problems of research and social policy. *Responsibility for Child Care* is his first book. His published articles deal with birth control policy, policy implications of programs for the elderly, child care on campuses, and the relation of the family and the social structure; they have appeared in *The Catholic Charities Review, Family Planning Perspectives, The Gerontologist,* and as chapters in several books.

Greenblatt began his professional career as a researcher with the Wisconsin Department of Social Welfare in 1954 and

moved on to administrative and grants management positions in
the U.S. Department of Health, Education, and Welfare in
1960. He has combined that practical experience with academic
work, starting at the Catholic University of America in 1966. In
1968 he joined the faculty at SUNY in Buffalo. He has directed
research projects on federal-state programs for the elderly
(funded by the U.S. Administration on Aging), on day-care
costs (funded by the U.S. Children's Bureau), and a survey of
juvenile law enforcement (part of a delinquency project conducted by the U.S. Children's Bureau and the National Institute
of Mental Health at the direction of Congress). Greenblatt has
served as a consultant on the Joint Commission on the Mental
Health of Children, on the Joint Commission on Correctional
Manpower and Training, and has given testimony at Senate
hearings.

     Greenblatt received an M.A. in sociology from the Uni-
versity of Wisconsin (1963) and a Ph.D. in social welfare from
Brandeis University (1975). He is married to Gail Bruder, a cognitive psychologist, has two daughters, Ruth and Sarah, starting
out on their careers, and a young son, David.

Responsibility for Child Care

The Changing Role
of Family and State
in Child Development

ONE

Child Care
in Family and State

In the mid-1960s, a significant change took place in the relationship between the state and the family in the United States. At that time, three laws were enacted. The Public Welfare Amendments of 1962 authorized federal grants of funds to the states for day care of children. Under the Economic Opportunity Act of 1964, project grants are made for day-care and nursery school programs. And grants-in-aid to the states for preschool programs are authorized by the Elementary and Secondary Education Act of 1965. This study focuses on the social policy bearing on preschool-age children contained in those pieces of legislation.

1

To determine the social and historical significance of those federal preschool enactments requires analysis and assessment of data gathered within a pertinent framework. That framework is presented in the first two parts of this chapter. The beginning, theoretical part was constructed from concepts and generalizations derived from sociological and historical works on the interrelations between the family as an institution and two broad institutional orders, the polity and the economy. The next part consists of a summary of specific features of United States history that served to impede enactment of a federal preschool policy. Based on that theoretical-historical construction, the last part of the chapter will identify the policy dilemmas that have confronted the policy makers. The factors that overcame the historical obstructions and the approach taken in the 1960s to resolve the dilemmas will be described in Chapters Four and Five.

Theoretical Framework

A state of tension between familial and political authority has been characteristic of modern times, especially during revolutionary periods or in totalitarian societies. The assimilation and acculturation of immigrant groups also heighten this tension, as was true in the United States in the past and in Israel, more recently. We are less likely to realize, however, the persistence of such competition and conflict in all industrializing nations.

The modern state seems ambivalent toward the family: It increasingly assumes "family" functions, but is repelled by the increasing costs of these functions. If decisions were made rationally, then, before assuming financial or other responsibility for this or that family function, the state would weigh the anticipated costs against the benefits presumed in the fulfillment. Among the possible costs are conflict with religious and other allies of familial authority, administrative and legal complications of implementation, the establishment of troublesome precedent in assuming a surrogate function, and, not least important, the drain on the public treasury. Major reasons of state that lead governments to assume family responsibilities include the easier assimilation of foreign elements; the achievement of demographic, military, and economic goals; and the maintenance of internal order.

In Western nations, the rationales for intervention by the state into family functions have been closely associated with the process of industrialization. Dissolution of medieval society witnessed the exit of the serf, with his feudal burdens and protections, while the rise of modern capitalism was accompanied by the entrance of legally free but unprotected labor. Much of the social legislation in the industrializing countries represents the effective expression of humanitarian ideals. Aside from the intentions of humanitarian policy makers—that is, from an objective viewpoint—such legislation may be characterized as attempts to cope with the problems stemming from industrialization, of regulating and financing what Weber termed, in another context, "responsibility for the reproduction of the working class" (1950, p. 175). (The word *proletarian,* it may be recalled, means a propertyless stratum unburdened of all civic responsibility except that of bearing children.) The poor laws, regulation of child labor, control of baby farming, and so on, can be understood in that light, as well as in moral and humanitarian terms.

Families may bear children, but providing at least for their minimal wants and protecting them from blatant abuse and exploitation are other responsibilities that the state could not or would not entrust or expect impoverished parents to perform adequately. The early political intervention into family matters suggests some noteworthy, interrelated features. The relationship between political and parental authority varies along lines of class and sex.

Parental-political friction rubs unequally on different social strata, even though statutes may be phrased in terms of formal equality. According to legal definition, upper- and middle-class children are as likely as those in the lower class to be delinquent, neglected, or abused. But, in the arena of social life, such characterizations almost always apply to lower-class children. Similarly, even with the transfer of functions more or less universally from families in all social strata, dissimilar consequences are likely. These effects of stratification are often overlooked in discourses on "the child and the state," on "the loss of family functions," or on "the family as an institution." As a result, much of the social science literature on these topics, including work otherwise cogent, paints a monochromatic family portrait; that is, the existence of social class is deemphasized or even overlooked (Mead, 1948; Parsons, 1949; Parsons, 1960; Wrong, 1950). For example, both Mead (1948) and Parsons (1949) acknowledge differences in class patterns, but consider lower- and upper-class family behavior as "deviant" cases from the urban, middle-class pattern.

The impact of political authority on parental rule has also been different for fathers than for mothers. The state in the Occident came into confrontation with a family institution whose historical base, since recorded time, was patriarchal. Surrogate state parenthood—*parens patriae*—in evolving, succeeded various types and degrees of paternal domination, of which the extreme form was *patria potestas* of early Rome—absolute patriarchal authority. Intervention in the family, therefore, meant a diminution of paternal rights and duties, and a relative increase in maternal sharing, communal concern organized in voluntary associations, or in the assumption of family functions by the state. In regulating such matters as physical punishment of children by parents, control over children's earnings, including the right to decide on the child's working at all, and the decision whether or not to provide education, the state took over what theretofore had been paternal prerogatives. Providing support for dependent children and performing services for which fathers would otherwise have to pay, such as health and education, are aspects of what Bertrand Russell termed the "process of substituting the state for the father" (1959, p. 139). Russell, focusing on England and Europe, recognized the differential effects of this process among the several social classes: "In the upper and middle classes this process has hardly taken place at all and consequently the father remains more important, and the family more stable, among the well-to-do than among wage earners" (1959, p. 140).

Aside from the effects of poverty or of economic power-lessness, paternal functioning is further attenuated by the less-ening of the father's authority that accompanied the emancipa-tion of women. During the past century or so, while fathers experienced divestiture of legal rights as *paterfamilias*, mothers received increments of familial authority. In empowering mothers with increased rights regarding themselves and their children, the law reflected and also facilitated the process of industrialization and its effects on the family. This process, by extending and intensifying the separation of work site and home site that had been initiated by the earlier workshop sys-tem of production, achieved the de facto emancipation of women and mothers from paternal authority in economic activ-ity. This same separation, in conjunction with urbanization and the nucleation of the extended family, has significantly affected many familial functions of employed mothers.

To appreciate fully the transformation of the family and the strong relationship between the family and economy would require an extensive discussion of the social history of the American family. Such an exposition, however, would lead us too far from the central aim of explaining and assessing the en-actment of federal preschool policy in the 1960s. Instead, we will assert that a social history of the American family would demonstrate: (1) the close kinship between the family and the economy (Calhoun [1919], 1960; Aries, 1962); and (2) the operation of economic forces that, in their progressive develop-ment, by the 1930s required federal intervention into the fam-ily circle, thereby advancing the extension, in Calhoun's phrase, of "social parenthood."

There is considerable acceptance in the literature of the first generalization, as well as the direction of the relationship. Schorr (1968, p. 146) has stated the case as a research meta-phor: "One might regard the United States as a vast experiment in which two variables have been economic development (in-cluding industrialization and urbanization) and the structure and internal relationships of families. It is apparent that, in the United States as elsewhere, the family has been the dependent variable." However, other variables than the economy impinge on the family, such as the state. Furthermore, the variables interact. As we implied earlier, the political acts of the state and the economic process of industrialization had mutually reinforcing effects on the family. The best fit to the data in this study was found in the trilogy of factors that Russell (1959) identified as bearing on the modern family: economic (the industrial revolution), cultural (religious doctrine, social theories, and what we call "theorhetorical" images), and political (action of the state). The objective here is to describe and analyze the actions of the federal government in establishing preschool policy, and the following chapters are devoted principally to that aim. Of course, relevant cultural and economic factors will be mentioned.

Particularly pertinent to this study has been the impact of the trilogy of factors on the one maternal function that, amid the seeming disintegration of the family, is often deemed to be fundamental—care and rearing of the preschool child (for example, see Burgess, 1942). Some illustrations of the way in which the political process works may be noted. Laws holding parents culpable for deficient performance or neglect of this function represent the state's assertion of the right to establish parental standards and its intention to enforce parental compliance. Mothers' pensions are efforts by the state to ensure care and rearing of children within the kinship group by subsidizing maternal performance. And provision of funding by the state of surrogate care arrangements represents degrees of substitution of the state for this "intrinsic" maternal function. This would have, Bertrand Russell believed, as the "logical consequence . . . the elimination of the mother as well as of the father from all importance in the child's psychology" (1959, p. 143). (Mayor Fiorello H. LaGuardia held this same attitude to public provision of day-care. Apparently he was as concerned that such programs would "make the state the 'father and mother of the child' " [Fleiss, cited in Mayer and Kahn, 1965, p. 34].) But, as we shall see, involvement in surrogate arrangements for the care of children under six years of age was avoided by the federal government, except for reasons of depression and war, until the 1960s. Until that time a number of historical features specific to the United States had operated, along with broad economic forces, to forestall federal action in periods of normalcy.

Impediments to Enactment of Federal Preschool Policy

Of primary interest here is the developing pattern of the transfer or assumption of family functions, particularly in regard to young children (under six), by *federal* authorities. Federal involvement in family matters can be very briefly summarized. During the greatest part of our history, the federal government shied away from encroaching on familial authority. Family law in the United States, until the 1930s, consisted of state statutes and court decisions, with federal courts providing appellate review of constitutional issues. A brief review of state law regarding the family is necessary before examining the later federal laws.

The dominance of state laws on family matters conforms, of course, to the constitutional assignment of residual powers (those not delegated to the federal government). States differed in whether and when family laws were enacted, in the specific provisions of statutes adopted, as well as in their enforcement. Viewed from a national perspective, laissez-faire in family affairs at the state level produced a patchwork quilt of social legislation.

Family law enacted by the states is defined as the rules and procedures for "establishing, administering, and reorganizing" family relationships (Goldstein and Katz, 1965, p. 1). Laws on marriage formation fall into the first category; on adoption, abuse, dependency, neglect, education, child labor into the second; and on separation and divorce into the third. So far as these laws bear on filial relationships, they exemplify the extension of "social parenthood" (Calhoun [1919] 1960, 3, p. 158).

Most pertinent here among the state laws governing administrative relations within the family were those removing education of children from parental responsibility and assigning it to the public authority. Several aspects of the evolution of those laws deserve notice. One is the social class dimension. The colonies in New England had widely adopted universal, compulsory education. After the revolutionary turmoil in the early nineteenth century, free schools were generally established, either exclusively or preferentially, for destitute orphans and poor children. Under the influence of democratic ideals and pressure from labor groups, public education then developed into universal, compulsory schooling. To be sure, it was first necessary to overcome opposition by some parents, especially in the South, to the egalitarian integration of social classes in free public schools.

The second feature of these laws is the emergence and response to the issue of authority over or responsibility for children. Some parents objected to compulsory education as an unwarranted interference with parental authority. Others assailed the principle that all the children be educated by the state on the grounds that "the people must educate their own children" (Calhoun, [1919] 1960, 2, p. 61). These and similar declarations of the spirit of familism echoed and reechoed during nineteenth-century debates on various statutory proposals bearing on the family. (Even in the twentieth century, such views were expressed in opposition to child labor laws.)

The high value placed on the family as a basic social unit probably reflected appreciation of the impressively independent and vigorous frontier family. The family came to be apotheosized, as may be seen from remarks by the President of Amherst College in 1840: "Families are so many divinely instituted and independent communities, upon the well ordering of which, the most momentous interests of the church and the state, of time and eternity are suspended" (Cited in Calhoun [1919], 1960, 2, p. 68). A state legislature understandably might hesitate to enact a statute that could bring church, state, and eternity crashing down.

State laws regarding the education of children, especially laws that established public schools and eventually made education mandatory, impinged on the interests of an institution other than the family. Religious organizations had essentially carried sole responsibility for educating children during the colonial period. As we shall see in the next chapter, however, a spirit of nonsectarianism began to intrude into charitable educational programs even as public education began to develop. But the most profound restriction on the ecclesiastic interest in educating the laity, as we shall see later (Chapter Five), had been embodied in the United States Constitution. The First Amendment prohibition against the establishment of (and infringement on) religion had also been incorporated in the constitutions adopted by many states.

The wall separating church and state meant that public funds generally were not available to parochial schools. Aside from religious concerns over education to the faith or over moral education, the restriction in state constitutions essentially placed religious institutions under heavy fiscal constraints in the field of education. Compared to the influence that church groups had exercised in education during the colonial period, the later entrance by the states into education could appear as an encroachment on ecclesiastic prerogatives. Religious clergymen in the United States thus had an allied interest with those parents who resented the movement of the state into matters previously governed by parental authority. Churches, especially the minority Catholic church, became an institutional ally of the family in resisting the advance of social parenthood.

For about 150 years, the federal government had no cause to fear attack by institutional allies and advocates of familism. In addition to the Constitutional issue and the geopolitical immaturity of the federal government until the twentieth century, enactment by state and local governments of laws and ordinances on family matters to a great extent made federal action unnecessary. When the child labor amendment to the Constitution was proposed in 1924, the criticism to be expected was not long in coming. A Catholic prelate charged that "For the parental control over children it would substitute the will of Congress and the dictate of a centralized bureaucracy, more in keeping with Soviet Russia than with the fundamental principles of American Government" (Cited in Bremner, 1971, p. 743).

A federated structure of national and state governments complicates the relation of political and parental authority in the United States. Up to the mid-1930s, the relationship was essentially bipartite. State law governed the interaction of family and political authority. From the mid-1930s on, beginning with the enactment of federal social security, welfare, and child labor laws, a tripartite relationship was formed. This now exposed the family unit to two entities of authority with partially distinct, partially overlapping jurisdictions.

Probably more traumatic than the impact on federal-state relations were other effects of the federal social legislation that grew out of the Great Depression. Mass unemployment accompanied that catastrophic breakdown in the production of goods and services. In turn, that led to a crisis in the family, the social mechanism for the reproduction and sustenance of human labor. Facing vast social unrest, the federal government abandoned the policy of laissez-faire in the economy and the household. Borrowing and expanding on measures from some of the more liberal or advanced states, the New Deal transformed the economy and the family. Examples of the latter include making economically dependent children in the family home financial wards of the federal government and establishing a "pension" system for retired, elderly members of the family. Earlier opposition effectively blocked the passage of federal child labor regulation until 1938. During the Great Depression, the first federally aided preschool programs in the history of the United States were established, under the Works Progress Administration (WPA), to provide employment to mothers. And during World War II federal funds were expended to provide day care for children whose mothers worked in war-impacted areas. That program was terminated shortly after hostilities ended. After 1945 there were no further federal preschool programs until the mid-1960s.

With the exceptions during the crises of the 1930s and 1940s, the impediments mentioned generally blocked federal involvement in the preschool area until the 1960s. Proponents of such a federal role ran up against the historic obstacles. To support any legislative proposal meant facing one or more policy dilemmas arising from the political and cultural impediments.

Policy Dilemmas

Whether or not recognized by the policy maker, the historical and structural issues we have discussed are involved in the various laws and governmental programs concerned with families and children. This study has as one purpose the attempt to determine the goals projected by recent legislative programs, which includes the task of identifying and clarifying how aware or self-conscious are policy makers and program planners of the social structure in which they act. This question itself is relevant to the second goal of the study—assessing the different policy formulations and dilemmas that confront those individuals who initiate and shape policy.

Our problem is to analyze the formulations that have been attempted to solve the policy dilemmas that confronted the preschool policy makers. They faced a number of major predicaments.

The first dilemma concerns the tension between familial and social parenthood. Even before the Aid to Dependent Children program was enacted, governmental policy generally had been to encourage mothers to stay home and rear their young children. Except when parental failure had been legally established, child rearing outside the home, particularly of preschool-age children, had never been officially espoused as generally desirable or as a function for which the state should assume positive responsibility (that is, regardless of the availability of parental supervision). The dilemma involved in legislation proposing day care for children of working mothers consists of (1) either opposing the measure and risking possible neglect of these children while the mothers work; or (2) supporting the legislation and then having to justify the assumption of federal responsibility without seeming to conflict with the high normative value ascribed to familial rearing of very young children.

The constitutional reservation to the states of powers not otherwise assigned created a second dilemma. Essentially, the predicament that confronted federal legislators considering aid to education consisted of either accepting the anticipated continuation of educational deficits and defects in state programs, or becoming vulnerable to the charge from jealous guardians of the states' prerogatives and strict legal constructionists of an unconstitutional exercise of federal power.

The third dilemma involves the constitutional prohibition against the establishment of religion. Prior to 1965, proposals for federal aid to education foundered on this dilemma: If aid to parochial schools was excluded, criticism of the proposed legislation by spokesmen for powerful religious groups would rally sufficient support from coreligionist legislators to block passage; inclusion of aid to private schools would rouse effective opposition from sectarian and nonsectarian advocates of an inviolate separation between church and state.

The choice in legislating day care or education for all children of a given age or for those who also meet other selective criteria stipulated in the legislation leads to a fourth set of dilemmas. The cultural norm stressing equality, as in the legal phrase *equality under the law*, found expression in the evolution of state educational programs toward providing universal coverage. Given that norm and such legal precedent, several dilemmas arise if policy makers consider legislation with selective provisions, such as day care for children of working mothers, or preschool programs for impoverished children. Such legislation seems to depart from the democratic value of formal equality. It also may appear to publicly establish or reinforce a dual track, along social class lines, for such programs. Selective provision may also imply acceptance of the inequality of the poor as unalterable. So legislators must be prepared to embrace these apparent legal and cultural contradictions, or they must consider legislating universal coverage. The latter, of course, would expand the financial cost astronomically, as well as heighten opposition from opponents of federal parenthood.

One or another of these dilemmas had to be dealt with in enacting the three pieces of legislation central to our study: the authorization and funding specifically provided in 1962 under the child welfare title of the Social Security Act to make grants to the states for day-care services, primarily but not exclusively for children of working mothers; the project grants made under the Economic Opportunity Act of 1964 for Head Start day-care centers and nursery schools as part of the Johnson Administration's War on Poverty; and the much larger program for the preschool education of young children, authorized by Title I of the Elementary and Secondary Education Act of 1965, also enacted as an antipoverty weapon. All three programs, one under a welfare title, the other two as educational measures, officially aimed to mitigate conditions of poverty. Also noteworthy, the federal government offered—family involvement being voluntary—to share with *parents in low-income families* the costs and responsibility for rearing the young child outside the home. These historic changes are taken here as the presenting problem for our analysis.

The selection of this presenting problem deliberately bypasses another series of problems of strategic urgency for practitioners and administrators in the field of education and welfare. One of the other questions is: How *do* day-care centers and nursery schools differ? Another is, what differentiation of expert roles and organizational responsibilities is indicated by different conceptions of day care and nursery school? As shall be shown, these questions were articulated decades ago. Since then, various attempts to answer these questions by specialists, administrators, and other conferees have been at issue in most discourse on those programs. Even in the mid-1960s, the various federal commissioners have felt forced to attempt to clarify these issues (see Chapter Five). But these issues of professional and organizational differences are primarily considerations aimed at implementation, mere matters of ways and means, when viewing the programs from the perspective of the relationship of the family to the social order. From that vantage point, broader social policy issues come into focus, connecting nursery and nation. Of course, the instrumental matters must be examined in policy analysis. The point here simply is to formulate the problem for analysis in societal and structural terms.

The central problem addressed in this study can be pinpointed now. We assume that the care and rearing of preschool-age children has been deemed to be the fundamental responsibility of the family unit. As we shall see, however, from time to time the state has intervened in that family function. Such intervention leads to tension between parental and political authority in a very sensitive area—the rearing of very young children. Hence the three pieces of legislation in the 1960s constituted an historical departure in shifting the traditional balance of familial and political authority. They represented a major role, historically unique during periods of normalcy, for the federal government in the rearing and education of very young children and directed those functions outside the home. (For some years now, working parents with low income have been entitled to deduct limited amounts of child-care expenses for federal tax purposes. This, of course, implies political concern over the child-rearing consequences faced by low-income workers. This tax law differs from the preschool legislation, however, in that it seeks to subsidize in part expenditures that parents decide to make and is neutral regarding care arrangements in or out of the household.) In describing and explaining the events of the 1960s, we hope to learn about the dynamics of the tension between familial and social parenthood. First, we will seek to learn the conditions under which the balance shifted from one side to another; specifically, our aim is to identify the conditions under which intervention into early child care by various surrogate agencies occurred. Second, we will attempt to explain the forms that intervention took in terms of sponsorship (philanthropic, proprietary, public) and types of programs (day care, kindergarten, nursery school).

The legal solutions to and perspectives on the policy predicaments were sought in official documents (statutes, reports of legislative hearings, and committee reports), newspaper accounts, journal articles, books, and in interviews with federal legislators, government officials, and other policy makers. The alternative policy assumptions and viewpoints associated with these legislative approaches constitute the primary focus of this study, and the attempt to ascertain the means and processes by which the various policy assumptions were formulated, through the analysis of these sources, constitutes the primary "operation" of this study.

In the next chapter, we present a history of preschool programs in the United States, to lay a basis for the examination of preschool perspectives.

TWO

Early Child Care Programs

The impediments to federal action in the preschool field and the related social policy dilemmas did not suddenly appear in the 1960s. They reflected cultural and institutional influences that had been at play for over a century. Furthermore, the policy makers giving consideration to federal preschool programs in the 1960s were not dealing with entirely new and previously unheard-of phenomena. Preschool programs had existed in the United States since the 1830s. The historical development of those programs formed a heritage that influenced subsequently enacted policies. The chronological narrative in this chapter is intended to contribute to an historical appreciation of preschool programs and policy. It will also provide a basis for

15

examining, in the next chapter, several problems in and perspectives on preschool policy of significance in the 1960s.

The various forms of preschool programs will be described in an essentially chronological narrative. The information to be presented falls into seven categories: (1) program
conception or type, (2) goals, (3) auspices, (4) clientele, (5) program content and techniques, (6) staff, and (7) program magnitude.

Gaps and unevenness in the chronology, as well as the
lack of uniform descriptions of the programs, result from infor-
mational, conceptual, and terminological difficulties. The available literature treats more sparsely certain types of programs,
such as infant schools, and certain historical periods, such as the
World War I period. Almost no information on programs under
proprietary auspices was found prior to the 1950s. Also, only
scant data on church-sponsored programs were located. Accordingly, a specific program feature, such as proprietary sponsorship, is treated extensively during that historical period for
which a significant source of information was available.

Conceptual difficulties made the specification of program
goals somewhat complex. Perhaps this should be expected of a
concept—program goal—that embodies philosophical assumptions regarding human nature, education, and valued social institutions. On a formal level, the complexity of goal analysis is
attributed to the multiplicity and intertwining of goals and to
resulting problems in the delineation, transformation, and agglutination of goals. On the substantive level, complications in goal
specification and transformation will be illustrated in this and
the following chapters.

The multiplicity of program goals and associated values
contributed to the profusion and confusion of program terminology. We will discuss the various preschool programs that
appeared in the United States: day-care centers, infant schools,
kindergartens, and nursery schools. In the course of describing
those programs, the program categories will be shown as far less
distinctive than the existence of diverse terms might suggest.
During the century from 1860 to 1960, the program types
apparently overlapped as to age of children enrolled, social class

of clientele, program content, and, except for the half-day session generally observed by kindergartens, program schedules. Hence the program names employed here should be understood as reflecting the nondistinctive, nominal usage in the literature. Given the terminological confusion, the program names employed would best be understood as though in quotation marks. We shall also show that the distinction that evolved over fifty years ago between day-care and nursery school programs manifested more than a confusion in terminology, namely, invidious social class comparisons.

The Antebellum and Civil War Years

A concern for the welfare of children endangered by the social and economic consequences of the industrial revolution impelled the development of the first type of *preschool* program in the United States. "Infant schools" were established around 1830 (Calhoun [1919] 1960, *2,* p. 60), even before day nurseries are mentioned.

The infant schools were organized by charitable sponsors and catered to children of poor and of immigrant families. Although charitable sponsorship was applauded by some, the nonpublic auspices and circumscribed clientele were criticized in labor circles: "Education is the right of every child, and it is in the interest of the community that the right should be possessed and exercised by all" (Cited in Calhoun, [1919] 1960, *2,* p. 60). Except for the philanthropic sponsorship and the lower-class clientele, little else *specifically* appears in the literature about this type of preschool program (Forest, 1930, p. 320). It is not known whether these were full- or half-day programs, nor what other differences or similarities they may have had to later types of programs, such as day nurseries and kindergartens. (Although programs named *infant schools* continued in England to the end of the nineteenth century, in the United States that term seems to have vanished after the midcentury.)

Several pertinent features, however, are reported or may be surmised from contemporaneous conditions. The name *infant school* implies an educational or child development goal.

Such goals involve a relative focus on and development of one or more of the emotional, intellectual, moral, physical, and social capacities of the child. Those goals reflect conceptions of the nature of the child as the raw material of the nurturing process. Those conceptions may also include ideas about the methods appropriate to the program for achieving the designated developmental objectives. Those goals, in other words, display variations of ideas about human nature and nurture.

A child welfare—"child rescue"—objective pertained to the infant schools. No doubt some of the humanitarian contemporaries were moved by genuine, unself-conscious concern for endangered children and sought to mitigate the social and economic hardships to which they were exposed. For others, an authority remarks, the impoverished "child was to be saved less for his own sake than because he was a potential threat to society" (Wishy, 1968, p. 16).

It has not been clearly established whether the infant schools represented a specific school of philosophy or of educational thought. Infant schools, however, developed at the same time in which significant shifts had occurred within religious thought. By 1830, theologians had begun to question explicitly the earlier Calvinist view of infant depravity. That view had informed religious education and established as its goal the conversion of children to the faith. At about the same time, interest in secular education had also begun to stir. Both the traditionalist (religious) and the reform (secular) educators saw the child as subject to a divinely ordained moral law. But secular educators and reformers explicitly challenged religion as the only basis of morality and asserted that "moral and religious education were distinct from each other" (Wishy, 1968, p. 69). The emerging distinction between moral and religious education, in addition to the constitutional restrictions on religion and egalitarian educational ideals, nourished a developing consensus that sectarian teaching was not compatible with public education. At best these new attitudes represented a challenge to religious *education*, not to the dominant religion per se. Neither Christian doctrine nor moral prescription were questioned.

The traditional, religious educators still projected as the

goal of education the conversion of the individual to prepare him for another worldly salvation; the reform educators, however, projected as the aim of education the application of the same moral injunctions on individuals in this world, in their role as citizen or moral individual. Both shared the ideal conception of the American Christian citizen; but one focused on the here and now, the other on the hereafter.

Not only did the goals differ; so did instrumental considerations that had bearing on later preschool developments or on interrelations between the family and other institutions. First, teachers (and parents, especially mothers), in addition to clergy, were seen as having responsibility for the moral education of the child. Reform educators claimed a "divine mission" for teachers—to guide "the progress of Christian civilization" (cited in Wishy, 1968, p. 54). Teachers came to represent serious secular competition for ministers as parent surrogates in the nurture of young children. This may be seen in the educational literature, which, from 1830 on, reveals a struggle between "partisans of religious or secular . . . education" (Wishy, 1968, p. 67).

Traditionalism and reform, religious instructors and secular educators, also differed in their respect for a well-known pedagogical tool—the rod. The "new nurturists" criticized whipping by schoolmasters and urged, instead, appealing to the child's "moral sense" (a tactic, Wishy points out, that induces guilt through that inner monitor, the superego). Orthodox religious teachers did not see the new light and continued to find spiritual merit in corporal punishment.[1]

On one pedagogical matter, however, most teachers and ministers apparently agreed. They, as well as many parents, rejected the strong emphasis on intellectual demands recommended by a minority of the newer educators. This may be illustrated in the warning by the educational reformer, Horace Mann, of "the dangers of insanity if intellectual training began while the child's emotions were immature" (cited in Wishy, 1968, p. 70). Others found the child's health or happiness endangered by attention to "analysis" and intellectual effort rather than to "real-life" matters.

These educational topics and considerations of pedagogy

were widely discussed in the popular and professional literature at the time infant schools were known in the United States. Parental interest in these matters was also high, because the schools explicitly aimed to compensate for "openly confessed deficiencies in training at home" (Wishy, 1968, p. 68). Parents were seen as inexpert and overly permissive. In the 1830s, the school was described as an aid to parental care, as "the great auxiliary of the fireside" (cited in Wishy, 1968, p. 73). Thus the infant schools also may have had parent education as a goal. However, from the standpoint of the family, the teacher—the principal agent of the school as an institution—was seen as a competitor, as a potential substitute for the parent. Aside from its other features, the infant school was a precursor of later interventions in family life.

The infant school presents several significant developments. Despite the apparent evanescent quality of the infant schools, they had paradigmatic importance. According to Wishy, they were the first American "agencies to share parents' work with young children" (1968, p. 68). More precisely, they were the first *secular* expression of social parenthood. Tension between familial and social parenthood arose. As a result of the subsequent establishment and proliferation of other types of preschool programs, involving ever larger numbers of children, this tension has continued. It may be found today, but it affects various groups differently.[2]

Moral education as an aim of child development, first projected as a nonreligious objective during the period of the infant schools, was also adopted in later decades and may well have become one of the most pervasive goals in education. Thus the infant schools may have represented the start—but were not the cause—of a long tradition that selects out the moral dimension as the educational focus in child development. In part as a result of that focal attention, of emphases on "health, happiness, or 'real-life' " concerns and fears of intellectual training, a notable flavor was imparted to subsequent education. "Existing American tendencies to invoke narrow 'real-life' or utilitarian standards of intellectual and moral judgment were thus reinforced ... [and, Wishy adds, strengthened an] antitheoretical, antiintellectual, anticritical strain . . . ." (1968, p. 71). These strains will be seen again.

The beginning of secularization of public education was another significant contribution of the infant schools. The monopolistic hold of the ministry on the morals of the laity was broken by secular teachers. It would have been impossible to foresee, hidden in that process, the bitter controversy between church and state over aid to education, a controversy that played a key role when peacetime federal preschool policy was enacted in the 1960s.

The charitable sponsorship of the infant schools also occasioned the first dispute over selective versus universal provision of preschool programs. That dispute, begun in the 1830s, reappeared a century later as a professional concern and then entered the public arena.

Another more hardy type of preschool program, the day nursery—as day-care centers were called until about fifty years ago—also were started before the Civil War. Most reports consider the day nursery established in New York City at the Nursery and Child's Hospital in 1854 to be the first in the United States.[3] It provided care (from nurses) for children of former patients who went back to work; the aim seemed to have been to assure the posthospital recovery of mothers harassed by work, motherhood, and illness.

The effects on children of maternal employment at this period may be gauged from a slightly later (1877) account: " 'Motherhood . . . brings to a poor mother, who has to go out to work, despair and often leads to infanticide, abandonment, dosing the children with narcotic cordials, leaving them to the charge of incompetent children, who themselves badly want watching, or to the cruelty of strangers, if not to shutting them up between cheerless walls, and converting them through this isolation . . . into semiidiots' " (cited by Calhoun, [1919] 1960, 3, p. 73). In the idiom of the day, such children were "day orphans." Their number increased with the pressure on poor mothers to go out to work, whether stemming from widowhood, separation, divorce, the husband's disability, or—as capitalism developed—from the husband's unemployment or low wages. As a result, in the United States, as elsewhere, according to virtually all reports, humanitarian concern over child neglect led to the establishment of day-care centers. Recognition of that concern, however, should not be construed as challenging the generalization that "The day nursery, or crèche, is primarily a by-product of the . . . industrialization of women's work" (Tyson, 1930, p. 13).

The earliest group day-care programs thus pursued two goals: preventing child neglect and alleviating the hardships faced by mothers employed outside the home. Both goals were telescoped into a broader aim, to strengthen the family. However, extrafamilial maternal employment deviated from traditional sex roles. It also departed from the widely shared conception of the conjugal family, a conception held to be divinely sanctioned, and on behalf of which, it was said, the " 'momentous interests of the church and state, of time and eternity are suspended' " (cited in Calhoun, [1919] 1960, 2, p. 68). At the beginning, day nurseries apparently accepted only fatherless children and children of permanently incapacitated fathers, for widowhood and paternal incapacitation could widely be accepted as dire circumstances—"acts of God"?—that justified maternal employment. In such tragic cases, departure from the normative family pattern could be condoned.

At the outset, day nurseries in this country were mostly philanthropic agencies. Ladies from the affluent classes were the first day-care staff. In the spirit of charitable voluntarism, they helped organize the early day nurseries in their towns and continued their work after the programs were established. Rather than being paid for what they did, they more than paid their own way. In addition to rendering service, they made personal contributions from family funds. In short, mid-nineteenth-century women of leisure from wealthy families living in cities expressed their humanitarian concern over child neglect through day-care activities. To a considerable extent, they imparted to the programs they had started a "charitable" image that continued in philanthropic day care for a century.

Some of the ladies may have devoted many hours to their good works. According to an "ancient record . . . 'the patronesses [were advised to] not content themselves with giving their money and names to the suppost [*sic*] of the work, but [to] exercise by their visits and counsel a personal influence' " (White House Conference, 1930a, p. 9). Friendly visitors from the day-care center, circumstantial evidence suggests, may have screened applicants deemed to be deserving, who would be admitted to the day nursery, from others, who would quite possibly be counseled to not seek or even discontinue employment outside the home. From the perspective of a postindustrial society in the 1970s, friendly visiting may well appear intrusive, haughty, and patronizing. Perhaps. But as performed in the United States in the mid-nineteenth century, it represented an attempt to apply principles of an emerging social science to existing social problems. The friendly visitor was an innovative successor to the then traditional Lady Bountiful bringing her charitable food basket to the poor. Traditional philanthropy apparently criticized the innovators (Becker, 1964, p. 59).[4]

Another important piece of information is known about the early patronesses of day care. Aside from friendly visiting, they also served on the board that set policy and assumed "responsibility for the details of management" as a "personal trust" (White House Conference, 1930a, p. 9). Because they were often spending their own donations and that of their social equals, indeed they were carrying out a personal trust.

The social perspective manifested by the ladies' day-care activities was certainly not radical or even that of militant reform. Child neglect resulting from maternal employment was to be deplored and remedies sought. But the industrial system, which led to unemployment and a nonliving wage for men, and therefore to maternal employment, was not challenged. Rather, it was assumed as given. Also, the normative model of the conjugal family was taken as (divinely) given.

That these philanthropists were females should not be overlooked. As women of means in a period of history when custom defined home as their place, they found a respectable way not to know their place, or to discover it. Moreover, their action implied an intricate irony: They were upper-class women liberating themselves from complete domesticity, acting in the interests of lower-class women "liberated" from the domestic life by economic necessity, and in the stated interest of a normative conception of the family that held women's place is in the home. The contradictions may have been lost on their contemporaries, but they placed on day care a lasting feminine touch. In fact, for about one hundred years, day-care policy and programs were almost wholly untouched by men.

Except for friendly visiting, the literature does not refer to a guiding programatic philosophy, program content, or techniques in the early day nurseries. However, as we shall see in later historical periods, a custodial orientation apparently prevailed in these programs for many decades.

In addition to the infant school and the day nursery, the kindergarten also appeared in this country before the Civil War. The program and its underlying ideas were brought to America by political refugees from the German revolution of 1848. Apparently it was Margarethe Schurz, wife of the well-known German emigre Carl Schurz, who, in 1855 and 1856, established the first kindergarten in this country, in Watertown, Wisconsin (Goodykoontz, Davis, and Gabbard, 1947, p. 59; Rowe, 1972, p. 4).

At its inception, the kindergarten had a clear educational focus. It not only constituted a program, but also reflected an educational theory and related pedagogical methods. All these represented the ideas of the German educator, Friedrich Wilhelm August Froebel, who coined the name *kindergarten*, meaning a "garden of children."

In emphasizing the education of children at a very early age, Froebel stood in a long line of philosophers and theorists extending back to Plato, who "insisted upon the importance of the earliest years in shaping the destiny of an individual" (Forest, 1930, p. 320). Another forerunner was the seventeenth-century theorist, Comenius, who also believed that early childhood education provided "the foundations of all later education" (Forest, 1930, p. 321). Comenius placed great value on play, an activity whose significance Froebel also appreciated. Hence, kindergartens are sometimes also known as "playschools."

Froebel's ideas also reflected those of another philosopher, Rousseau. For the earlier belief in original depravity of man, Rousseau had substituted the notion of man's natural goodness. Given his inherent goodness, man was seen as self-sufficient, as able to steer his own course without supernatural guidance provided through revealed religion ("Education," p. 126). Froebel's theories were built on the philosophy of naturalism that Rousseau had articulated.

For Froebel, instruction as the imparting of knowledge was not the way to educate. Rather, the proper aim was "to draw out [from the pliable child the] capacities of feeling and thinking, and even of inventing and creating" ("Kindergarten," p. 802). Recognizing intuition or direct experience as "the true basis of knowledge," Froebel avowedly claimed to "teach the children not what to think, but how to think." Children were seen as individuals with the right of self-expression. One of the chief mechanisms of that expression, play, became recognized as having a pedagogical potential.

Although he disclaimed teaching children what to think, Froebel saw as the purpose of education helping children gain understanding of " 'the laws of unity and interdependence'— which, he believed, governed the universe" (Forest, 1930, p. 321). The kindergarten curriculum and pedagogical techniques were designed to help the children recognize these laws. That curriculum consisted of a series of games involving the use of very specific playthings, called *gifts*, which were to be used in carefully prescribed sequences. The children were to be outdoors as much as possible, where each was to have his own little garden. The name *kindergarten*, therefore, had several meanings; it served as a metaphor of the innate human capabilities to be nurtured by means of education, and also referred to the plot of ground that each child was to cultivate. As conceived by Froebel, then, the kindergarten was a playschool for assisting the physical, moral, and intellectual development of children from the ages of three to seven.

The earliest American kindergartens were privately sponsored. The sponsors apparently were disciples of Froebel, such as Margarethe Schurz and Elizabeth Peabody, Horace Mann's

sister-in-law and a member of the Concord School of Philosophy, whose interest in Froebel's metaphysics led her to establish a kindergarten in Boston, in 1860. In the absence of information, we can only speculate about the clientele of the early
kindergartens. Probably the programs attracted parents who
also found the Froebelian ideas and ideals on education congenial. Most likely they were from the middle or upper classes.
It is not impossible, of course, that the earliest sponsors also
held philanthropic views and may have organized programs to
educate children from the lower classes.

From an educational perspective, the kindergarten was
clearly the most impressive of the earliest types of preschool
programs in the United States. It reflected an elaborate educational theory and related pedagogical techniques and rested on a
profound philosophical base. Not surprisingly, it eventually
grew into the most extensive form of preschool education in the
nation. As we shall see in the course of its subsequent historical
evolution, however, its theoretical sophistication miscarried and
its rigidities gave rise to the theory that became so dominant in
American preschool education as to be called a *movement*,
namely progressive education. The kindergarten itself was
caught up by that movement.

The few developments pertaining to preschool matters
during the Civil War that are mentioned in the literature concern the day nurseries. The war accelerated trends set in motion
by peacetime industrialization. It continued the influx into factories of women who, it has been estimated, already were performing one fourth of all manufacturing when the war started
(Calhoun, [1919] 1960, 2, p. 191). It also hastened the entrance of middle-class women into office and professional work.
To cite a dramatic example, almost overnight the war feminized
school teaching.

Very probably, most of the wartime female labor force
did not consist of mothers with young children. Nevertheless,
the war apparently spurred maternal employment outside the
home and, as a result, the demand for day nurseries as well.
During that war, of course, social legislation in the developing
nation was as yet underdeveloped; public support for day care

then would have been unthinkable. Philanthropic funds and voluntary labor seemingly were not adequate to meet the demand, for industrial and proprietary programs sprang up. (Proprietary preschool programs are defined here as day-care centers, kindergartens, or nursery schools operated to obtain profits *directly*. They differ from industrial day-care centers, which seek profits *indirectly* through the preschool program by facilitating recruitment of maternal employees.) Thus one reference suggests that the first industrial day nursery was a by-product of the Civil War, a program established in Philadelphia in 1863 for children whose mothers made soldiers' clothing or worked in hospitals (Whipple, 1929, p. 91).[5] Of these day-care developments, as we shall see later, the proprietary or commercial programs increased to become a major sector of the day-care field, while industrial programs in this country have never become more than curiosities that arise at special times or places.

From the Postbellum Era to the
Turn of the Twentieth Century

If the period from 1830 to 1865 may be characterized as one of preschool program inception, diffusion and development of preschool innovations mainly typified the last third of the century. The history of kindergartens exemplifies these processes.

Originally, Froebel may have aimed to "train mothers to teach their own young children in the home" (Whipple, 1929, p. 247). And it is conceivable that the earliest American kindergartens were conducted in private homes with mothers of the children as the staff. Nevertheless, by the postwar years kindergartens operated as extrafamilial educational programs. Moreover, a major shift in goals had occurred. Religious and philanthropic organizations "eagerly sought" to establish such programs "as the most hopeful form of social regeneration" (Whipple, 1929, p. 247). Those groups viewed the programs as useful for dealing with the poverty of immigrant cultures and the social disorders of the slums. Not only did kindergartens aim to begin the education of immigrant children, they also had a parent education objective. The staff of early kindergarten programs, many of which were located in urban slum areas, reportedly taught the children, did social welfare work with the parents, and also gave them instruction in regard to child rearing, such as on nutrition and hygiene. Philanthropic funds were insufficient to pay both a teacher to work with the children and a social worker to assist the parents, so the tasks were combined —child education in the morning, welfare and parent education in the afternoon.

As an aside, it should be noted that interest in parent education on the part of kindergarten sponsors coincided with a host of related developments in the latter part of the century. Popular journals flourished, clubs for child study and parental education were formed, and eventually national associations were established, such as the Child Study Association of America (Wishy, 1968). In addition, professional associations also devoted attention to such subjects as the family and child rearing (Calhoun, [1919] 1960, 3, p. 8).

Philanthropic advocates of kindergartens must have recognized the limits of charitable funds, for they soon sought to have kindergartens incorporated within public schools. Seeking permission to use empty schoolrooms served as the "opening wedge" (Whipple, 1929, p. 248). Of course, this contrivance still required private funds for salaries and other operating expenses. Then, in 1873, the advocates' efforts succeeded in gaining establishment of the first public school kindergarten, in St. Louis. Support in this achievement came from W. T. Harris, also an associate of the Concord School and, not unimportant, a one-time United States Commissioner of Education (Forest, 1930, p. 322). Demonstration of a kindergarten program at the Centennial Exhibition in Philadelphia in 1876 also gave impetus to the spread of this type of preschool program. These developments and the efforts of advocates such as Elizabeth Peabody are credited with having given momentum to the kindergarten movement in the United States.

The movement advanced considerably. By 1898, forty years after the first kindergarten had opened, there were about

2,900 such programs throughout the nation with 144,000 children enrolled (see Appendix, Table 5). Over half of these children attended privately sponsored kindergartens; less than half were in public programs. For the kindergarten movement, the year 1900 marked an auspicious turning point. Not only had enrollments increased by more than 50 percent over the preceding two years, but public sponsorship overtook philanthropy. Since the turn of the century, a large majority of kindergarten children have attended programs under state auspices (see Appendix, Table 6).

The relatively rapid growth of this type of preschool program had been achieved, however, at a cost of some substance. By 1888, criticism had developed of the rigidities in the Froebel programs. Included were criticisms of features such as the fixed repertoire of playthings and their use within a rigidly prescribed sequence. Adherents warned that " 'the spirit of Froebel's utterances may be smothered beneath the letter of his methods' " (cited in Wishy, 1968, p. 141). Under the influence of adult interests and concerns, the warning continued, the programs were developing in an unnatural and unhealthy direction.

Dissatisfaction with Froebelian kindergartens, which had become stilted and rigidified, contributed to the development of a different theory of and curriculum for preschool education. This was stimulated by two American educators, Anna Bryan and Patty S. Hill, who established the private "progressive" nursery and kindergarten around 1888 (Forest, 1930, p. 322). Their ideas won support from the psychologist G. Stanley Hall and the philosopher John Dewey. Out of the work of this group developed what has since been called the *progressive education movement*. As we shall see later, during the twentieth century that movement influenced both the kindergarten and a newer form of preschool program, the nursery school (and, eventually, elementary and secondary education in general).

Compared to the kindergarten, day nurseries experienced a much slower increase in the last part of the nineteenth century. By 1892, only 90 "regularly organized" nurseries were reported (see Appendix, Table 1). A model day nursery exhibited at the World's Fair in Chicago, in 1893, is credited with having stimulated expansion of such programs (White House Conference, 1930a, p. 9). Whether or not that credit is deserved, by 1897, 175 "regularly organized nurseries were listed." The lists apparently included formally organized, charitable programs, and, it can be assumed with virtual certainty, excluded proprietary programs (Whipple, 1929, p. 92).

The slow but continued influx of married women into the labor force circumstantially suggests the possible growth of the proprietary nursery sector at the end of the century. Other, indirect evidence of the continued presence of commercial nurseries may be found: abuses by proprietary day nurseries, especially those connected with "baby farms,"[6] and the ensuing notoriety toward the end of the century resulted in the first municipal and state regulation of day care (Tyson, 1930, p. 15).

Public regulation paralleled the promulgation of day nursery standards. Proposing, setting and advocating adoption of such standards were among the self-assigned functions performed by local and regional associations of day nurseries. These organizations also convened conferences: The first such was held in New York City in 1892, and another in Boston in 1897. Formation of the National Federation of Day Nurseries followed, in 1898.

These events at the end of the century reflected and were part of broader historic developments. Formation of organizational associations for standard setting, self-regulation, and coordination of day care resembled the orientation toward rationality and systemization of the charity organization movement (Leiby, 1971, p. 1466). Proliferation of the settlement houses contributed to the expansion of and—as we shall describe later—changes in day nurseries. Aside from the objective conditions that the social settlements addressed, such as the poverty and social disorder of the immigrant-laden urban slums, the settlements represented a "subjective necessity" (Jane Addams' phrase). The settlements "gave form to the interests of a college-trained elite," young ladies such as Addams who rejected the "patronizing and undemocratic role" of the friendly visitor in favor of "a dignified and paid career" (Leiby, 1971, p. 1470). No doubt this changed orientation also reflected the advance of the women's suffrage movement. But, above all, these various events, trends and movements flowed into the widening stream of social reform that formed, in the 1890s, the period that Commager called "the great watershed" in American history.

During this decade, the "reform Darwinists," as Eric Goldman referred to the liberals then in American sociology, raised the banner of education in the name of social reform. Lester Ward spoke of education in such terms as "the mainspring of progress," the "piston of civilization," and the "great panacea" for all social problems (Cremin, 1964). Albion Small, Dewey's colleague at Chicago, declared education to be the most radical means of social reform known to sociology. He urged on education the task of informing the next generation of the major realities of the day—those of interdependence, cooperation, and progress. However, the "conservative Darwinists" in sociology, such as William Graham Sumner, did not agree with the meliorative uses of education. Rather, they viewed the spread of public education as leading to a deterioration of parental responsibility. Although the conservative view generally prevailed in regard to the education of very young children, the reformers' ideas had important bearing for the relatively few preschool programs that did develop.

The Early Twentieth Century and World War I

The ideas of the reform Darwinists were closely embraced by the early leaders of progressive education, Jane Addams and John Dewey. Dewey's ideas proved to be truly seminal and unquestionably made him *the* theorist of the progressive education movement.[7] As an introduction, it may be said that Dewey essentially held the Rousseauian and Froebelian point of view in education. This is not to say that Dewey was uncritical of Froebel, especially of the later interpretations made of his ideas.

Dewey posited as the aim of education "development of a spirit of social cooperation and community life." The objective from the standpoint of the individual child was stated in phrases reflecting the naturalist philosophers: "growth of the

child in the direction of social capacity and service," and "fullness of realization of his budding powers" ([1900] 1956b, pp.
16, 91-92, 119).

To that naturalist, Froebelian aim, Dewey fused a social
reform goal reflecting conditions in industrial America at the
beginning of the twentieth century. For Dewey, the grievous
shortcoming of industrial work was its meaninglessness. "How
many of the employed are today mere appendages to the ma-
chines which they operate! . . . it is certainly due in large part to
the fact that the worker has had no opportunity to develop his
imagination and his sympathetic insight as to the social and scientific values found in his work" (Dewey, [1900] 1956b, p.
24). By pointing to the meaninglessness of industrial work,
Dewey revealed his idealist analysis of the problem, but it also
implied the solution. Education was seen as the process by
which the worker's consciousness could be enlarged, so that
"his activity shall have meaning to himself" (Dewey [1900],
1956b, p. 23). Through education, the growing child and ado-
lescent would gain a scientific and humane understanding of the
industrial world and the meaning of work. In short, Dewey projected as a goal of progressive education the image of an ideal
personality: the industrial worker as applied scientist.

In passing, Dewey's idealistic analysis also may be noted
in the view he held of work in the earlier agrarian period
([1900] 1956b, p. 11). But his idealism shows even more in his
belief that "the genuine community standard of value" is the
"quality of work done" ([1900] 1956b, p. 16). That belief
stands in sharp contrast to another vision of contemporary community standards, published in 1899, namely Veblen's *Theory
of the Leisure Class.*

Dewey believed that his educational aims could not be
achieved within the home. The home did not expose the child
to sufficient numbers of adults nor to as many children as is
necessary for the "freest and richest social life" (Dewey
[1900], 1956b, p. 36). Moreover, the main activities and relationships within the home did not have as their principal aim,
nor were selected for, facilitating the growth of the child. What
the child got out of these activities was "incidental." But within

the school, the ideal school—such as the University of Chicago Elementary School—"the life of the child becomes the all-controlling aim" (Dewey, [1900] 1956b, p. 36).

Dewey's educational focus clearly rested on another principle that he acknowledged had derived from Froebel: "the primary root of all educative activity is in the instinctive, impulsive attitudes and activities of the child, and not in the presentation and application of external material, whether through the ideas of others or through the senses . . . accordingly, numberless spontaneous activities of children, play, games, mimic efforts, even the apparently meaningless motions of infants—exhibitions previously ignored as trivial, futile, or even condemned as positively evil—are capable of educational use; nay, are the foundation stones of educational method" (Dewey, [1900] 1956b, p. 117). The task of education is thus to give direction to the child's impulsive expressions.

So far, then, Dewey's position consisted of a set of philosophic aims and principles to be achieved through an educational process. The home could not accommodate that process. For the progressive educators, neither could the traditional schools, so they also set out to change those schools. Dewey identified the major defect in the "old education" and pointed to the radical meaning of the new education: "the center of gravity is outside the child. It is in the teacher, the textbook, anywhere and everywhere you please except in the immediate instincts and activities of the child himself. . . . Now the change which is coming into our education is the shifting of the center of gravity. It is a change, a revolution, not unlike that introduced by Copernicus when the astronomical center shifted from the earth to the sun. In this case, the child becomes the sun about which the appliances of education revolve; he is the center about which they are organized" (Dewey, [1900] 1956b, p. 34).

Dewey advocated that education be not only child centered, but also future oriented. He compared the educational condition in traditionalist "primitive" societies with that of modern industrialized societies. The traditionalist societies required bringing up the young in conformity with the customs of the elders. Not so in progressive societies, where "life customs" are constantly in flux. Such societies, therefore, " 'endeavor to shape the experiences of the young so that instead of reproducing current habits, better habits shall be formed and thus the future adult society be an improvement on their own' " (cited in Lasch, 1967, p. 88).

Doubtlessly Dewey realized that a fervent belief and faith in those principles was insufficient to achieve a revolutionary redirection of education. Teachers sharing that belief, and practical educational devices, techniques, and procedures would be required. Development of those educational means within a school defined in his perspective was the exact aim of the experimental school he directed. Two educational techniques illustrate Dewey's approach to achieving the aims of progressive education.

One technique has already been implied. Dewey saw clearly the educational implications of play that Froebel had earlier recognized. The importance of play was not in its external manifestation. By *play*, Dewey meant "the psychological attitude of the child," "the free play, the interplay of all the child's powers, thoughts and physical movements in embodying, in a satisfactory form, his own images and interests." Play also means, negatively, freedom from adult responsibilities. "Positively, it means that the supreme end of the child is fulness of growth" (Dewey, [1900] 1956b, pp. 118-119). It may be noted that by emphasizing the internal or psychological nature of play, Dewey was able to identify the error into which the followers of Froebel had fallen. That error was the identification of play with external performance, either in a fixed sequence of activities or with a specified collection of toys.

Dewey expanded on another Froebelian pedagogical technique, called *occupations*. He defined *occupation* as "a mode of activity on the part of the child which reproduces, or runs parallel to, some form of work carried on in social life" (Dewey, [1900] 1956b, p. 132). For example, the children at the Chicago experimental school worked at a year-long textile project. They started with raw cotton and wool and freed the fibers from the cotton seed. The children built a wool-carding frame and devised a simple spinning process (a pierced stone twirling through the fibers). From this, they learned the limitations of early devices and gained an appreciation of the necessity for and advantages of subsequent inventions. Later phases of the project involved weaving cloth and dealt with geographic aspects of cultivating the raw materials, development of the textile industry and the distributive system for the finished products, and so on. Thus, occupations in the school, for Dewey, were not merely practical activities or "modes of routine employment" for gaining technical skills, but were "active centers of scientific insight into natural materials and processes, points of departure whence children shall be led out into a realization of the historic development of man" (Dewey, [1900] 1956b, p. 19).

Two categories of information pertinent here, auspices and clientele, essentially were not discussed by Dewey. The University of Chicago sponsored the school he directed. Presumably children from the university community, that is, mainly middle-class children, attended. If so, progressive education theory, which sought to develop a "cooperative commonwealth" of industrial workers as applied scientists, certainly did not mandate such a social composition. Also, Dewey's writings imply that progressive education theory applied universally to all children.

Furthermore, that Dewey agreed the theory applied to lower-class children may be surmised from his relations with the nearby settlement house, Hull House, and its founder, Jane Addams. She shared Dewey's hopeful vision of the new education as well as his critical assessment of the old (Cremin, 1964, p. 62; Lasch, 1967, pp. 12-13). The similarity of views held by the philosopher and by the settlement house worker is attributed to their close association at Hull House. Jane Dewey, named after Addams, wrote of Addams' deep influence on her father's educational aims (Cremin, 1964, p. 63). Thus Addams may have been the godmother of progressive education.

She also had faith in the naturalist assumption of the inherent sociability of the "inner self," in the new educational aims, and in Dewey's fascinating vision of humanizing industrial work. Addams added several grandiose touches, as well as considerations reflecting closer proximity to the world of work. Humanizing the industrial *system* was her educational objective. (Properly educating workers, the settlement house worker realized, was insufficient; workers educated in socially conscious schools would also need to be associated in labor unions in order to invert the demeaning and dehumanizing subordination of man to machine.) By embracing progressive education and establishing a preschool program at Hull House, Addams, who was widely known, lent encouragement to such programs.

Because the pertinence of developments in progressive education for the federal preschool policy enactments in the mid-1960s will be elaborated on in the next chapter, here mention need only be made of a few points important for the historical chronology. Even at the outset, critics objected to various elements of progressive education theory. Most critics questioned whether the child in a progressive school gained the knowledge that adults believed desirable. Dewey's attack on the older education for identifying learning with "exclusively intellectual pursuits," his emphasis on the social and artistic capacities of the child, and stress on "learning by doing" fed suspicions that progressive education disparaged knowledge. Given these divergent educational orientations, it should not be surprising that Dewey recognized the need for continuity between (the progressive) kindergarten and the elementary grades (Dewey, [1900] 1956b, p. 131).

Neither the early nor the later criticism of the progressive education movement should blind our recognition of its long-term influence. It failed to achieve the "cooperative commonwealth" of "humanized industry," but its child-centered educational ideas and ideals were widely diffused. For example, progressive education popularized the naturalist tenet of helping the child to the full realization of his inherent capacities. Those ideas dominated preschool theory and curriculum development in this country for at least sixty years, perhaps still dominate, and were widely incorporated into the schools generally (Cremin, 1964, p. 349). Moreover, by contributing a theory, an intellectual base, to preschool education, it furthered the professionalization and advance of early childhood education, especially of nursery schools.

While the progressive education movement was gathering momentum, conditions affecting poor children were creating wide concern. Those concerns were to lead to another movement that later produced indirect, but weighty consequences for preschool programs, especially the day nurseries. The focus of concern were the large numbers of children of the poor being placed in institutions. Even at the start of the twentieth century, few cities had any form of "outdoor relief," that is, public financial assistance outside an institution. Poverty-ridden parents—inadequately paid or disabled fathers, deserted or divorced or widowed mothers—faced the alternative of institutionalizing their children or seeing them starve. Increasing numbers of parents chose the former, at public expense. The Bureau of the Census reported almost 93,000 children throughout the United States in orphan asylums on December 31, 1904, and estimated another 50,000 dependent children in what today are called *foster homes* (Stretch, 1970, p. 367). In New York City alone, in 1899, 15,000 children had to be cared for, at a cost to the public of $1,500,000.

Increasing the number of day nurseries, to facilitate employment of mothers of such children, was recommended by "relief agencies . . . as a more humane and less costly method of mitigating these evils" of institutionalizing poor children (Whipple, 1929, p. 92). Day care, then, was being advocated as a means of reducing the costs of "indoor" relief, that is, residential care. Such advocacy may have accounted for a great increase in day nurseries. In the decade from 1905 to 1915, the number of such programs "nearly doubled" (White House Conference, 1930a, p. 9). But, as shall be seen shortly, an alternative policy to day care was adopted to ameliorate the problems of dependent children.

A related problem also troubled philanthropists, social workers, and other child welfare allies. Not only did the practice of institutionalization result in increased taxes. Too often, proprietary child-caring agencies, including profit-seeking day-care programs, provided minimal care or even abused the children. Public expense, parental anguish resulting from the tearing apart of poor families, and reports of child abuse stirred humanitarian feeling. These reasons led President Theodore Roosevelt to convene a meeting at the White House in 1909 to discuss the care of dependent children. That conference—the first White House Conference on Children—declared in its first resolution, " 'Home life is the highest and finest product of civilization. . . . [unfortunate children of worthy parents] should as a rule be kept with their parents, [with] aid being given as may be necessary to maintain suitable homes for the rearing of the children. . . . Except in unusual circumstances, the home should not be broken up for reasons of poverty, but only for reasons of inefficiency or immorality' " (cited in Bremner, 1971, p. 365). In this resolution, the earlier religious sanctification of the family had become secularized, but otherwise the glorification of that institution continued. Now it informed public policy, which apparently took as its goal to protect and safeguard family life.

The conference did not recommend a program of federal aid, but called for community programs of aid for dependent children in their own homes, " 'preferably in the form of private charity rather than . . . public relief' " (cited in Bremner, 1971, p. 365). This preference reflected the social philosophy of the more traditional "philanthropists," in contrast to the stance taken by the "economists"; reformers, such as Addams, and adherents of the Progressive movement who "abandoned dogmatic laissez-faire to advocate positive state action" (Leiby, 1971, p. 1465). Over the bitter opposition of social service traditionalists, especially in private agencies, the reformers succeeded in advancing passage of mothers' pension laws.

Once enacted in 1911, mothers' aid legislation spread rapidly. Within a decade after passage of the 1911 law, forty states made similar provision, generally for widows and their families. In many states, wives and children of permanently incapacitated, insane, or imprisoned men also were eligible. The potential earning capacity of the mother also was considered in determining eligibility; unskilled or semiskilled mothers were likely to be granted aid, but not skilled mothers, who, if employed, could earn a good wage or salary. A class distinction, in other words, was built into the mothers' pension programs.

The provision of mothers' aid seriously affected day-care programs and policies. Admissions policies changed significantly: Day nurseries, which were established originally to care for the children of widows, experienced a noticeable decrease in the proportion of such applicants as the pension programs spread. Moreover, as a result the nurseries began accepting the child whose parents both worked. Mothers' aid caused a major shift in the social purpose to be served by day nurseries.

In addition, the development of mothers' aid profoundly altered the way in which day care was perceived. For eligible mothers of young children, mothers' aid provided a choice: to not work and receive such aid, to work for low wages, or some combination of both. In providing alternative child care for eligible mothers who worked instead of taking a mother's pension, day nurseries were viewed as a substitute for the new form of public relief. Day care continued to be funded by philanthropic donations. But its sponsors began to define their programs as a substitute for or even a form of relief. By becoming attached to the relief system day care came to share the stigma of that system. This produced lasting effects on day-care programs and public policy in subsequent epochs. For these reasons, the decade of mothers' pension programs decisively influenced the development of day care. Furthermore, the aid legislation also established the subsidizing of mothers to stay home and rear their children as the predominant public policy in the various states.

Several fragmentary pieces of pertinent information on the World War I period can be reported. Circumstantial evidence strongly suggests the federal government did not entertain aiding or establishing day-care centers for mothers in war production. When the United States entered the war, federal officials believed an ample supply of male workers was available and that women workers were not needed. For example, early in 1918 the Secretary of Labor reportedly said the supply of labor was sufficient for the armed forces and industry; his administration aimed, an authoritative source stated, "to prevent the introduction of women into new occupations as long as men were available" (National Industrial Conference Board, 1918, p. 69). By September of that year, Bernard Baruch, Chairman of the War Industries Board, said more women workers were needed to achieve maximum production of war materials, and, early in November (a week or so before the war ended), the Department of Labor called on women to enter the labor force. Such volatile federal policies and a wartime involvement lasting only eighteen months rendered federal support for wartime day care unlikely.

When the nation entered the war, nearly ten million women (single and married, mothers and childless) already were in the labor force. They made up almost one fourth of the forty million persons gainfully employed at that time. From 1915 to the end of the war, the number of women workers increased by about one million (Hobbs, 1920, pp. 156-157). (We should note in passing that when the war ended, some public speakers reverted to peacetime views. One said, " 'The women have responded with fine patriotism to the appeal to take part in industry during the war. It now becomes their duty to withdraw' " [cited by Van Kleeck, 1920, pp. 151-152].)

It seems reasonable to assume an increased need for day care in general during the war. The demand for maternal employment, however, must have been acute in certain localities, for some industrial day-care centers were established. A professional source states, "there was a threatening increase of this type [of day care]" (Whipple, 1929, p. 89).[8] (Most of the wartime factory centers closed after the war, apparently being too costly to operate in peacetime.) Sectarian day nurseries also may have developed as a reaction to the wartime day-care vacuum. We conjecture that for the most part, however, whatever day-care demand arose during the war probably was filled to the largest extent by the sector of day care most responsive to the marketplace, the proprietary programs. Both wartime pressures and consequences of compulsory *school* attendance reportedly led the Los Angeles Board of Education in 1917 to establish day nurseries. These were the first public day-care centers in the nation. (Enforcement of the compulsory school attendance law in 1910 resulted in immigrant school-age children leaving infant siblings unprotected at home or bringing the tots to school and leaving them in offices and corridors. So the Board of Education furnished the room for a nursery with

Parent Teachers Association (PTA) members serving as staff. By 1917, the Board of Education undertook full operational responsibility. About ten years later, when the board operated twenty nurseries enrolling over 1,400 children monthly, the program goals were listed as: Americanization of immigrant infants and mothers; and preventing school absence of older children with infant siblings. Educators criticized the program as one that only served the "preschool" children in an instrumental way and for having presumed to do the work of private charity or public welfare [see Whipple, 1929, p. 90].)

Between World Wars

Although it is somewhat arbitrary, the 1920s may be regarded as the beginning of the modern preschool period. The social, philosophic, and programatic (curricular) bases had been shaped earlier. Subsequent preschool development built on the earlier base and sometimes reshaped it, but in considerable part the issues that were to concern later policy makers already were becoming visible.

The history from this period forward departs from the past for another reason. Immeasurably more documentation came into being; books and booklets on many aspects of preschool education began to appear, as well as studies and surveys of existing programs. For example, in 1923 the federal government conducted an institutional census covering day nurseries (White House Conference, 1930a, p. 22). (Characteristically for the preschool field, proprietary programs were not counted.)

Such activities reflected the enlarging professionalization of preschool work as well as popular interest. The child and child nurture began to receive ever wider recognition as appropriate subjects for study and education. Research centers on child development and on "child welfare" were established. Beginning in 1923, the Laura Spelman Rockefeller Memorial Fund gave a powerful impetus to the establishment of research centers to study child development at universities, by providing grants for that purpose (Alschuler, 1942, p. 7).

.Early in the twentieth century, but especially after 1920,

programs were also established for the purpose of training teachers in early childhood education. Sometimes both functions, research and teacher training, would be conducted within a single institution that had developed a preschool program. National scholarships for training researchers and instructors of child development, awarded by the National Research Council beginning in the mid-1920s, provided additional support and incentive for such activities. The seven institutions at which those scholarships were then available (for example, Columbia University, State University of Iowa, the Merrill-Palmer School, and Yale University) all conducted a preschool laboratory to provide research opportunities (Whipple, 1929, pp. 285-296).

Other evidence of the pursuit of research objectives through preschool programs is provided by fourteen nursery school profiles, a sample of eighty-five surveyed in 1929; a majority of the programs described were engaged in research, either because they had been established to conduct research or, as a result of affiliation with nearby research and training institutions. (The sample of fourteen purportedly is representative of the total of eighty-five known schools with a "trained nursery-school teacher in charge." Day nurseries were explicitly excluded from the survey. Most likely, proprietary nursery schools were not even considered for possible inclusion [see Whipple, 1929, pp. 137-235].) Another measure of the extent to which research was pursued by preschool programs is provided by data on nursery schools under the auspices of institutions of higher education. In 1929, a different (enumerative) survey reported approximately fifty-six laboratory nursery schools, constituting over one fourth of the known "nursery" schools.[9] (See Table 1 on the following page, and Appendix, Table 4. Again, we must mention the nondistinctiveness of program terms.)

Some of the research centers did not engage in training of nursery school teachers. Others, such as the Merrill-Palmer School, performed both functions. In 1929, thirteen centers for the training of nursery school teachers had been identified. Whether on an intramural or extramural basis, all of these teaching centers provided practical experience in child care within

Table 1. Preschool Programs in the United States by Auspices and Type, 1929 (in Percent)

Auspices	Total	Type				
		Day Nursery	Relief Nursery School	Nursery School	Nursery School and Kindergarten	Kindergarten[a]
All Auspices	100.0[b] (N = 1236)	100.0 (516)	100.0 (60)	100.0 (169)	100.0 (114)	100.0 (377)
Philanthropic						
Sectarian	14.9	20.5	20.0	5.9	3.5	13.8
Nonsectarian	20.8	30.4	41.6	11.2	4.4	13.5
Proprietary						
Individual	37.9	39.5	28.3	49.1	26.3	35.4
Private School	12.4	–	–	–	53.5	24.7
Industrial	1.9	2.5	1.7	–	0.8	2.4
College/University	7.6	0.2	8.3	30.2	7.9	7.5
Public	3.4	5.4	–	2.9	1.8	2.1
Miscellaneous	1.1	1.4	–	0.6	1.6	0.9

[a] Survey purported to exclude public kindergartens.
[b] Figures may not add to 100.0, because of rounding.

Source: Adapted from White House Conference (1930b, p. 158).

preschool programs for their teachers in training (Whipple, 1929, pp. 421-422). (Most of these teacher training centers were conducted under private auspices or as units of home economics departments of state colleges and universities. Teacher colleges had not as yet begun to provide training in early childhood education. [See Henry, 1947, p. 432].)

Some results of the programs of research and teacher training in child development may be mentioned, even if several are somewhat self-evident. First, the agencies of social parenthood could at last support the claim implicit in the earlier assessment of parents as inexpert at the nurture of very young children. That claim rested on the assumption that other (nonparental) experts existed. Yet, for almost a century after the first infant schools—that is, until the 1920s—expertise on early child nurture was more a claim staked out than a professionally developed competence. Second, the researchers and teachers trained at the research and training centers provided knowledge, skills, and the man- and womanpower that served as further stimuli for the development of preschool programs. This probably accounts in part for increases of most types of programs in the 1920s, especially nursery schools. However, institutions for training early childhood educators had proliferated and grown to the extent that soon they were turning out more teachers than the existing number of nursery schools could employ (Beer, 1938, p. 47). This overproduction had interesting consequences, as we shall see shortly.

Table 1 presents data on all auspices of the nursery schools enumerated in 1929. By then, proprietary programs in the several nursery school categories held a plurality or even majority position. Philanthropic organizations—that is, social agencies and church groups—did not sponsor nursery schools to as large an extent as colleges or proprietors, although their charitable purpose would appear to explain a heavier involvement in "relief nursery schools"; still, the existence of nursery schools under philanthropic auspices merits notice.

The sample survey mentioned earlier reveals some surprising findings on nursery school clientele. Almost one half of the sample (six out of fourteen programs) reported clientele *pri-*

marily of low-income, immigrant families, including numerous one-parent families (Whipple, 1929, pp. 137-228). Alschuler, who directed one of the schools in the 1929 sample and who later was Chairman of the National Commission for Young Children, provided some confirmation in her report, perhaps hyperbolic, that *all* the "experimental" nursery school programs in the 1920s "cared for children from more as well as less privileged homes" (1942, p. 6). (A respondent interviewed for this study, who founded and directed one of the earliest nursery schools in the United States, reported the program was designed primarily for children from poor families. However, middle-class black families dwelling in the slum area where the school was located applied for nursery schooling for their children in such large numbers that a quota of 50:50 was established as a "quiet policy.") Consistent with such clientele, more than half the sampled nursery schools mention having social workers on the staff or as cooperating professionals, cooperative arrangements with social agencies, or home visiting by staff. Staff visited the homes either for purposes concerning the health and welfare needs of the parents, or for parental education. The editor of the nursery school survey writes proudly of the "admirable work done in parental education," adding that "through the influence of the nursery school parental responsibility has been increased rather than lessened" (Whipple, 1929, pp. 233-234). In a consistent vein, the author of a chapter on parent education in *The Twenty-Eighth Yearbook* noted that "Directors of nursery schools and others interested in the nursery school movement maintain that the organization of a nursery school is not justifiable unless accompanied by a program for the education of the parents of the children enrolled in the school" (Whipple, 1929, p. 313). The heavy emphasis on parental education as an indispensable function of preschool programs led another specialist later to conclude that such forms of early childhood education as the nursery school and kindergarten have been formed "primarily as a device for parent education" (Anderson, 1947, p. 98). One may quarrel with that as the priority in functions performed by preschool programs, yet the indications are indisputable that parent education has been a significant aim of early childhood education programs. At least this conclusion is warranted on the basis of available evidence up to the 1930s.

Data from the 1929 surveys contain somewhat unexpected findings on the length of the daily schedule observed by nursery schools. Of the eighty-five nursery schools surveyed for *The Twenty-Eighth Yearbook*, 55 percent operated full-day rather than half-day programs. (Whipple, 1929, pp. 238-241). The enumerative survey in 1929 preparatory to the 1930 White House Conference on Children reported full-day programs for 35 percent of the nursery schools; 67 percent of the relief nursery schools maintained full-day schedules (White House Conference, 1930b, pp. 157-158). Still another survey, in 1932, found 53 percent of the nursery schools operating for five or more hours per day (Forest, 1930, p. 323).

Information on the program content was obtained, in self-described profiles, on the nursery schools in the 1929 sample survey. The detailed descriptions evidence extensive educational content in these relatively new nursery schools (less than ten years old). The profiles clearly reveal the imprint of progressive education, one facet of which is noteworthy. All but one of the fourteen profiles describe their educational emphases in Deweyan terms: Seven explicitly write of habit training, while the other six programs are described in terms of social development, character development, or providing an environment for the optimal development of the child (Whipple, 1929, pp. 137-235). Thus, a little more than one decade after Dewey published his suggestion that habit training be addressed to an emergent future, perhaps as many as one half of the extant nursery schools were trying to follow his advice. However, it appears that Dewey's ideas were becoming translated too mechanically, for the need was seen (by the editor of the survey report) to warn against an undue "emphasis on routine habit-building" (Whipple, 1929, p. 230).

By the late 1920s, kindergartens had come to share with nursery schools this progressive education emphasis on the social capacity of the child, this aim to nurture socially adjusted personalities. Also during this decade, the kindergartens, with half a century head start over the nursery schools and nourished by public sponsorship, that is, by state and local tax funds, continued to expand. By the year 1929 to 1930, the ratio of children in kindergartens to those in nursery schools was about 150:1 (778,000 to 4,900). With understandable pride, progressive educators proclaimed in 1929 that kindergartens had become an integral component of the school system. More likely than not, kindergartens were part of the public school systems in cities with a population over 30,000. Still, in the early 1920s only about 27 percent of the nation's four- and five-year-old children were in kindergartens.

In part, the greater expansion of kindergartens compared to nursery schools may be due to considerations of cost. An early report (1921) in New York City found per pupil costs of an experimental, research-oriented nursery school to be from four to six times greater than the unit cost in the public kindergarten. However, there were problems associated with the spread of kindergarten incorporation into public schools. One effect of that incorporation, noted in 1929, was that the public kindergarten classes became "much too large and it became impossible to give children the amount of individual attention which they had received under earlier [philanthropic] conditions." The report goes on to express regret over another effect: "little or no opportunity to carry out the welfare work" of the earlier kindergarten period (Whipple, 1929, p. 249).

We turn now to the day nurseries in the 1920s and will first present information on program sponsorship. The available statistics indicate a decrease in day nurseries by about one sixth during the 1920s, but it is not known whether changes had occurred in program sponsorship. For the first time, in 1929, national data on auspices appear in the literature. Not surprisingly, given the philanthropic impetus to (if not initiation of) day nurseries, it is evident from Table 1 that such sponsors occupy the commanding position (51 percent of all known programs). Those sponsors, however, apparently had reason to worry about their ability to hold that position. The conduct of local studies of day-care costs indicates a heightened consciousness of costs and suggests financial worries (White House Con-

ference, 1930a). (In undertaking cost studies, the early local
associations of day nurseries set a research fashion for community funding groups that continues to the present). Even philanthropic day nursery care, provided it met adequate standards,
became widely understood to be an expensive service.

In acknowledging the preeminence of charitable day care
in 1929, we must not fail to note that the proprietary sector
held a major place (42 percent). Little else about this sector is
reported, except for the existence of about twelve industrial
day-care programs.[10] One of these was established by a men's
clothing factory in the South around 1920. It was reportedly
started "when management discovered that many of its employees' children were sleeping on rag piles" in the factory, and
that day care was unavailable. This center remained in operation
until 1970 (U.S. Department of Labor, 1971, p. 29).

Program auspices carry an implication beyond their mani-
fest meaning. They may convey implications about the social
position of the clientele. The information on this period of history, sparse as it may be, may help to provide a factual base to
our chronology and to assess later the accuracy of such implications.

During the 1920s, the indirect effect of the mothers' aid
programs on day care continued and broadened. In the last half
of the decade, "a very definite and growing increase" (White
House Conference, 1930a, p. 24) was noted in day nurseries of
children with both parents in the home, the mother working because the father was unemployed, only seasonally employed, or
employed at an inadequate wage; and of children whose parents
were separated or divorced. Families with children in day nurseries were characterized as not functioning "normally." Day-
care eligibility was now defined essentially as for "the economically handicapped family" (White House Conference, 1930a, p.
47).

These shifts in clientele and in how they were characterized .contributed to the transformation of the philanthropic
day nursery from an enterprise of private charity to a private
form of relief. In an era when day care was viewed as a functional substitute for the new form of public relief, the mother's

pension, the lowly paid mother who could not afford the full cost of day care was seen also as receiving relief: "The nursery, as an agency supported by the community, should either charge [the mother] what it costs to give that service to her children or look upon the sum by which the fee fails to meet it as definite financial relief. [The mother] should . . . recognize that the subsidy is a form of cash relief" (White House Conference, 1930a, p. 44). Thus an authoritative association of experts wrote, "The day nursery is primarily a relief institution" (Whipple, 1929, p. 104).

This conception coexisted with knowledge that middle-class mothers who were entering the labor force in the first third of the twentieth century were approaching the philanthropic nurseries for child care. "The secretary of the National Federation of Day Nurseries reports . . . numerous requests for nursery care for the children of business and professional women who were able and willing to pay the full cost for such service. Whether this will result in the establishment of [high standard proprietary day nurseries] or whether the nursery school and the progressive private school will take its place is a matter which comparative convenience and expense will probably determine" (Whipple, 1929, p. 88). The statement is curious. It assumes the National Federation of Day Nurseries either should not or could not accommodate middle-class mothers. This may reflect a preconception that charitable programs should be used exclusively for impoverished families, even if middle-class clients were willing to pay their way. Perhaps it indicates a belief that the philanthropic day nurseries could not provide what the other types of programs had to offer. Or it may reflect the tension between the conception of the day nursery as a relief institution and "a new type of need . . . of nursery service for the children of working mothers . . . able and prepared to meet more nearly the cost of that service" (White House Conference, 1930a, p. 47).

In other words, shifts and strains had developed between, on the one hand, the conception of the day nursery as a relief agency and of clientele deemed appropriate to that conception, and on the other, desires of a middle-class clientele for nursery

care. No doubt concerns about the fiscal limitations of philanthropy, high costs of day care, and payment of fees representing
less than full costs, especially by families with two wage earners,
contributed to a wish for clients who could pay full fees. This
wish, however, was not matched by an expectation that such
clients would indeed end up using the day nurseries. But the
extent of attitudinal stirrings, as the 1930s began, may be
sensed by juxtaposing to the conceptions and wishes cited a
view novel to *day-care* professionals: "If the grouping of little
children for a few hours each day for educational activities and
for habit-training through nursery schools is found to be desirable in itself, then this service should be extended on behalf of
children generally, regardless of the economic status of their
families" (White House Conference, 1930a, p. 47).

If some middle-class and other mothers able to pay fully
sought to arrange for day nursery care with sectarian and nonsectarian social agencies, others apparently did not. Some un-
impoverished mothers avoided the philanthropic day-care program, one document notes, in the belief it carried "the taint of
charity or because they infer that [such] nursery service, being
cheap, must be inferior" (White House Conference, 1930a, p.
44). Still other affluent women or families with adequate income may have found social agency staff less "tactful" than
what fee-paying customers expected (Beer, 1938, p. 215).
Those who avoided the charitable nursery or felt repelled by the
staff may have patronized proprietary programs. Unfortunately,
data do not exist on the social class composition of the families
paying for proprietary nursery care. We surmise that the commercial day-care centers were less homogeneous as to the class
composition of their clientele than the philanthropic programs.
Further, the fee-paying basis of attendance suggests the proprietary customers would rank higher on a scale of socioeconomic
status than the beneficiaries of private charity.

The changes in day nursery clientele and client expectations suggest a period of transition or even a potential turning
point. Developments pertaining to day nursery staff more clearly point to a time of change. Career-seeking professionals, it
may be recalled, had begun to enter the day nurseries, in part

replacing the philanthropic ladies toward the end of the nineteenth century. That trend advanced during the early twentieth
century, and accelerated during the 1920s.

Partial replacement of volunteers with paid staff could be
expected to result in friction. Such staff, despite shared concerns for the children and program, have vitally different interests. Usually volunteers work intermittently, while paid staff—
especially full-time—work regularly. The latter would understandably resent the volunteer who does not show up at the
scheduled time: "It never enters her head that she is incon-
veniencing the Day Nursery" (Beer, 1938, p. 115). Volunteers,
by definition not subject to the discipline and sanctions of paid
work, cannot be as readily ordered about; so they "want to
choose" their tasks by preference rather than by program needs
(Beer, 1938, p. 115).

Very galling, however, were the social attitudes manifested by the twentieth-century successors to the nineteenth-
century charitable ladies: "Untrained young women from the
leisure class . . . turn to voluntary service as a stop-gap between
social events [intrigued] because there is a certain glamour in
serving poor children [but their] great zeal . . . gradually fades"
(Beer, 1938, p. 112). Patty Smith Hill, a progenitor of progressive education in the nineteenth century, in the introduction to
Beer (1938, pp. 10-11) remarked that Beer, the author, hurls
"strictures with a singular sureness of aim at 'Ladies Bountiful.'
The sentimental and oft disturbing efforts of debutantes and
their ambitious mammas seeking an emotional outlet for their
own starved lives are also bitterly assailed for attempting leadership in a philanthropy for which they are utterly unprepared."
(Both Hill and Beer were middle- or upper-class women who
became professionals in the preschool field. Beer entered the
field via membership on the Board of Trustees of a day nursery,
Hill through college education.)

Trained teachers seeking jobs in day nurseries doubtlessly
seemed preferable to glamour seeking amateurs. Moreover, the
college, university, and other centers for preparing teachers in
early childhood education had blossomed, and those graduates
who could not find nursery school jobs turned to the larger

number of day nurseries for employment. The teachers brought with them educational values, ideas, and techniques that no doubt invigorated their day nurseries. But now staff relations involved different professions rather than just volunteers and paid staff. Differing conceptions of the job, status distinctions, and interprofessional rivalry arose. Teachers, more often than not accustomed through their training to the often shorter nursery school regimen, at first "would not stay all day" at their day nursery jobs. Their training did not prepare them for the child care aspects of day nursery work (such as supervising tooth brushing and toileting) and they considered such "routine duties beneath them." Also, because the program was "mainly custodial" until they had introduced educational content, they "looked down on the day nursery." "Rarely were [they] proud of their association with a social agency" (Beer, 1957, pp. 23, 39).

Probably more injurious to the feelings of staff identified with social service was the educators' bid for leadership. By about the late 1920s or early 1930s, the nursery school teachers made up a majority of the staff in many day nurseries. Their discipline, being newer and more popular, was accorded more prestige. Apparently they were also zealous in trying to extend their professional "doctrine." As a result, from the older social service viewpoint, it appeared that "the Nursery School more or less usurped the whole Day Nursery program" (Beer, 1957, p. 162). The disappointed social worker somewhat exaggerated the teachers' victory—social welfare organizations and staff retain considerable authority and jurisdiction in the day-care field to the present. The victory of the early childhood educators was not only conditional—it was barely visible to the public.

Prior to the influx of the preschool teachers, day nursery programs, even those not motivated by pecuniary motives, such as the philanthropic nurseries, apparently were mainly custodial. Educational ideas and ideals may have been stressed as aims in early National Federation documents, the authoritative yearbook notes. Then it acknowledges that "For a long time the children . . . were given practically no education in the day nursery." Then, reflecting a familiar education orientation, educational omissions are identified: "The children were given little training in specific habit-formation. There was practically no effort to provide experiences which would be educative and enriching. The play materials were meager and ill-suited to constructive child activity" (Whipple, 1929, pp. 98-99).

The earliest educational efforts involved the introduction of Montessori and kindergarten (presumably progressive) practices to the four- and five-year-old children in some day nurseries. Then the increased infusion of educational perspectives into the program content of day nurseries through the teaching staff, and perhaps through the general diffusion of knowledge of early childhood, initiated an important, but limited transition process in day care.

The "more progressive day nurseries," seeking to upgrade their programs, opened "a nursery school within the day nursery" (Whipple, 1929, p. 99). Then a number of those programs underwent a transformation that had nominal, educational and probably social dimensions. To choose one example, the evolution of the Hull House day nursery to the Mary Crane Nursery School, in 1925, may be representative of that process. The name change clarified the conceptual and terminological confusion revealed in the awkward phrase "nursery school within the day nursery." The school's affiliation with the National Kindergarten and Elementary College of Evanston symbolized the central educational focus of the program. On the social level, it probably presaged the upward mobility of its clientele. Some nurseries modified their programs by incorporating preschool educational content without altering their name; for example, the Cleveland Day Nursery and Free Kindergarten Association.

Statistics on the number of transformed and modified nurseries probably do not exist. We believe only a minority of day nurseries underwent the transition during this period of history. Most likely the majority of day nurseries essentially remained custodial programs. Day nurseries as a whole retained the "taint of charity" and the designation as "relief institutions," in spite of the large proprietary sector and some programs with substantial educational emphases. An educational focus, that of progressive education, was adopted more typically by nursery schools, it is widely believed.

A summary of these preschool developments in the 1920s

may be useful. By 1929, about at the start of the Great Depression, the comparison between day nurseries and nursery schools in the professional literature only selectively reflected these developments in the preschool field. Despite differences in goal and program expectations, confusion reigned in the public mind, so the literature states, over the distinction between day nurseries and the nursery schools. Experts offered clarification. They explained that, despite some common features between the program types, their ultimate aims differ. Relief for the economically dependent family is the day nursery's goal, necessitating an important social service component. "A nursery school," on the other hand, "has a definite educational goal limited to the needs of the preschool child and emphasizing the education of his parents in intelligent child guidance" (Whipple, 1929, p. 104; see also Beer, 1938, pp. 43-51). Most probably this relief versus education distinction dates back no further than about 1920. But it had a long and popular future ahead of it: It entered so firmly into the conventional wisdom that for decades it has appeared in public utterance, professional literature, and as we shall see later on, in federal statute and definitions in the 1960s.

Prior to 1933, the federal government had an implied policy on maternal employment. For over a century, it had tacitly acquiesced in the operation of the social and economic forces that resulted in the industrialization of women's work. The old policy of seeming to have no policy changed in 1933. An economic depression with mass unemployment of historic magnitude had created a climate in which many past policies and associated values were discredited. The Works Progress Administration (the WPA, established in 1933 as the Federal Emergency Relief Administration) was enacted to give employment to needy, unemployed workers. According to an authoritative history (Campbell, Bair, and Harvey, 1939, p. 107), apparently without legislative language explicitly authorizing preschool programs, day nurseries and nursery schools were established to create jobs for unemployed teachers and nutritionists, among others. The preschool programs were not designed principally to provide child care for working mothers, but to provide employment for preschool teachers and other personnel. The preschool programs for children served only as a secondary purpose.

Another important feature of the policy was the criterion of admission to these depression-created federal preschool programs. By explicit policy, the WPA program was intended for children from families on state or federal relief or from "similar" low-income families. This criterion is notable for several reasons. It appears to be a continuation of the past conception of day care as a form of relief. Further, it extended that conception to the nursery school. But in a period of mass unemployment and widespread poverty, the impoverished were in the majority. A survey of the WPA nursery schools in the year 1933 to 1934 reported the children as having come " 'from all socioeconomic levels in approximately the same proportions as the general populations with some tendency to come in greater proportions from the slightly skilled and laboring groups' " (cited in Campbell, Bair, and Harvey, 1939, p. 38). A self-image shared by the majority would carry a different meaning than one arising among an impoverished minority.

There was another difference from past day-care programs. Despite the employment *purpose* of the programs, their *content* was clearly defined as education. Purpose and content were fused in the person of the teachers for whom the program was established. The locus of two thirds of the programs within school buildings symbolized the educational focus.

In spite of the explicit program emphasis on education, most of the WPA units operated for a full day, from 8 A.M. to 3 P.M., five days a week, the year round. Insofar as the *program schedule* is concerned, the WPA programs resembled day-care centers. Indeed, the distinction between nursery school and day-care center within the WPA program seems to have been sufficiently blurred as to have created confusion in the program data. During the WPA period, therefore, the differentiation of nursery school as a half-day program and day care as full-day apparently fit even less neatly than in the 1920s.

A wide range of types presents another unexpected feature of the WPA program. Four overlapping types of nursery school programs were to be found: (1) programs conducted by

the WPA as an "integral part of a public school; (2) [those serv-
ing] as observation and training centers attached to universities,
colleges, and normal schools; (3) [programs functioning] as
high school laboratories in connection with courses on child
care and training"; and (4) those conducted by local agencies
but not housed in public schools (Campbell, Bair, and Harvey,
1939, p. 109). Doubling of the campus-based, laboratory nursery schools between 1929 and 1942 may well be attributable
to the WPA (see Appendix, Table 4). During the Great Depression the influence of a national relief employment program, the
WPA, thus extended to programs not usually associated with
relief, but with a middle-class clientele. Perhaps even more surprising were the laboratory nursery programs established in high
schools.

The WPA administrative arrangements departed from traditional federal practice in the fields of child welfare and education. The laws governing federal welfare and education programs required administrative arrangements with counterpart
agencies in the states. Except for about the first two years, the
federal WPA administrators bypassed the federal- and state-level
organizations and dealt directly with those in the localities conducting the programs with federal funds.

Several problems emerged from the WPA preschool program. Not all the women hired as teachers had preschool training or experience. Those who had the requisite training feared
the detrimental effects from untrained nursery teachers. Other
difficulties arose from dealing directly with local project staff
without going through federal and state channels in education
and welfare. Competitiveness arose between the respective agencies, the Children's Bureau and the Office of Education (both of
which had extensive relations with state agencies), and the
WPA. The child welfare and educational agencies partly expressed this competition in statements about the program *purpose*. Three policy conceptions were advocated for the preschool programs. These were: (1) social services to needy
children; (2) primarily educational programs; and (3) a program
to facilitate employment. According to the published record

and witnesses' recollections, the WPA seemed to have distinguished between the prime employment objective and the subsidiary issue of program content as education without jeopardy to the latter.

Not only did the WPA bypass federal counterparts and state officials. The WPA also detoured around the "organized education profession" (Cremin, 1964, p. 323). This led to charges by the National Education Association that the federal government was taking over the school system.

Another consequence of the fiscal and administration arrangements has been suggested. In part, the disinterest by local schools in continuing the nursery schools after the WPA program was terminated may reflect the absence of a vested interest and sense of responsibility for nursery school education (Goodykoontz, Davis, and Gabbard, 1947, pp. 60-61).

Assessment of the WPA program will be combined with that of a later program that apparently inherited the former after World War II broke out, namely the Lanham Act program. However, a quantitative measure of the WPA achievement may be given at this point. The WPA program provided preschool experience to an unprecedented number of American children. During a one-month period in 1937, 40,000 children attended 1,500 WPA nursery schools. After almost one century of miniscule development, preschool programs in the United States were no longer infantile in scope.

World War II

Even before the United States entered World War II, mothers in increasing numbers gained employment in war production. Reports came to the Children's Bureau of "latch-key" children, children left on their own, with a house key on a string around the neck, and of children who were locked in parked cars while their mothers worked (Oettinger, 1962). The bureau convened a national conference of experts in child care in the summer of 1941, after which the federal child welfare authorities attempted to establish as national policy a statement discouraging employment of mothers with young children (information from a respondent* who participated in shaping that policy proposal).

In 1942, after the country entered the war, child care was swept along in the wartime rush of government activities and expenditures. Funds and responsibilities were divided among a handful of agencies with jurisdictional interests in child care and preschool programs: The WPA was allocated $6,000,000 in July 1942 to "reorganize its nursery school program in order to meet the day-care needs of employed mothers" (Kadushin, 1967, p. 304); the Children's Bureau and the Office of Education were assigned to assist states in promoting and coordinating preschool programs. All three agencies were to be coordinated by the Office of Defense, Health, and Welfare Services (ODHWS). (A respondent who had worked in that office, said its climate could be inferred from an acronymic rendition, "hot house.") At the top of this network, policy was set by the War Manpower Commission. This commission altered the proposed policy statement seeking to discourage maternal employment, which child welfare specialists had recommended, and enunciated as federal policy that the decision to work or not should be made by each mother.

Shortly thereafter the WPA was abolished, and the preschool program was continued under revised funding and administrative arrangements. The Community Facilities Act of 1941 (Lanham Act), "concerned primarily with defense housing and public works for defense, was reinterpreted so as to permit the allocation of funds to communities in support of child care facilities and services" (Kadushin, 1967, p. 305). That reinterpretation may have resulted in part from an influential article in the *Washington Post*, by Agnes Meyer, on the effects on children of their mothers' absence while at work on the war effort (Perlis, 1965, p. 83).

With the two aims of stimulating maternal employment in war industries and preventing neglect of children, the Lan-

*The word *respondent*, here and hereafter, refers to a person interviewed for this study.

ham program provided federal funds to the states on a dollar-for-dollar matching basis to establish and expand day-care centers and nursery schools in officially designated, war-impacted areas. An organizational division of labor assigned to the Office of Education responsibility for the development and extension of nursery schools operated by or under the auspices of local schools. The Children's Bureau was given the apparently analogous responsibility for day-care programs run by nonschool agencies. However, the WPA had emphasized education in its preschool program. Furthermore, almost 6,000 new school buildings had been built with its funds and an additional 12,700 had been built by the Public Works Administration (PWA). As a result, 95 percent of the Lanham programs came under educational auspices. Even the bulk of the Lanham day-care centers operated in school facilities.

The record is not clear as to the exact admissions criteria to preschool programs under the Lanham Act. Because the mothers were ostensibly employed, the former WPA requirement of low income simply could not have been continued. Fees were charged, on a sliding scale of family income (Cremin, 1964; Mayer and Kahn, 1965; U.S. Department of Labor, 1971; and Zeitz, 1959).

In quantitative terms alone, the Lanham program was impressive. In two-and-a-half years of operation, $52,000,000 had been allotted to the states. Presumably, then, a total of $104,000,000 of federal and state funds were expended for Lanham preschool programs. By July of 1944, 129,000 children were enrolled in 3,102 Lanham *day-care* centers. A much larger total number of children received care throughout the duration of the Lanham program—between 550,000 and 1,600,000.[11] About 60 percent of the children attended preschool programs. Not included in this fiscal and statistical portrait of the Lanham program are the "notable" efforts by the Farm Security Administration (Department of Agriculture) "in developing day care facilities in rural areas" (Lundberg, 1947, p. 290).

Before proceeding to a qualitative assessment of the WPA-Lanham programs, we will describe briefly another day-care program that received federal wartime aid. Day-care centers for children of employees were established by Curtiss-Wright in Buffalo and by Kaiser in Portland to facilitate their production of planes and ships. These were industrial preschool programs. The available information pertains to two centers in Kaiser shipyards. Federal funds from the U.S. Maritime Commission were provided to construct and equip the centers. The program operated around the clock: "The centers located at the shipyard entrances were open 7 days a week, 24 hours a day, 364 days a year. The day and swing shifts had large enrollments, but the night shift involved small numbers of children" (U.S. Department of Labor, 1971, p. 32). A large staff of trained specialists were employed at each center consisting of a director, teachers, and assistant teachers, nurses, social workers, and nutritionists. The centers also provided an unusual service: "as a result of studies concerning needs of working mothers, a special home food service was inaugurated. While not utilized widely, this service allowed a mother to pick up a take-home dinner from the center kitchens at the end of a work shift" (U.S. Department of Labor, 1971, p. 32).

These industrial centers operated on a large scale. In the first year of operation, 1,000 children were enrolled; an accumulated total of 4,000 children were cared for during the twenty-two months the centers were in operation. (The centers terminated when war ended in September 1945.) Costs exceeded fees by approximately $7 to $8 per child per week. Because the centers were considered a business expense, costs were included in the cost-plus-fixed-fee contractual arrangement with the government. In short, the federal government largely subsidized these industrial centers.

The Kaiser center, and others operating swing and nighttime shifts, received criticism. Location at the job site was also questioned by social workers, who favored neighborhood location because of proximity to the children's homes and avoidance of transportation (respondent; Lundberg, 1942, p. 283). Otherwise, reactions to the Kaiser centers appear to have been very favorable. To some, those centers might signify the possibility of achieving large-scale but quality day care and intimate the high financial cost of that achievement.

The WPA-Lanham programs represent the first federally supported preschool programs in the nation's history. As such, they deserve an evaluation in their own right, as well as for the implications they carry for the history of federal preschool policy. First we will consider several problems that were encountered.

The social work profession and the Children's Bureau were never enthusiastic about day care under WPA and Lanham auspices. They had misgivings about group day care for children under three years of age, but, according to several respondents, failed to convince the WPA to develop family day-care programs for those children. Nor could they overcome their main concern about familial and child-rearing consequences of mothers working and ambivalence about programs—even during a world war—that encouraged such employment. The core of their concern was that "the Federal stimulus to day care would in the long run be destructive of the family and contrary to basic American values" (Mayer and Kahn, 1965, p. 27). The fear of social parenthood was genuine and deeply ingrained. Twenty years after these events, one of the chief federal officials (a respondent) remarked that perhaps the child welfare professionals had erred in "resisting maternal employment," and added quietly, "although, years ago the working day was long."

Bureaucratic competition was perhaps the most divisive problem reported. Competition between experts was tied not merely to jurisdiction, but also to the policy goal and content of the program. Content of the program, it was said by one child welfare official (a respondent), should depend on the purpose of the program, its daily duration, and clientele. A mother who works full-time requires a full-day program for the child, who is made vulnerable by her absence from the home. A social service purpose was implied, yet many of the children were in day-care centers under educational auspices. From this viewpoint, one may conceivably understand the opposition, from a state welfare department responsible for licensing day-care centers, to efforts by those who sought to develop strong educational components in those programs. For their part, public school educators, some of whom were not enthusiastic about nursery schools and cared even less about day care, nonetheless were housing, advising, or supervising such programs. Their training led them to identify the programs as educational in nature. In retrospect, the fact that 95 percent of the programs were under the aegis of educators lends an unreal quality to the doctrinal dispute.

The WPA administrative arrangement of direct relationships between federal officials and local project staff may have set a precedent. It bypassed other related federal- and state-level agencies. By so doing, it may have served as a model in the mid-1960s for how to rapidly develop and expand local programs on a national scale.

Other problems faced by the Lanham program, probably more onerous for day care, stemmed from shortages of the two most critical resources for preschool programs, adequate physical facilities, and trained, experienced staff. Lack of teachers with the usual academic qualifications was acknowledged by the WPA; inservice training, however, was said to have compensated largely for the "preservice" deficits (Campbell, Bair, and Harvey, 1939, p. 107). But for the earlier, large-scale construction of school buildings by the WPA and PWA, the Lanham program could not have expanded to the magnitude it achieved. Nevertheless, according to a preschool expert (respondent), shortages of space and staff in part reflect the precipitous, unplanned nature of both federal programs.

In evaluating the WPA-Lanham programs, one must consider the several goals and their implementation. The evidence suggests the programs were successful in achieving the major goal, employment. Although it is not known what proportion they constituted of the total number of unemployed teachers, in November 1937, 3,200 teachers and 200 supervisors were employed in WPA nurseries (Campbell, Bair, and Harvey, 1939, p. 110). The available literature does not mention the number of employed mothers whose children attended Lanham centers. Manufacturers and business managers, however, are said to have "testified" to the "great value in reducing absenteeism and turnover in their plants" (U.S. Department of Labor, 1971, p. 32). It would seem, then, that at least worker retention and stability of the work force were increased.

Most assessments accord high praise for the standards applied to the WPA program, despite its having hired untrained staff. To choose one example, according to Fleiss, the WPA " 'enlisted the leadership and guidance of outstanding persons in the field. Intensive inservice and preservice training programs for staff, parent education and community interpretation did much to promote standards and to focus attention on the value of nursery education' " (cited in Mayer and Kahn, 1965, p. 24).

The WPA program clearly conceived of a well-rounded *preschool* program as one that integrates health and welfare components around an educational core. The record does not explicitly state, but implies, that this conception was carried forward by the Lanham program. Furthermore, created during national crises, the WPA and Lanham programs were able to overcome the relief-versus-education distinction between day-care and nursery programs and affirmed the relevance of educational content to children in either type of program.

All in all, there seems to be little basis for rejecting the widely held impression that the federal WPA and Lanham programs provided a strikingly large number of young American children with a quality of preschool experience considerably higher than that generally available in preceding years. They also may have surpassed many subsequent nonpublic programs.

The WPA and Lanham programs had long-term policy implications. They represented a major shift of national policy on preschool programs. The federal government had essentially declared that (1) if the national interest is served, public funds should help wage-earning mothers carry the burden of the cost of day care; and (2) that the education of very young children may be a legitimate public responsibility (Zeitz, 1959, p. 173). Here, too, a precedent had been set; in the future, preschool advocates might understandably look to the federal government as a possible source of funds. Moreover, the policy represented another step in the advance of social parenthood.

That public policy on maternal employment had changed during the depression and the war has been previously noted. The policy during national emergencies may well have stimulated subsequent mothers to take outside work who otherwise might not have entered the labor force. However, the precedent it set that legitimatized public encouragement of maternal employment was established under highly specific conditions.

Termination of the Lanham Act in February, 1946, after the war had ended, highlighted one of those conditions. New York State then discontinued its city- and state-funded day-care program. Women in New York City organized and brought strong pressure to bear on Governor Thomas E. Dewey to resume state aid for day care. They picketed his residence; he called them communists (Mayer and Kahn, 1965, p. 38). Maternal pressure to continue Lanham programs in Michigan after the war also led to charges of communism. Representatives of nine professional and women's groups met with and presented a series of recommendations to President Truman; for example, favoring federal aid to public schools, including provision for nursery schools and kindergartens (Gans, 1947, pp. 8-9). The meeting proved fruitless (Goodykoontz, Davis, and Gabbard, 1947, pp. 56-57). Apparently the mothers and preschool advocates had failed to understand that social parenthood was only patriotic during a war or national emergency. To overcome the ambivalence toward maternal employment, and to resolve conflicts between the norm of strengthening the family and the interests of the economic and political orders, seemed to have required national crises.

After the war, ambivalence toward maternal employment returned to the forefront of federal policy. Without a justification couched in terms of the national interest, mothers were not to be encouraged to leave their child-rearing responsibilities for outside employment. Besides, as after World War I, state and federal policy makers apparently deemed it patriotic to place priority on ensuring jobs for the millions of demobilized soldiers and sailors.

The Postwar Period to the 1960s

While the dynamics of a world war in an industrial age had especially magnified the public day care sector of preschool programs, the postwar period produced marked changes in virtually all sectors, particularly the private programs. Despite public policy, mothers went to work in unprecedented numbers after the war. "In the ten years, 1948 to 1958, the number of mothers in the labor force increased by 80 percent and the proportion by almost 50 percent" (Herzog, 1960, p. 2). By 1960, eight million mothers with children under eighteen were in the labor force. Three million of these mothers had four million preschool-age children. These trends continued unabated after 1960, when the number of mothers of preschool-age children going to work even accelerated. In assessing this vast outpouring from home to office and factory, Herzog noted there had been a " 'quiet revolution' in women's employment over the past few decades" (1960, p. 1). As a former chief of the Children's Bureau commented, " 'the hand that rocks the cradle must often also punch the time clock' " (cited in Kadushin, 1967, p. 314).

From 1946 until 1962, national policy generally remained in the earlier position of not supporting preschool programs. A military program constituted a minor exception. Beginning in about 1956 day-care centers were established on Army posts in this country and abroad. The purpose is to enhance the morale of servicemen and their families. The Army provides the building and land; operating funds derive from Post Exchange profits and day-care fees. The programs are used almost exclusively by enlisted men. By 1966 programs were operating on most posts, enrolling an estimated 20,000 children here and abroad. (This information was provided by an Army official, a respondent.) Although minor in size, existence of this federally-aided preschool program prior to the 1960s was not consistent with national policy. The Army program did not require maternal employment outside the home to establish eligibility for day care. While the program catered mainly to enlisted personnel, some number of whom were sufficiently impoverished to be eligible for public welfare, poverty was not an eligibility requirement for day care on Army posts. Federal aid to day care to sustain family well-being apparently served the national interest only in the armed services. This exception shows that social policy in the military sector may be more liberal than national policy at large.

During the postwar period, insofar as the federal government had a dominant policy relating to mothers, the aim was similar to the earlier mothers' pensions—subsidizing mothers of dependent children to stay home and rear their children. That policy was incorporated in the Aid to Dependent Children (ADC) program, later renamed Aid to Families of Dependent Children. Public preschool programs continued during the postwar years only in New York City, Philadelphia, and the state of California (Mayer and Kahn, 1965; Moustakas and Berson, 1955). Except for the absence of federal funds, these programs essentially continued the WPA and Lanham policies. A vacuum in public preschool support at the national level combined with the absence from the home during the workday of large numbers of mothers of very young children produced a buildup of pressure for surrogate care programs.

Kindergarten programs, which had decreased in the depression, began to increase during the war, and by the war's end probably had returned to the 1930 level. Still, the enrollment in 1945, seventy-two years after the first *public* kindergarten was established, represented only about 25 percent of all five-year-olds in the population (Almy and Snyder, 1947, p. 229).

Kindergartens appeared to be increasingly popular. Local policy makers had become relatively partial to that form of preschool education. A poll of school boards in 1946 showed three times as many urban school boards preferred to include kindergartens, rather than nursery schools, in their public school systems. Public kindergartens grew considerably: The 1960 enrollment of 1,900,000 was more than three times that of 1940 (see Appendix, Table 6). Private kindergartens—those under philanthropic and proprietary auspices—increased at an even greater rate than the public programs. Private enrollments in 1960 were more than six times greater than in 1940. However, in spite of the rapid growth of kindergarten enrollments in this period, by the 1960s over one third of the eligible five-year-olds were not receiving a kindergarten education. (Given the relative lack of distinctiveness between kindergartens, nursery schools, and daycare centers as to age of children in attendance, however, some part—presumably small—of the five-year-olds not then in kindergartens may have been attending nursery schools or day-care centers.)

Kindergarten expansion during the postwar years, as in other time periods, led to problems. The class size problem in public schools apparently grew even more aggravated over the years. A survey of early elementary education in the year 1960 to 1961 found that "On the whole, kindergarten classes are larger than first-grade" (Gore, 1965, p. 37), which means many kindergartens do not meet the professional standards pertaining to class size and pupil-teacher ratio.

Differences between the curriculum objectives of "progressive" kindergartens and those of traditional elementary grades, a problem Dewey had addressed in 1899, continued and probably became exacerbated. Kindergarten teachers, increasingly imbued with the perspective of progressive education, not infrequently faced administrators and supervisors who did not share their ideas. The most damaging of the old-fashioned educational ideas to the progressivists was the stress placed on reading readiness. If the kindergarten teacher accommodates to the expectation of such superiors, "at its best, her program loses some of the spontaneity and depth of interest to the children; at its worst, the children become, for all practical purposes, slaves to the reading-readiness workbooks" (Almy and Snyder, 1947, p. 243). Instead of emphasizing "formal school work," the progressivists called for stress on "general adjustment, social relations, personality development, and zest and enthusiasm for living" (Anderson, 1947, pp. 96-97). This opposition to disciplined learning by the progressive education movement played a part, during the postwar years, in hastening its own demise (Cremin, 1964, pp. 347-353).

Industrial day care appears to have returned from the wartime period to its usual miniscule proportions. (How large a decrease occurred when the war ended is not known. Oddly, nowhere does the literature mention the total number of wartime industrial programs in operation. It is difficult to challenge the acknowledgment by the pertinent federal agency that "authoritative information" on industrial day care is scanty [U.S. Department of Labor, 1971, p. 29].) In 1950, seventeen

industrial programs were reported in existence. In general, industrial day care in the United States has been a miniature
curiosity, either in comparison with the magnitude of domestic
day care or even more so in contrast to industrial day care in
Western Europe and the U.S.S.R.

Several other points about industrial day care deserve
incidental mention. Cotton mills and textile manufacturers
seem to have been the dominant types of businesses involved.
This is to have been expected on the basis of the heavy reliance
of that industry historically on female employees. Not only
does that industry employ many women, but also large numbers
are concentrated in the factories. Typically, industrial day-care
centers have been housed within the factory building or in another building adjacent to the factory. As for the quality of
such programs in the postwar period, one authoritative professional assessment reported they tend to meet "only minimal
requirements" (see Moustakas and Berson, 1955, pp. 159-160,
the major source on the postwar period).

Little is recorded regarding the degree of success or failure
of peacetime industrial day care in encouraging maternal employment. Although it may be simplistic, it is difficult not to presume
that the day-care program was initiated and continued as long as it
was deemed to be serving the company's pecuniary interests. The
advantages it provided to employers apparently operated only
in periods when demand was high and the labor supply short.
The reverse situation appears to have led to abandonment of the
industrial day-care center. All in all, their rarity and seemingly
short life span suggest that industrial day-care programs served
temporary, localized, and particularistic labor shortages.

After the initial massive enlargement of nursery schools
by the WPA, the known number fluctuated somewhat, reaching
about 1,500 the year the war ended. By 1951, the last year
prior to the 1960s for which data were located, just over 2,000
programs had been enumerated. However, important dynamics
lay hidden in the overall figures. Data on nursery school auspices illuminate the influences at work (see Appendix Table 4). In
1951, about two thirds (64 percent) of the nursery schools
were under proprietary management. Moreover, this represented
a doubling of proprietary programs, in number and propor-

tion[12], although during the preceding decade the total number of nursery schools had only increased by about 7 percent. In that decade, in a major sponsorial shift, the proprietary sector replaced public programs as the dominant portion of the nursery school field. In fact, during the decade, the public sector experienced a decrease by twenty fold (from almost 1,000 to about 50), a drop reflecting termination of the WPA-Lanham program without a federal successor. Concurrent with proprietary ascendancy, the philanthropic sector decreased by one fifth while laboratory schools almost doubled (from 6 to 11 percent).

The nature of the postwar proprietary growth requires clarification. The postwar growth was part of a long term trend. As early as 1929, it may be recalled, proprietary nursery schools constituted a large plurality (or, if combination nursery schools and kindergartens are counted, a majority) of such programs (see Table 1). Between 1934 and 1942, when the public programs exploded in number, profit seeking programs also continued to increase, but less expansively than the publicly funded nursery schools (see Appendix, Table 4). The postwar cessation of federal support gave a boost to the long-term proprietary trend. By 1951, both the short- and long-run factors propelled the profit seeking programs to a clearly dominant position in the nursery school field. We believe proprietary dominance continued or even expanded up to the mid-1960s. Absence of national data specifically on proprietary nursery schools after 1951 makes it impossible to confirm our conjecture. (It also prevents ascertaining exactly what were the statistical effects on the proprietary sector of federal nursery school policy in the mid-1960s.)

The sociological implications of the proprietary expansion deserve notice. Faced with the cutoff of federal preschool funds and a diminution of philanthropic support, unfilled demand for preschool education and/or surrogate care created the market vacuum that historically attracted proprietors. Social parenthood of very young children spread; now, however, individual vendors rendered surrogate service that public school teachers had largely provided a decade earlier.

This apparently involved a corollary shift in nursery school clientele. Despite the absence of clear, solid information on families with children in the WPA and Lanham nursery schools, we can comfortably assume they differed, for the most part, from the proprietary clientele of 1951. According to a survey covering 1,300 proprietary nursery schools located in thirty-five states (Moustakas and Berson, 1955, pp. 62-63) 70 percent of the parents paid fees in amounts estimated to require middle- or upper-class income: The 62 percent who paid from $6 to $15 weekly were described as business and professional people; customers paying the highest fees ($15 or more) represented a suburban, upper-class clientele of business executives. Their children attended the private day schools that were part of larger exclusive educational institutions.

Several other features of the postwar proprietary nursery schools are noteworthy, such as the facilities, staffing, and programatic elements. A majority of the commercial nursery schools were housed in converted residences, which ranged from rooms in the director's home to luxurious estates leased or owned by the exclusive schools. Most of the programs run by the husband-wife teams were housed in their own homes. Only about 15 percent of the private nursery schools were estimated to operate in structures specially designed for nursery school purposes.

The educational training, length of preschool experience, and personal qualities of the principal program staff, especially the director or head teacher, are widely considered the most influential factors affecting the content and quality of preschool programs. A profile of the postwar proprietary nursery school staff follows. The director-owners of private nursery schools displayed a wide range in their training. All, however, had prior teaching experience, usually gained in their present position. Husband-wife teams generally lacked prior experience with children and professional training, particularly in child development. It should be noted, however, that the husbands in commercial nursery schools (as in day-care centers) provided a male presence usually absent from noncommercial programs. A majority of the directors or head teachers in the private nursery schools were college graduates, 38 percent with a baccalaureate, 17 percent with a master's degree. (By this indicator, perhaps a majority of the private nursery schools would rate well. As is shown later, within the proprietary sector the nursery school teachers, as a group, show a markedly higher level of education than their day-care counterparts. Partial corroboration of the quality private nurseries are capable of achieving is suggested by findings of a survey in the early 1960s; the proprietary nursery programs were rated by qualified observers as of higher quality than voluntary nurseries. However, only a small number of those programs were studied [see Ruderman, 1968, p. 116].) This staff profile of the private nursery schools would be incomplete without mention of the personnel in the luxurious, exclusive programs; in addition to a headmistress (director) and teachers, the staff included butlers, chauffeurs, and maids (Moustakas and Berson, 1955, p. 56). Almost one out of every six private nursery schools comprised this type.

A few programatic effects of profit seeking by proprietary nursery schools have been remarked on. Moustakas and Berson regard the readiness of proprietors to cater to their clientele—for example, as to the child's arrival or departure time—as one of the major advantages to parents of such programs. Professionals criticize another result of the proprietary priority on being a successful business establishment. They note that private nursery schools have made almost no contribution to the literature of early childhood education. Finally, even the proprietary nursery schools, as a group—which, at least on one objective factor, namely staff education and experience, rate comparatively well—do not entirely overcome their dependence on fiscal solvency. Moustakas and Berson concluded that high tuition does not necessarily purchase high educational quality because educational requirements often are subordinated to financial aims (1955, p. 62).

After the war, the day-care field experienced an even more traumatic decrease of free or low-cost public programs than had occurred among nursery schools. So far as the available data indicate, the philanthropic programs also decreased, from 1,500 in 1951 to 1,109 in 1960, a 25 percent drop (see Appendix, Tables 1 and 2). The existence of demand for day care by an increasing maternal work force that was unfilled by the voluntary and public sectors produced the familiar result.

By 1960, 64 percent of the centers were proprietary, holding 51 percent of the aggregate capacity of licensed day care. (Philanthropic day care, despite its decline, comprised 29 percent of the centers and 37 percent of licensed capacity.)

Again, data from the 1951 survey, on about forty-five proprietary day-care centers in twenty-one states (Moustakas and Berson, 1955), permit sketching some features of those programs. Business and professional families were reported to be the patrons of the more expensive proprietary day care centers; these charged $15 or more per week, an amount paid by a handful—2 percent—of commercial day-care users. (But a larger number of commercial centers were more "exclusive" than that small percentage might suggest: Over one half of the commercial day-care programs surveyed excluded black children and a few did not accept Jewish and Catholic children.) The overwhelming majority of clients paid less than $15: 18 percent paid $5 or less per week, 77 percent from $6 to $15, and 3 percent paid an hourly rate. It should be understood, in thinking about such fee charges, that almost all the centers operated for eight or more hours a day.

The survey provided an unflattering portrait of the education of those heading the commercial day-care programs. On the basis of the data gathered, the majority of directors and teachers were evaluated as lacking adequate education, training, and experience for work with young children. Only 27 percent of the persons in charge of the programs had completed college study; 18 percent had undergraduate degrees, and 9 percent graduate degrees. If the effect of staff education and training on preschool programs was as critical as generally believed, the quality of commercial day-care centers *in general* would have been grounds for considerable concern in 1951, as earlier. Of course, there are exceptions to that generalization. For example, another study noted that some "commercial centers had equipment, supplies and ideas superior to most public or nonprofit facilities" (Prescott, 1965, p. 35; see also Ruderman, 1968, p. 113).

Nevertheless, Moustakas and Berson (1955, p. 156) report great inadequacies among the commercial day-care programs in their survey. The professional surveyors faulted the physical facilities, play space, equipment, training and experience of staff, and the medical and mental health care. The majority of these commercial day-care establishments were said to simply provide custodial care. A few exceptional places struggled to improve their standards; reportedly even these places, however, had to be concerned with survival, which meant placing emphasis on fiscal viability. Making a profit and achieving a quality child-care center were deemed by professionals to be antithetical. As a result, according to the experts, needs of the children remain unfilled (Moustakas and Berson, 1955, p. 160). Data from more recent studies lend some support to that antithesis. A study in the Boston area found that "One of the most striking results of this study was the sharp contrast . . . between the Proprietary Center and the other five facilities, all of which were nonprofit. The Proprietary Center had the lowest costs, but also the most minimal program, the least staffing, and the most marginal of services" (Gurin, Guberman, Greenblatt, and Thompson, 1966, pp. 113-114). Ruderman also compared proprietary day-care centers with centers under other auspices (1968, p. 113). Twenty-one programs were involved in the observational part of her study. In general, voluntary programs were rated by experienced observers as of higher quality than proprietary centers. The data from all these studies converge to indicate that the clientele of proprietary centers did not get what they paid for.

The social and economic policy implications of such findings warrant citation: "If families of low income who need day-care services are to obtain services that meet the program and staff standards of responsible agencies in this field, this can come about only through substantial financial subsidy. If our data are any indication of the general situation, the bulk of the working class population that uses [proprietary] day-care services at the present time are purchasing a service that they can ill afford and one which is grossly inadequate by the standards of both the social welfare and educational professions that claim jurisdiction in this field" (Gurin and others, 1966, p. 116; compare with Moustakas and Berson, 1955, p. 160).

Proprietary day-care programs also displayed a feature previously mentioned in regard to commercial nursery schools. The dependence on parents' fees motivated proprietors to accommodate to their customers' needs and desires. This willingness to adjust policies and program schedules has been generally noted by observers. One researcher contrasted this consumer orientation of proprietors to the unconcern of staff in public and nonprofit programs, which provide partially or fully subsidized care: "These [nonprofit] centers may therefore not be as concerned with pleasing parents but rather see themselves as benefactors" (Prescott, 1965, p. 6). Professionals understandably may be concerned that the consumer orientation could mean a willingness in the interest of pecuniary gain to make adjustments detrimental to the program and the needs of the children. On the other hand, we should add, it is far from clear that the lack of professional responsiveness to parental requests necessitates detrimental effects.

In conclusion, the postwar growth of the proprietary sector may be attributed to the absence of effective competitors, to consumer preference for accommodative programs, and, possibly, to a modest level of profitability. After all, if the antithesis of profit and program quality is accepted, then the reputedly inadequate level of proprietary day-care programs could conceivably mean that profit is made. (The proprietary program in the Boston area apparently made a modest profit [see Gurin and others, 1966, p. 106].) However, evidence is substantially unavailable on the profitability of proprietary programs. Another feature of proprietary programs implies either a modest level of profits or profitlessness. Proprietary preschool programs in the 1951 survey had a far shorter life span than programs supported with public or community subsidy (Moustakas and Berson, 1955). This should not be surprising. Proprietary programs appear to have the same characteristics as all small businesses. While easily started, usually they are undercapitalized, underequipped, understaffed, inadequately staffed in terms of training of personnel, programatically deficient, and have a high failure rate.

Summary

We will now summarize the main points that emerge from this historical chronology. First, it is now possible to identify the conditions under which social intervention into familial rearing of young children occurred prior to the 1960s. Those conditions are economic necessity associated with industrialization and economic and military emergencies on a national scale. Second, intervention displayed several forms of sponsorship. Philanthropic sponsorship was primarily associated with mitigating the familial effects of chronic social conditions—secular trends of maternal employment and acculturation of immigrant groups. By contrast, the need to stimulate maternal employment during national crises led to public sponsorship. The insufficient supply of philanthropic or public programs in the face of increased demand for preschool programs apparently instigated the growth of proprietary programs. Third, the types of program that developed reflected the influence of several factors. These include the varying social purposes (such as preventing neglect, acculturating immigrant children and parents, and fulfilling the potential of early childhood), social class dynamics, and the diffusion of programatic innovations across cultures (such as the kindergarten and possibly the infant school and day-care center).

Whether history repeated these conditions and forms of intervention in the 1960s remains to be discussed in Chapters Four and Five. Before examining these preschool policy developments, however, we will consider several emergent themes from the chronology that bear on the preschool policies formulated, enacted, and implemented in the 1960s.

Notes

[1] Perhaps this pedagogical orthodoxy reflected the strict Calvinist belief in infant depravity. The vigor of that belief is captured in Jonathan Edwards' characterization of unrepentant children as " 'young vipers and infinitely more hateful than vipers' " Jonathan Edwards (cited in Wishy, 1968, p. 11).

[2]Some middle-class parents may object to child-rearing standards practiced in their child's preschool program, but most such families probably share the middle-class orientation generally held by preschool teachers. In the past, this did not rest easily with immigrant parents, nor does it now with black parents in the slums. For a recent study examining this tension, see Prescott (1965).

[3]For example, see Tyson (1930) and also Kadushin (1967, p. 303). An earlier nursery is reported, however, to have been established in Boston, in 1838, for children of employed widows or of mothers employed because their sailor husbands were away at sea (see Beer, 1957, p. 35). This nursery may have been one of the "infant schools" reported in Boston at this point in time (see Calhoun, [1919] 1960, 2, p. 60).

The suggestion has also been made that the woman paid to take in and care for children of neighboring mothers who went out to work probably provided the first form of day care (see Whipple, 1929, p. 88). (Today such an arrangement is called *family day care*. It is defined as the care for part of the day of a small number of children, usually six or fewer, under age three, within a family residence. Because only group day-care programs have been selected for study here, family day care will not be dealt with further.) The absence of written public records makes it difficult to prove that such commercial day care was the earliest form of day care.

[4]The innovation was lasting—the day-care literature mentions friendly visits by day nursery staff in the twentieth century (White House Conference, 1930a, p. 20). As a professional activity, it developed into social casework.

[5]The literature is not entirely clear as to when the first industrial program was established. Confusion may arise from differing definitions. As employed here, the term *industrial day care* means a day-care program primarily or exclusively for children of mothers employed by the company or organization that established the program. Other definitions include programs sponsored by an organization for children of nonemployees, such as the 1854 Nursery and Child's Hospital center developed for children of former patients (see U.S. Department of Labor, 1971, p. 29).

[6]The term *baby farming* means "the taking in of infants to nurse for payment, but usually with an implication of improper treatment" (see "Baby Farming," p. 97). Some parents brought their children to such places for indefinite boarding care, others for day care during working hours. (For other pertinent references see Bremner, 1971, pp. 191, 195-196; Deardorff, 1930, p. 373; and Falconer, 1930, p. 410.)

For the most part, the subject of preschool regulation will not be dealt with in our chronology. The reader interested in the subject would find the history of such regulation to be revealing. Fragmentary evidence suggests it would show enactment of legislation generally at a snail's pace, often insufficient funds and staff for enforcement, and great variety in laws and in their enforcement in the several states. An interesting differential in legal requirements of day care and of nursery schools would also become evident. (For a detailed discussion, see Moustakas and Berson, 1955, pp. 199-218. For a more recent survey of day-care licensing, see U.S. Department of Health, Education, and Welfare, 1968a.)

[7]Dewey's early work on education, *The School and Society*, was published in 1899. The first several chapters were delivered as lectures before parents of children attending the University of Chicago elementary school, which school Dewey directed for some time. (Dewey and Bertrand Russell thus had in common careers as eminent philosophers of the twentieth century and as nursery school directors. For the latter's nursery school activities, see Russell, 1951.) Another of Dewey's early writings is *The Child and the Curriculum*, which first appeared in 1902. The edition cited contains both documents: *The Child and the Curriculum and The School and Society* (Chicago: University of Chicago Press, 1956). However, because of discontinuous pagination *The Child and the Curriculum* will be cited hereafter as [1902] 1956a, *The School and Society* as [1900] 1956b. Problematic aspects of Dewey's educational ideas and the transformation that occurred as those ideas were applied in progressive preschool programs will be examined in Chapter Three.

[8]The increase in this country never approximated what many industrial European nations experienced. Government sanction and funds in England, France, Germany, and Italy led to the opening of many centers at munitions plants. In Italy, 800 factory nurseries were set up (Tyson, 1930, p. 14).

[9]The figure *56* combines "Relief Nursery School" and "Nursery School," and excludes kindergartens, whether separate or combined with nursery school. The survey definitions reveal a struggle to accommodate distinctions to a reality more complex than the extant concepts: "Day Nurseries A. Purpose—relief of unsatisfactory economic or unwholesome social conditions in the home. . . . Relief nursery school. . . . A. Purpose—relief of unsatisfactory or unwholesome social conditions in the home and the education and training of children. . . . Nursery School A. Purpose—education and training of young children" (White House Conference, 1930b, pp. 152-153). The term *relief nursery school* has not been encountered elsewhere.

[10]Perhaps more noteworthy is the only factual mention found in the literature to an industrial alternative to day care—modification of work hours for married women. One manufacturer willing to modify his policy to attract such employees "found it necessary to delay the beginning of his week until Monday noon as his workers refused to come in until the week's washing was on the line" (Whipple, 1929, p. 90).

[11]The larger figure is said to represent the number "receiving care in [Lanham] nurseries and day care centers" in July 1945 (Mayer and

Kahn, 1965, p. 27; see also Zeitz, 1959, p. 188.) That figure is not consistent with an accumulated total estimate of "between 550,000 and
600,000 children" cared for in Lanham schools and centers (U.S. Department of Labor, 1953, p. 9, cited in Kadushin, 1967, p. 305). The seeming
incompatibility between the statistics could not be reconciled.

[12]The change between 1942 and 1951 may not have been quite
that large; another source than the one we relied on reported 1,000 private
nursery schools out of a total of 2,500 in 1942 (Alschuler, 1942, p. 8).

THREE

Problems
and Perspectives of
Child Care Programs

The history of preschool programs to the 1960s covered a profusion of events and issues. In this chapter the emphasis changes from the chronological to the thematic. Four themes contained in the historical detail are examined and their relevance to preschool policy in the 1960s indicated.

Several of the themes concern aspects of preschool programs and policies as expressed from a particular perspective. The first theme involves the distinction that developed in the 1920s between day care as relief for economically dependent families and as custodial in orientation, and nursery schools as programs for educating children presumably of economically

independent families. We analyze this distinction and point to
the bearing that the reputation of day care and its custodial
orientation had on the enactment and implementation of the
1962 day-care legislation.

The second theme deals with the general omission from
the literature of reference to proprietary preschool programs in
spite of their numerical significance from 1920 to 1960. This
we attribute to professional antipathy and the nature of these
programs as business entities at a low stage of development. As
a result, these programs played no part in the formulation and
enactment of federal preschool policy in the 1960s.

The third theme concerns a contribution of the progressive education movement, the principle that stressed the maximum fulfillment of the individual's inherent capacities. We
examine the ambiguity of that principle, and the transformation
from its naturalist presuppositions that allowed policy makers
in the 1960s to employ the same phrase with different meanings. Yet that credo was one of the most frequently encountered rationales favoring enactment of federally supported preschool programs in the 1960s, and became part of federal
statute.

The last theme touches on the preference on the part of
public educators for federal funds to expand kindergartens rather than to support nursery schools in the postwar period. We
suggest reasons for that preference, indicate its antagonizing
effects on those policy makers who advocated nursery schools
in the 1960s, and also note its contribution to an antieducation
posture in the implementation of nursery school policy at that
time.

Relief versus Education

No doubt many influences fed into the evolution of this
distinction between the goals of day care and nursery schools.
Certainly economic factors were operative, such as the costs of
preschool programs and the source and amount of funds involved. The focus in this chapter is on social class and professional dynamics involving clientele, staff and their normative

and associated viewpoints. Specifically, attention is given to upper- and middle-class valuation of the family as an institution and the strain on that norm caused by day care, and to the differential application of that norm across class lines. First, we attempt to demonstrate that those factors were major determinants of the conception and content of those preschool programs. Second, the accuracy of the distinction is questioned in light of the history detailed in the preceding chapter. Then its pertinence for federal policy will be discussed.

During the nineteenth century, the emphasis on sanctity of the family in religious doctrine became secularized and occupied a prominent position in the moral value system of Americans generally. One family form was assumed as the normative ideal, the self-reliant, intact, two-parent family with the mother in the home. The beneficence of that normative model was taken for granted. Impoverished one-parent families and similar lower-class departures from the normative model were considered deviant cases and characterized as incomplete, endangered, inadequate, ineffective, dependent, or otherwise deficient. Incidentally, middle- and upper-class nonconformance was not as likely to be labeled as a deviation from the family model.

Because of widowhood, desertion, or their husbands' illness, women in the lower classes were forced by economic necessity to support their children by seeking employment outside the home. The resulting dangers to and neglect of children aroused the charitable concern of well-to-do ladies who established and staffed day-care centers as a means of intervention or prevention of deviancy (child neglect). From the literature, we infer that the ladies in the early day nurseries were confronted by a normative dilemma in establishing an admissions policy.

It was understandable or even acceptable if a day nursery made outside employment easier for a poor mother compelled to work by dire circumstances, such as widowhood or a permanently incapacitated husband. But it was another matter to encourage work outside the home by a mother whose employed husband was poorly paid, or whose husband had been laid off or was temporarily disabled, for that appeared to endanger the

integrity of the family as normatively defined. The more that
cases admitted to day nurseries conflicted with prevailing opinions of appropriate departures from the family norm, the
broader the eligibility rules, the greater was the likelihood of
self- and other criticism of day nurseries as endangering the
integrity of the family unit. Distinguishing between deserving
and undeserving cases may have implicated complex factual and
normative ambiguities. Neglect cannot always be objectively
defined or ascertained. Furthermore, a case may not clearly
have fit existing eligibility rules, and the family nevertheless
may have been judged victimized by circumstances and truly deserving of help from the day nursery. Those who made or evaluated such judgments would not always have agreed. Thus, for
example, in the twentieth century the broadening of eligibility
to include children whose parents both worked in charitable
day care led to "criticism of the effect of day nurseries upon
the home" (Whipple, 1929, p. 93). Warnings of the "danger of
lessened parental responsibility" came from social workers and
others "concerned with the values of family and child life"
(White House Conference, 1930a, p. 6). Polemic criticism appeared in the professional literature: "The use of private philanthropy to relieve an irresponsible mother of her duty to her
children . . . or to help industry to avail itself of cheap labor, is
contrary to all recognized social principles" (White House Conference, 1930a, p. 27).

    As a result of the dilemma, ambivalence arose to torment
those who sought to strengthen the family unit and also prevent
child neglect. Upper- and middle-class ambivalence toward the
anomalous trinity of strengthening the family, preventing child
neglect, and providing day care appears and reappears in the
course of day-care history. In passing, we should note another
effect of the quintessential concern of charitable day care with
protecting the family unit and preventing neglect; so far as the
literature indicates, emphasis was placed not on the programatic
activities for the children in the day nursery, but on determining and monitoring eligibility and on parental instruction.

    Friendly visiting was the measure first advocated for over-
coming the dangers to the "basic social unit" by nullifying the

unprincipled use of day nurseries. The well-to-do philanthropic ladies served as the earliest friendly visitors in day care. What that charitable technique involved may not be self-evident. Exemplifying a tradition in charitable work dating back to the sixteenth century, namely individualization in place of mass methods, friendly visiting consisted of investigation and a personal service across social class lines. The latter meant establishment by someone in a "socially superior position" of a friendly relationship with a social inferior. The theory underlying the practice held that "poor families would learn that the well-to-do were not enemies, and the wealthy would come to appreciate the fortitude of the poor as they observed how they coped with life's hardships" (Lewis, 1971, p. 97). By investigating the home conditions and possessing knowledge of local resources, the day nursery friendly visitors applied the prevailing eligibility criteria to determine whether the case was deserving or undeserving of charitable help. Friendly visiting served to resolve the ambivalence of the well-to-do ladies toward the normative conception of the family, preventing neglect, and day care. That technique enabled the philanthropic donors to put their imprint on admissions to the day nursery—their social class ideas and attitudes as to the clientele appropriate to the program.

Paid staff began replacing the well-to-do volunteers in day nurseries beginning in about the last quarter of the nineteenth century. We assume the day nurseries experienced the same insufficiency of volunteers in relation to the volume of work to be done as the charity organization societies in recruiting their friendly visitors. The literature docs not indicate whether the women who took paid jobs in day nurseries were, like the reformers in the settlement house movement, imbued with the spirit of the women's suffrage movement or graduates of liberal arts colleges. However, the day nursery staff very likely shared with the feminist reformers and the paid agents of the charity organizations middle-class origins. This meant the paid nursery staff differed from the patronesses in social status. In part, a status differential was associated with the pursuit of vocational careers in contrast to an affluent avocation of good works and civic responsibility. However, the paid staff and the philanthropic ladies shared other beliefs and values. Specifically, the middle-class workers also valued the normative family ideal and were torn by ambivalence toward departures from the norm. The paid day nursery staff, as their counterparts in the charity organization associations, carried forward the practice of friendly visiting that the volunteers had performed. That practice provided the "inspiration" for social casework (Pumphrey, 1971, p. 1451), as the technique came to be called in the twentieth century. That change in terminology reflected the professionalization of social work. The social service staff in day nurseries, along with the more numerous charitable organization workers, among others, formed the fledgling social work profession.

The literature unceasingly emphasizes the importance of casework as a professional technique for case decisions. Some decisions resulted in approving provision of day care as a "support" or "supplement" of the family.[1] Other decisions meant attempting to discourage mothers from seeking employment by denying admission, and by counseling.[2] By deciding to whom philanthropic day care, recognized more and more as a scarce resource, was to be available, caseworkers sought to resolve high-minded ambivalence and to implement the goals of preventing neglect by admitting appropriate cases to the day nursery and of strengthening the family by discouraging maternal employment in other cases.

The focus of casework concern fell not on maternal employment per se, but on "irresponsible" or "inefficient" mothers. The former included mothers with employed husbands for whom work out of the home may not have been deemed compelling; the latter meant mothers whose low pay could not cover the full cost of day care. Excluded from those categories were mothers in professional or better-paying jobs, perhaps with someone at home to provide child care, or able to afford proprietary day care.

Aside from its use in making case decisions, casework had institutional utility. Nurseries that accepted, without casework screening, children whose parents both worked were criticized by social workers and others for "indiscriminate use" and lessening parental responsibility. The defense that such dangers were not inherent in day care relied on the prescription that casework be employed (Whipple, 1929, pp. 93-94; White House Conference, 1930a, p. 27). Its diagnostic efficacy was taken for granted.

It may be supposed that by criticizing the absence of casework screening, caseworkers were merely engaging in a form of professional advertisement, were only attempting to create a demand for their service within day nurseries. We will deal with that supposition and several other facets of casework in day care, although doing so will divert us briefly from pursuing the relief-versus-education distinction. The significance of that technique in the field of social work, however, justifies the diversion.

The supposition would be supported if social workers concerned with day care, child welfare workers, had been seeking simply to broaden day-care demand for their casework expertise and really were not concerned with the presumed familial effects of maternal employment. The historical evidence does not indicate such unconcern, but the opposite.

Social workers were so strongly imbued with the goals of strengthening the family and preventing neglect by discouraging maternal employment that the onset of World War II did not readily shake their value position. Perhaps at the risk of diminishing demand for casework services in relation to day care, child welfare officials, as we mentioned previously, attempted to gain adoption of a federal policy discouraging maternal employment in wartime.[3]

It may be tempting to smirk at professionals more concerned with strengthening the family than with strengthening the war effort. Most political statesmen resolved the ambivalence of the comfortable and affluent classes by giving priority to the nation, rather than the family defense. However, for some a problem may have arisen in determining priorities, as may be seen from the following anecdote (possibly apocryphal). During World War II, New York City faced a complicated day-care problem. In large part, it is said, the question was one of choosing which of several departments to administer the day-care program. Mayor LaGuardia selected the Welfare Department. His decision "was undoubtedly strongly influenced by his

often stated opposition to . . . women [leaving] their small children to go to work. . . . In order to limit such assistance to
those who really required it, he felt that appropriate study of
each case was necessary and that the Welfare Department, with
its investigatory procedures, could properly carry out this policy. . . . In accordance with LaGuardia's philosophy, the staff
. . . often counseled mothers to stay at home rather than work
(Mayer and Kahn, 1965, pp. 34-35).[4] As a politician, LaGuardia
differed from social work professionals in possessing authority
and a willingness to exercise it. He also manifested a deeper—
more conservative?—commitment to the older, peacetime policy
of discouraging maternal employment by use of casework counseling. Apparently even in wartime, LaGuardia believed the
interest of the state must be secondary to the well-ordering of
the family. Or perhaps the fact that New York City had not
been designated nationally as a war-impacted area—hence was
ineligible for federal Lanham funds—led LaGuardia to see no
tension between familism and patriotism.

Returning to the main line of argument, we may ask rhe-
torically, What is the significance of the ambivalence stemming
from tensions between the normative conception of the family,
preventing neglect, and day care, and the techniques advocated,
at least in peacetime, to lessen that tension? We have already
pointed to the institutional utility served by those techniques;
by extension, they also served to assuage concern over normative ambiguities and conflicts, to make it possible to live with
such value conflicts. However, and more to the point here, they
helped make real the charitable conception of day care as a program for the deserving poor, for dependent families worthy of
charitable concern, by restricting the clientele to generations of
families who were identified in similar social terms despite distinguishable differences in their circumstances. Day-care clientele were given a common social identity as "needy." This identity contributed to the program conception of charitable day
care as a "relief institution."

Mention was made earlier, in passing, that upper- and
middle-class departures from the normative conception of the
family were less likely to be viewed as deviant than lower-class

divergences. For example, because the charitable friendly visitors from the day nursery were also mothers, their avocational activities outside their homes implied an inconsistency regarding the family norm that their day-care efforts sought to safeguard. More generally, the family norm applied differentially across class lines. The mothers' pension laws became the watershed issue in regard to the uneven application of a norm supposedly classless in scope.

The state laws authorizing mothers' pensions made several significant changes in social policy. First, the aim of preventing child neglect by not encouraging maternal employment became public policy authorized by state law, rather than a part of the mores or social policy of voluntary associations. The mothers' pension laws aimed to assist widowed mothers struggling to be both homemakers and breadwinners. Based on the normative conception of the family, on the belief that "The mother is the best guardian of her children" (New York State Report of the Commission on Relief for Widowed Mothers, Albany, 1914; cited in Bremner, 1971, p. 379), the laws intended to help preserve the family by providing an option to widows to stay at home and rear their children. The mothers' aid laws may be seen as efforts by the states to provide lower-class, widowed mothers with a choice between child rearing and outside employment similar to that available to mothers in other social classes.

Grace Abbott emphasized a second significant point about mothers' pension laws that is most pertinent here. The laws established as public policy that the "contribution of unskilled or semiskilled mothers in their own homes exceeded their earnings outside the home and that it was in the public interest to conserve their child-caring function" (New York State Report, 1914; cited in Bremner, 1971, p. 385). Mothers' pensions did not establish a clear-cut policy of influencing mothers to retain or helping mothers to carry out their child-rearing responsibilities regardless of income. Perhaps the income qualification in the laws was caused by limitations of charitable or public generosity; or perhaps it was assumed that the well-paid mother could afford adequate child care in her absence.

But the qualification implied a social class distinction in public policy: The laws were based on the ostensibly universal family norm that emphasized maternal child rearing, yet they only focused on child rearing by mothers in the lower classes. Maternal child rearing in middle and upper classes was outside the scope of those laws. The laws aimed at preventing child neglect by making it unnecessary for mothers to take low-paid jobs that would not offer enough pay to purchase substitute child care, but were silent about the possible effects on child rearing of employing mothers who could command higher earnings or of socially busy, unemployed middle- and upper-class mothers. This statutory silence reflected a concern with families believed to be a danger to the community as a result of neglect or delinquency, families that placed a fiscal or philanthropic burden on their communities. It also reflected a presupposition of the family norm embodied in the pension laws—the beneficence of child rearing in the middle and upper classes.

Thus, in their conception the mothers' aid laws intended to make more equal the choices available to widowed mothers in the several social classes. However, the presupposition about child rearing in affluent families and the perceived threat to the domestic order and tax rates only from lower-class departures from the dominant values suggest a different assessment. We view the mothers' pension laws as implying a publicly sanctioned differential between the child-caring function of low-paid and more highly paid employed mothers. The mothers' pension laws established a minimum cost measure of the value of full-time maternal nurture based upon the lesser skilled who could get only low-paid outside work.

The position taken here is based on the belief that the supposedly classless family norm was applied differentially across class lines. Evidence on the implementation of the mothers' pension laws supports a view contrary to that of mothers' pensions as equalizing life chances across class lines. The level of aid generally provided was inadequate: The standard of aid generally established in the pension laws was "approximately from one third to two thirds the amount found requisite [in the 1920s] by agencies for boarding children in family homes" (Lundberg, 1921, pp. 103, 105).

The development of mothers' pension programs also created a new context within which day-care policy was considered. Women eligible for a mothers' pension now had a choice—to work full-time for low wages, to not work full-time and accept public aid, or to combine part-time work with public aid. Day care made up the other side of the alternative to take a lowly paid, full-time job. It also provided a possible child-rearing supplement for other women—sick mothers, those not eligible for a pension—and other families.

Comparison of the mother's low pay with the per capita cost of day care for her child served as a simple formula for comparing costs and benefits. This provided a useful gauge to day nurseries, one that explicitly acknowledged "the fallacy of spending community funds in nursery service for a single family often as large as or in excess of the wages of the mother [which would] much better be utilized in subsidizing the mother in her own home" (White House Conference, 1930a, p. 41). A corollary formula—accepted as a "general principle"—held that day-care costs far exceeded the benefits in cases of employed mothers with three or more young children.

These cost-benefit considerations reveal the general cost consciousness that developed over fifty years ago in day care. They also imply, as did the public policy in mothers' pension laws, a social class differential in estimates of the value of such home goods as raising children in various strata.

For charitable day-care centers, the mothers' pension laws resulted in a more sharply articulated and developed policy. First, they provided a fiscal calculus for deciding the respective costs and benefits in a given case, of providing a mother with day care for her child, so she could take outside employment without the risk of neglecting her child, or of subsidizing her to stay home to rear the child. Second, indirectly the pension programs profoundly altered day-care admissions policies. Widows who accepted pensions and no longer needed full-time work also no longer needed day care for their children. Enrollments of such children decreased and, in order to operate economically, day nurseries began admitting children of two-parent families. A husband's unemployment, seasonal employment, or inadequate wage became an acceptable reason for a mother to seek employment and for admitting their child to the day nursery. Increased numbers of children of separated and divorced mothers also were accepted for day nursery care. Parenthetically, this by-product of mothers' aid greatly heightened ambivalence toward the anomalous trinity. Third, professionals and philanthropists increasingly conceived of philanthropic day-care programs as a substitute for cash relief. They viewed charitable day care largely as a fiscally calculable alternative to public assistance, as an adjunct service linked to maternal employment to compensate for insufficient paternal earnings, and as a service considered more than ever before as a subsidy from charitable neighbors.

We attribute the conception of the day nursery as a type of relief program to the two factors discussed earlier. Efforts by affluent volunteers and middle-class staff to resolve their ambivalence to the tension between the family norm, preventing neglect, and day care resulted in an identification of the clientele as "economically handicapped." This reinforced the potent effect of the discriminatory application of the family norm to produce a perception of day care as a "relief institution." The staff of philanthropic amateurs and paid professionals was an influential determinant of the designation of day care as a socially differentiated service.

To avoid a facile and historically inaccurate analysis, we must not overstate the case. That conception was not inherently and immutably affixed to philanthropic day care. The *possibility* of a different conception is evidenced by a historically significant and paradoxical occurrence. The conception of day nurseries not merely as philanthropy but as a form of relief matured at about the same period in which employed middle-class mothers approached philanthropic day nurseries in search of child-care programs oriented to education. It may be recalled that the secretary of the National Federation of Day Nurseries rejected any prospect that high-standard, philanthropic nurseries would develop to satisfy the middle-class market. This occurrence indicates that philanthropic day nurseries per se were not repulsive to middle-class mothers in the early twentieth century, but that *repulsion by the day nurseries preceded the middle-class search for education of their children in nur-sery schools.* (We surmise from the evidence presented in Chapter Two that middle-class mothers then turned to nursery schools for reasons in addition to having been rebuffed by day nurseries. Day nursery staff had become too accustomed to dealing with lower-class clientele. Well-established attitudes of middle- and upper-class day-care staff and volunteers towards lower-class beneficiaries of charitable largesse probably explains behavior that middle-class mothers reportedly found tactless. Probably most influential, middle-class mothers seeking educationally oriented programs, such as the progressive education programs, were repelled by those day nurseries that remained unalterably oriented to custodial care. We believe this was a critical juncture in the history of day care and nursery schools. An opportunity existed then for day nurseries to discard the relief image by serving a broader clientele and developing in other programatic directions. As we mentioned previously, some day nurseries in the 1920s did evolve into education-centered nursery schools. Apparently, however, most charitable day nurseries did not shift at that time. As a result, middle-class mothers, other groups, and perhaps the general public eventually adopted the perspective in which day care was deemed a form of relief for needy families.

Why many well-meaning day-care professionals and boards of trustees were unable to alter their programs may appear self-evident. From the insiders' perspective, middle-class mothers would not have been deemed appropriate clientele for a "relief institution." Incidentally, those holding the charitable conception of day care seldom acknowledged explicitly—probably were unaware—that it was based on a class distinction. (Beer [1938, p. 212] stands out among the very few who saw the class dimension clearly: "The trouble is that though social service [day care] may be a step above old-fashioned charity, it still smacks of class distinction.") Still, to retain that class-bound perspective meant resisting the temptation to accommodate full fee-paying clients at a time when concern over day-care costs was high. However, to assume that class biases overwhelmed that temptation and rationalized the adequacy of a custodial orientation for children from impoverished families, to assume that class bias provides a sufficient explanation, leads to overlooking other factors involved in the widespread retention of that orientation from the 1920s on. The evidence suggests that cultural, professional, and bureaucratic pressures also helped shape and prolong the dimension of the relief-versus-education distinction pertaining to program content: that the program content of day care is custody; that of the nursery school, education.

The economic forces and class attitudes at play that led to conceiving of day care as relief were bound, of course, to partially mold the content of those programs. However, the cultural factor of the state of knowledge about children also had some effect. During the nineteenth century, when (nonprofit) day care was conceptualized as a charitable service, program emphases apparently were placed on the activities oriented to the parents, such as admissions, friendly visiting, and parental guidance, and, for the children, on "a regime based on health standards" (Whipple, 1929, p. 98). Probably the children received, at best, supervision from adults, a clean place in which to play and rest, health inspection, and nutritious meals and snacks. In short, well-meaning custodial care.

For a long time, as was mentioned in our historical chronology, practically no effort was made to educate the children, and the best that the day nurseries could have claimed to provide was healthy child care. Before the spread of kindergartens, let us say before the last quarter of the nineteenth century, the custodial orientation may be attributed to the cultural unawareness of the educational potential of early childhood and to untrained staff. By 1900, the approximately 3,000 kindergartens in existence were providing living examples of that potential. In the 1900s, the early professional day-care literature recognized educational possibilities of the day nurseries. By the 1920s, popular interest in child study, the progress of progressive education, and other professional and scientific advances into early childhood education and research led to the proliferation of nursery schools, progressive kindergartens, experimental schools, research centers, and institutions for training early childhood teachers. From that time on, the absence of an educational focus in day nurseries could no longer simply be attributed to unawareness of the possibilities of early childhood education.

The trained early childhood educators who went to work in day nurseries after the smaller number of nursery school jobs had been filled had an appreciation of the educability of very young children, as well as ideas and skills in how to do it. That educational perspective, newer conceptions of preschool programing, enthusiasm for those ideas, and eventually their larger numbers led to professional rivalry with social workers in the day nurseries. The latter, threatened by the more numerous competitors, resentful of the superior attitude of modernity manifested by the perhaps younger teachers, and suspicious that their professional position in day nurseries was being challenged, had ample reasons to resist incorporation into the program of the educators' "doctrine." It is not necessary for us to imply a principled affirmation of the custodial orientation in supposing such professional resistance occurred.

Not long after the professional rivalry began, it extended into competition at the state and federal levels. In the early 1930s, when the WPA began to plan a preschool program to employ unemployed teachers, statesmen and stateswomen of the preschool professions offered their advisory services. The offer was accepted, and the WPA preschool program was guided by the experience, knowledge, and curricula materials that had begun to accumulate from the experimental programs, child development research centers, and teacher-training programs. Even during the 1930s, bureaucratic problems arose between the centralized WPA program, the state child welfare and education agencies, and the federal allies of those state agencies, the Children's Bureau and Office of Education. Each agency also had its constituencies of the relevant professions, child welfare and education. The two federal agencies were assigned to supervise the wartime Lanham program after the WPA had been disbanded. Disputes between the agencies soon followed.[5] The disputes involved the facilitative and substantive facets of jurisdiction—budgets, staff positions, prestige, influence, and views on policy and programs. Contention spread to the counterpart state organizations.

The contending educators and social workers sought to resolve the doctrinal difficulty and reach an agreement. Late in 1945 the Office of Education and the Children's Bureau issued a joint statement advising that " 'School authorities should be responsible for such activities as nursery school and kindergartens . . . and school lunches. Social agencies should administer day-care programs, day-nursery service' " (cited in Lundberg, 1947, p. 295). The terms of that agreement parallel the conceptual distinction between day care and nursery schools in terms of relief versus education.

The bureaucratic *doctrinal* dissension had long-term consequences. The imprimatur of the highest governmental organizations in the respective fields was placed on the distinction. Their influence and prestige was found to extend a perspective that artificially segregated disciplines and activities bearing on the rearing of young children. Consequently, efforts to infuse educational content into day care later had to contend with high-level bureaucratic resistance. Also, it divided professions and organizations that, if allied, might have been able to press more effectively for preschool programs and funds. (A different assessment of the administrative aspects of the Lanham experience than that presented here was reached by federal officials: " 'Perhaps one of the more lasting effects was that the planning and operation of the program brought educational and welfare authorities to a better understanding of each other's policies and objectives' " [cited in Kadushin, 1967, p. 305]. The preponderance of evidence is contrary to that assessment. None of numerous respondents we interviewed in private supported that public claim. And subsequent events in the mid-1960s also give contrary indications.)

Summarizing to this point, we have attempted to explain the evolution and diffusion of the relief-versus-education dichotomy. Reflecting class distinctions, the associated conceptions of the programs and their content were articulated by day-care volunteers and staff and by others in the preschool field. Amplified by professional and bureaucratic dynamics, those distinctions appeared in the professional literature and then spread into the culture at large. That explanation admittedly deals only with several of the influential determinants of those issues and excludes potent social and economic factors.

It should be emphasized that we have been examining a distinction, a conception, the ideational and symbolic expression of perspectives on aspects of preschool reality. Now we will review evidence pertaining to empirical referents of that distinction. Those referents fall into three categories, each of which contains a dichotomy that parallels the basic distinction. By extension of that distinction, the clientele of day-care programs presumably falls into lower-class groups, the clientele of nursery school programs presumably into middle- and upper-class groups. What light does the historical evidence throw on these polarities? Are they accurate?

Day care as a relief institution presumably served segments of the lower class from 1860 to 1960. That presumption appears to be reasonably accurate only if it is qualified as limited principally to the clientele of philanthropic day care and if certain exclusions are made explicit. The most significant exclusion concerns the proportion of proprietary day-care clients who did not come from the lower class. That proportion is generally unknown and may have varied in different epochs. In 1951, we assume some sizable part of the 77 percent of the parents who paid proprietary fees of from $6 to $15 per week, plus very likely most of the 2 percent who paid more than $15 a week, were from comfortable or affluent families.

Other qualifications seem indicated, although they may well involve smaller proportions of day-care clients than those who paid relatively high proprietary fees. "The" lower class of day-care clientele included families in sufficiently distinguishable circumstances as to make dubious the ostensible homogeneity of clients in that social stratum: Compare the family with both parents working, or the family whose graduate student or professional student father would soon be earning a decent salary, with the widow or deserted wife working to support her children, or with the wife of an invalid husband, in the days before workmen's compensation and Medicaid, working to support her husband and children. The day-care literature mentions two-parent and student families, but not the proportion they constituted of day-care users. Nor are data available on the percentage of nonpoor families with children in the WPA day-care centers, or the possibly larger share of such families in the Lanham centers. Again, however, the presence of nonimpoverished families in those programs is asserted in or may be reasonably inferred from the literature.[6]

These reservations regarding the social class composition of day-care centers may not be sufficient to invalidate the generally held view of day-care clientele, but should serve to caution us against exaggerating the extent to which that clientele is "economically handicapped" or socially and/or psychologically inadequate. Developments in day care from the postwar period into the 1960s lend weight to that caution. By 1960, the proprietary sector—accommodating an unknown, but presumably sizable proportion of nonimpoverished children—dominated the field. It represented just short of two thirds (64 percent) of licensed day-care centers, and a bare majority (51 percent) of the aggregate capacity of those day-care programs (see Appendix, Table 2).

The conventional wisdom that holds day care to be a relief program for economically dependent families and nursery schools for the education of very young children has been construed to imply that nursery schools serve the middle or upper classes. One authority went beyond implying such social backgrounds and asserted that "the American nursery school served first the needs of the professional and economically favored groups" (Forest, 1930, p. 323; compare Moustakas and Berson, 1955, p. 180). The available evidence indicates such implications and assertions were seriously inaccurate for the period from 1920 to 1945.

Almost half of the nursery schools in the 1929 sample survey reported clientele largely resembling those supposedly exclusive to day care (low-income, immigrant, one-parent families). Especially because that sample included only a small number of programs, doubt about its representativeness may understandably arise. The sizable extent of philanthropic sponsorship (about 30 percent) of all known nursery schools at that time in part may offset those doubts. A contemporaneous observation by preschool authorities may also add weight toward counter-balancing disbelief; alluding to the philanthropic sponsorship of nursery schools, the analogy is made that "The nursery school of today is in much the same sociological position as the kinder-garten of two generations ago" (Whipple, 1929, p. 262). (Many kindergartens, it may be recalled, had been initially established under philanthropic auspices in the late nineteenth century to serve immigrant children in slum areas.) The data strongly sug-gest that during the first decade of substantial nursery school growth in this country, the 1920s, the children attending were not mainly from the middle class. The proportion of lower-class children in attendance may have been substantial.

Compared to the 1920s, the WPA and Lanham programs are more widely recognized as exceptions to the generalization that holds nursery schools essentially enroll children from mid-dle- and high-income families (for example, see Radin, 1971, p. 128). Although the WPA and Lanham programs are more widely known to have constituted exceptions to the ostensible middle-class composition of nursery schools, several points should be made. The magnitude of that exception was itself exceptional. Between 1933 and 1945, the federal government created and supported an increase of approximately six- to sevenfold in the number of nursery schools. This means that the number of lower-class children attending nursery schools in *any one of the depression years after 1933* probably exceeded the number of middle-class children in such schools during *the entire decade of the 1920s* (see Appendix, Table 3). Additional thousands of lower-class children attended Lanham nurseries during the war years. We can say with confidence that from 1920 through 1945, which is essentially the first quarter cen-tury of nursery schools in the United States, those schools accommodated significant, if not dominant numbers of children who were not middle or upper class. Thus the available evidence fails to sustain *for that time period* what has become the con-ventional wisdom on the social class composition of nursery schools.[7]

After World War II, however, with the ending of federal support for nursery schools, a major shift of sponsors and clientele apparently occurred. A massive increase of the proprietary sector occurred in the nursery school field; by 1951, it may be recalled, about two thirds of the known nursery schools were under proprietary management. Assuming that proprietary preschool auspices generally, but not exclusively indicate a middle- or upper-class clientele, the evidence would mean that to a much greater extent than ever before nursery schools then accommodated predominantly middle-class children. Data for 1951 on proprietary school clientele support the assumption of an association between commercial auspices and middle-class composition; 70 percent of that clientele paid fees estimated to require substantial family income, 30 percent paid lower fees. It seems clear that after the war middle-class children made up, at the very least, the majority in nursery schools. Thus in the postwar period, the generalization that nursery schools catered largely to middle-class families appears to be accurate, for the first time in nursery school history. This postwar pattern probably continued uninterrupted into the mid-1960s. By 1965 private nursery schools accounted for three fourths of the total nursery school population (Schloss, 1966, p. 6).

Several conclusions emerge from our examination of the available facts about day-care and nursery school clientele. The widely held characterization of day-care clientele as economically dependent stands in need of two modifications. First, although that description may have provided a loose fit with the clients in philanthropic nurseries, it probably did not fit with families that purchased proprietary day care. Second, many families served by the WPA and Lanham centers would probably have been difficult to recognize from the conventional portrait of day-care clients. Likewise, comparisons of the view of nursery schools as preschool enclaves of middle-class children with the available evidence points out a major distortion. That view misrepresents the social class composition of nursery school families from 1920 through 1945.

In ignoring the proprietary day-care centers, overlooking evidence from the 1920s, and treating admittedly critical years from 1933 to 1946 as exceptions, the conventional wisdom implanted social class and professional biases into what then was taken as a proven historical generalization. By implying clear social class distinctions, when the actually existing differences were far less sharp, social class stereotypes became congealed in the relief-versus-education formula.

Another category parallel to the relief-versus-education formulation on which data are available relates to the length of the program day. By inference from that formulation, day-care programs presumably cover a full day, six to eight or more hours, and nursery schools half a day, three to five hours. The inference may be attributable to the association of day care with lower-class working mothers and of nursery school with educating middle-class children. What does the evidence show?

Data on reports from virtually all historical periods consistently confirm the full-day schedule as a general pattern in day care. Several postwar references report a minor variation within that pattern connected to program sponsorship. To accommodate the parent-customer, some proprietors extend the program day well beyond schedules established by other, professionally staffed philanthropic programs (Gurin and others, 1966, pp. 37-41; Prescott, 1965, p. 6).

According to the evidence on nursery schools, however, the implication of essentially half-day operations is misleading. In 1929, 35 percent of "nursery schools" and 67 percent of "relief nursery schools" in a national enumeration conducted full-day programs (White House Conference, 1930b, p. 157); 55 percent of another national listing also reported having whole-day programs (Whipple, 1929, pp. 239-241). A national survey in the year 1931 to 1932 found 43 percent of the nursery schools in session from five and a quarter to eight hours a day, with another 9 percent from eight and a quarter to twelve hours (Forest, 1930). Most of the WPA nursery schools were in operation for a full day. And in 1951, between 16 and 41 percent (depending on auspices) of the nursery schools enumerated had programs of from five to twelve hours a day (Moustakas and Berson, 1955, pp. 53, 69, 85, 95, 116, and 151); cooperative schools (N = 116) reported a percentage of 16, proprietary (N =

200), 41; 22 percent of laboratory nursery schools ($N = 130$) held to elementary school hours.

The information on program schedules can be summarized simply. Day-care centers have almost invariably conducted full-day programs, but the evidence up to the 1950s indicates that considerable modification is called for in the traditional view of nursery schools as half-day programs.

Distinctive program orientations have been linked customarily with day care and with nursery schools: custodial care in the former, preschool education in the latter. In turning to the available evidence, we must acknowledge the greater difficulty authorities confront in objectively assessing this dimension than in categorizing the social background of the clientele or in classifying the length of the program day.

The literature very generally supports the view of a custodial focus in philanthropic and proprietary day care, especially before the 1930s. During the early period, 1860 to 1930, however, the evidence not only is sparse, but also most often is indirect and tenuous. (For an exception, providing a few specific details, see White House Conference, 1930b, p. 170.) Generalizations about the content of early day-care programs, therefore, cannot be definitive. Furthermore, such generalizations only apply after 1930 with several notable exceptions.

Earlier, in Chapter Two, we reported the infusion of educational content through the efforts of teachers trained in early childhood education and affiliation with training institutions. Presumably this occurred in a small proportion of philanthropic day-care centers. Most accounts of and reports on the WPA and Lanham day nurseries agree that their program content was primarily educational. Programs of such large magnitude covering a twelve-year time span constitute a conspicuous qualification to generalizations about day care as custodial care. They also have been credited with having advanced the idea of preschool programs and the importance of implementing professional standards. We offer as a conjecture that in this respect they served as a paradigmatic model for some later day-care programs.

Whether or not the WPA-Lanham programs set an example by incorporating education content in day care, several authorities report a qualitative change in the postwar years. In 1951, the national survey by experts with the Merrill-Palmer School reported the professional preparation of directors and teachers in the public day-care centers in California and in centers under the aegis of social agencies generally "compared favorably" with their counterparts in nursery schools (Moustakas and Berson, 1955, p. 190). The educational programs of those day-care centers were judged also to be moving in professionally desirable directions. Another study in 1956 provided corroboration: "One of the most interesting findings of the study was that nursery schools and child-care centers [virtually all nonprofit day-care centers] had more similarities than differences. . . . There were no significant differences either in theory or practice. This homogeneity of nursery schools and child care centers [indicates] that earlier distinctions between day nurseries, day-care centers, and nursery schools are no longer valid, and that care and education have become inseparable aspects of any good program for young children" (Moustakas and Berson, 1956, pp. 60-61; see also Allen and Campbell, 1948; Swift, 1964).

No evidence was found to warrant a claim by proprietary day care to educational progress approaching that apparently made in the postwar years by philanthropic and public programs. Rather, the studies referred to earlier, in Chapter Two, assessed the profit-seeking programs as generally deficient and inadequate. This suggests that the tradition of a custodial program orientation may have been maintained during the century of day care, from 1860 to 1960, by proprietary programs in general. If true, the dominant position occupied by the proprietary sector in 1960 could mean that the majority of day-care centers at that time still provided simply custodial child care. In the absence of substantial evidence, however, we must stress the conditional nature of such propositions.

The educational claim for nursery schools inherent in the relief-versus-education formulation remains to be assayed. Granting differences among various types of nursery schools, the information in the professional literature supports that claim in general, with one qualification. As judged by an objective indicator, the educational training and experience of the principal program staff, in 1951 a considerable minority of proprietary nursery schools did not meet the standards presumed necessary for a sound educational program. Additionally, professional experts suspect that too frequently the profit motive superseded educational requirements. If the objective indicator of professional education were validated, then the middle-class children in a minority, perhaps as large as 45 percent, of private nursery schools did not receive a quality education.

To recapitulate, evidence bearing on the program content of day-care centers and nursery schools reveals that the distinction between custodial care and education applied only partially and unevenly. The distinction bypassed historical exceptions, differences between programs under varied sponsors, and emergent trends. Finally, both our review of evidence and the history presented previously show generally that neither program nomenclature nor auspices offer assurance of program content, let alone quality, in a loosely regulated service industry.

What conclusions can be drawn from our examination of the relief-versus-education distinction? What pertinence did the distinction have in the day-care policy arena in 1962? We attribute the distinction to the social origins and associated normative and social viewpoints of preschool staff and experts, and to competition between contending professions and bureaucratic organizations. As applied by the program staff, the distinction influenced the conception and content of the respective programs. When examined in light of available evidence, the formulation appears at best misleading, at worst quite inaccurate. In failing to recognize numerous historic circumstances and influences the distinction seemingly took on timeless meaning. Ensuing generations of staff, parents, and the general public were guided by the stereotyped conception of reality and later generations then found the invidious distinction appealing, convenient, and seemingly too accurate to question.

The distinction became the epitome of the major, if not dominant perspective on day care among professionals and policy makers. Thus a broad survey in 1962 of welfare and civil opinion (welfare staff, board members, businessmen, labor officials, and clergy) found that many respondents conceived of day care as a service to needy, incomplete, or disturbed families (Ruderman, 1968, pp. 68, 73, and 80). Accepting the stereotype of day care as providing merely custodial care, United States senators in the 1960s reportedly opposed day-care legislation as authorizing federal funds for babysitting. This dominant perspective on day care, the child welfare perspective, was incorporated eventually into federal statute and regulation, as we show in Chapter Four.

The child welfare perspective may have played a part in obstructing diffusion and acceptance of a different vision, that of universally available day care. These two perspectives pose a basic normative choice with wide ideological ramifications for social or public policy—whether socially or publicly subsidized day care should be selectively or universally available (Bensman and Lilienfeld, 1973, pp. 240-242).

When explicitly defined as a program to prevent neglect or as a relief institution, day care applied selectively to those who would fit that definition. When defined as child care that higher-paid or career-seeking mothers could afford, the paycheck defined selectivity. Definitions in terms of universality required different presuppositions. Progressive education theory had provided a philosophical and pedagogical rationale, child development theory, a scientific rationale for universalizing the presuppositions of preschool educations. The Great Depression and World War II contributed an ideological rationale.[8] All these sources fostered the espousal of universal preschool programs. In the postwar period this ecumenical tenor continued to be heard, particularly from a few academicians in child welfare. For example, Kahn urged that day care, and other social services, be considered a "social utility" (1959).

When viewed in terms of the social structure, the distinction between universality and selectivity raises fundamental questions:[9] Should public day-care programs be made available to all social classes? If yes, would that not mean establishing a claim on public services for the rich, who can afford to pay, possibly at the expense of the poor? In a stratified society, the universal orientation can be challenged on the very ground that orientation seeks to bypass or overcome. As we shall see, this objection was raised in the 1962 deliberations on day-care policy.

On the other hand, if public programs across social class lines are not advocated, the questions arise: To which social strata should the policy apply? How does a policy of benefits to selected strata serve the general or public interest?

The child welfare perspective, as we have seen, answered these questions by defining day care as a service to prevent child neglect and to strengthen "the family," and by selecting "underprivileged children" and the "child of poverty" as the appropriate clientele. In the next chapter, the ramifications of that perspective in the policy arena are discussed.

The Invisible Majority

The literature makes reference to proprietary preschool programs beginning at the time of the Civil War. Toward the end of the century covered in our history, 1860 to 1960, proprietary day-care centers and nursery schools became numerically dominant in those fields. Yet by contrast to the philanthropic and public programs, infinitely less is known about profit-seeking preschool programs. We now examine this anomaly. First, data on the magnitude of proprietary programs is recapitulated and illustrations given to support our contention that the proprietary sector is symbolically invisible. We undertake to explain the anomaly in terms of professional antipathy, the nature of these programs as business entities and their stage of development. Finally, that explanation is related to the place taken by the proprietors in the preschool policy process in the 1960s.

We have taken some liberty in referring to proprietary day-care centers and nursery schools as a majority. Whether proprietary programs were ever in the majority during the period from 1860 to 1920 cannot be determined. Prior to the 1920s, no systematic information appears in the literature on preschool programs, including those under proprietary management. Therefore, any claim about the position in the preschool field held by proprietary programs in those years would be conjectural. In 1929, data presented earlier show that the proprietary preschool programs made up either a sizable minority or plurality compared to programs under other auspices. We assume the sector made little headway during the WPA and Lanham periods. The evidence cited earlier, however, clearly establishes that the profit-seeking programs in the day care and nursery school fields reached their majority after the end of World War II and held that position into the early 1960s.

For the early period of preschool programs, the available literature tells little more about proprietary programs than that they existed. Toward the end of the nineteenth century, child abuse in commercial day nurseries associated with "baby farms" resulted in public notoriety and professional hostility. The later professional literature treats proprietary programs with a mixture of enmity and disdain. For example, the authoritative yearbook of the National Society for the Study of Education refers to commercial day nurseries as "the lowest and least desirable form [resorted to] in localities where organized nursery service is inadequate or does not exist. . . . They contribute nothing to childhood but extra dangers" (Whipple, 1929, p. 88).

More often, professional disdain for proprietary programs was manifested by ignoring their existence. A federal survey covering day nurseries in 1923 failed to include proprietary programs, a failing also to be noted in the lengthy discussion of nursery schools in the authoritative yearbook (Whipple, 1929) and in the *Encyclopedia of Social Sciences* (Forest, 1930). Even in more recent times detailed descriptions of proprietary programs rarely appear in the professional literature. (There are two major exceptions: the 1951 national survey of preschool programs [Moustakas and Berson, 1955] and the 1961-1962 survey of day care and nursery schools conducted in seven communities across the country [Ruderman, 1968]. The Boston area study [Gurin and others, 1966] included data on one proprietary day-care center. Prescott's study [1965] in one community also obtained data on proprietary day care. Aside from these studies and reports on program statistics for 1929 and 1960, only fragmentary items on proprietary programs may be found in the literature examined for this study.) Impressionistically, it seems that national newspapers such as the *New York Times* were not any more attentive. Professional scorn extended to not inviting day-care proprietors to national day-care conferences in the 1960s and, according to several proprietors, to a condescending "chip on the shoulder" attitude.

For their part, however, the proprietors have made no contribution to the nursery school or day-care literature. As a result of long-term professional antipathy and the proprietors' even more extensive failure to write about their programs, that sector remained almost invisible symbolically during the periods when such programs have been a major, at times dominant, sponsor of preschool programs. Nor have the commercial programs received full recognition as the basic mechanism, over the span of a century, for balancing demand for and supply of preschool programs.

We suggest that several factors may explain the proprietors' apparent reticence. At least in the past, proprietary programs have differed typically from philanthropic and public programs by implementing their aims without declaration or doctrinal elaboration. The search for profits needs no extensive rationale in our society. Other reasons for the paucity of information on these types of programs also stem from their purpose. As with other profit-seeking enterprises, information could conceivably be useful to a competitor, the tax collector, or licensing authorities. Perhaps the consumer, too, might become better informed, and so be able to consider alternative possibilities. To these resistances to providing information must be added the inexpertness of small enterprises and the effort required to maintain records. (The flavor of proprietary reticence was captured in the report of a study: "A constant problem in . . . [dealing with the proprietary day-care center] was the inadequacy of records, and an unwillingness to share information about finances, families [clients], or anything else" [Gurin and others, 1966, p. 40].) If there has been a proprietary literature, it consisted of advertising brochures or leaflets. This form of the written word used by commercial centers also reflects their objective—eliciting consumer demand for the service. In short, the insufficient staffing, inadequately trained personnel, and secrecy characteristic of small businesses may account in part for the absence from the public record in the past of material on proprietary programs.

Other economic and collective attributes of proprietary programs may have heightened this symbolic nonpresence. For the most part, the sector has consisted of a large number of small, scattered program units. Programs could be established only with a minimum or modest capital investment. Until recently, while small conglomerate groupings may have been formed, operations for the most part out of the proprietor's home did not lead to economic benefits from large-scale operations. Furthermore, proprietary programs have been reputedly economically unstable—go into and out of business rather quickly. As a result of these economic traits, for decades proprietary programs apparently did not rationalize the protection of their collective self-interest by forming associations. The threat perceived from municipal and state licensing laws and standards did induce such collective action, at least in some cities and states (Mayer and Kahn, 1965, pp. 92-95).

At least until the 1960s, however, associations were not formed, nor business conferences held, nor journals published at the national level. Aside from the economic impediments to collective action nationally, apparently the proprietary sector did not perceive any possible threats or benefits to its self-interest in the nation's capitol. The unorganized nature of the proprietary preschool sector meant a lack of influence as an interest group in the national policy arena. Without an effective voice or representation in that arena, the dominant preschool sector was also invisible when federal preschool programs were enacted in the 1960s. Its interests unprotected, proprietary participation was excluded from the programs then established. (Developments in proprietary management in the late 1960s, however, may presage greater visibility and political influence. Those developments are taken up in the concluding chapter.)

Fulfillment of the Individual's Potential

In our earlier discussion of the progressive education movement, its major preschool contribution was noted. Progressive education had a decisive influence on the aims and content of nursery school, kindergarten, and, by the postwar period, day-care programs. As an illustration of its seminal influence we mentioned the wide diffusion of the progressive education ideal of facilitating the maximum realization of the child's inherent potential. Here we examine the transformation of that tenet of naturalist philosophy and of other goals of progressive education.

The theory underwent a remarkable evolution. Many factors at play in that process, such as the loss by the progressive education movement of its reformist zeal after World War I (Cremin, 1964, p. 183), are not taken up. Here the focus is on several features of Dewey's theory that contributed to its transformation.

We briefly recapitulate the pertinent goals and educational emphases in Dewey's writings, identify parts that proved fragile, describe the ensuing transformation, and relate its legacy to preschool policy in the 1960s. The purpose in doing so is to present our contention that the process whereby Deweyan principles were drained of their original meaning rendered them noncontroversial and thus useful in the policy process.

Dewey, it may be recalled, posited several goals for education. From the standpoint of the individual child, progressive education aimed to facilitate the "growth of the child in the direction of social capacity" and "fullness of realization of his budding powers." From the communal perspective, education should seek to develop "a spirit of social cooperation and community life" (Dewey, [1900] 1956b, pp. 91-92, 119, 16, respectively). These aims and the terms in which Dewey formulated them reflected his explicit adherence to the philosophic naturalism of the German educator, Friedrich Froebel.

Dewey added a corollary aim in applying that philosophic point of view to the industrial society around him. Education was to be the means to overcome the meaninglessness of factory work. It should aim to impart to the individual a scientific understanding of the industrial world and to help the individual apply that understanding to his work.

Acceptance of Froebel's educational ideas led Dewey to

place the focus in education emphatically on "the life of the child." That emphasis warrants reiteration: "The primary root of all educative activity is in the instinctive, impulsive attitudes and activities of the child, and not in the presentation and application of external material, whether through the ideas of others or through the senses" (Dewey, [1900] 1956b, p. 36). For Dewey, teaching meant giving direction to the child's impulsivity. In doing so, the child is to be the center around which the processes and means of education are to be organized.

This meant to Dewey that ideas in books be recognized as "formulated statements of experience," valuable to the student not in and of themselves but as reincorporated into his immediate experience. The progressivist challenge to teachers is precisely to induce a "vital and personal experiencing" of the received subject matter. Received wisdom is important if it enables the student to interpret and expand his experience, but educationally dangerous if permitted to serve as a substitute for experience.

Addressing himself to a progressive industrial society, in contrast to traditionalist "primitive societies," Dewey urged that education be future oriented. Instead of helping students reproduce received customs, teachers should endeavor to help students develop "better habits," habits by which the existing society would be improved (cited in Lasch, 1967, p. 88).

Finally, in completing our review of the pertinent parts of Dewey's educational theory, one technique to be employed by the progressive educator needs to be mentioned. Rather than ignoring or condemning the "impulsive attitude" and "spontaneous activities" of the child, they are to be nurtured. Play, defined as a "psychological attitude" allowing the "free play ... of all the child's powers" is seen as a fundamental educational technique (Dewey, [1900] 1956b, pp. 118-119).

Dewey's theory contained a number of troublesome difficulties, three of which are pertinent. Dewey's distinction between external impositions or materials and "the child's interests" was vague. He had classified those interests as involuntary, voluntary, and reflective. These definitions were so ambiguous that by as early as 1899 Dewey noted they had been "radically perverted" by followers. Some of them, he wrote, treated the word *"voluntary* . . . as meaning the reluctant and disagreeable instead of the free, the self-directed" (Dewey, [1900] 1956b, p. 149). Given such conceptual obscurity, discernment of the child's interests in a given situation, by Dewey's admission, required highly discriminating judgment: "Only by watching the child and seeing the attitude he assumes can we tell whether [the teacher's suggestions to the child] are operating as factors in furthering the child's growth, or whether they are external, arbitrary impositions interfering with normal growth" (Dewey, [1900] 1956b, pp. 129-130). Any educator will appreciate the difficulty in making that discrimination. Cremin (1964, p. 348) concluded that to implement this "commitment to build upon student needs and interest demanded extraordinary feats of pedagogical ingenuity [and] in the hands of too many average teachers [it] led to chaos."

Dewey could not clarify the distinctions in part because of an inability to depart from or qualify Rousseauian and Froebelian assumptions as to the nature of human nature and education. Try as he might, Dewey remained fixed to the assumption, in Wishy's phrase, of the "supremacy of self-activity."

The second and perhaps greatest difficulty in Dewey's theory, mentioned earlier in the history of preschool programs, concerned his attitude towards knowledge and its place in the process of education. The ambiguity stems from the complex and delicate construction, as precarious as a tightrope, which Dewey had made of the use of knowledge other than the child's direct experience for purposes of education. On the one hand he (and other progressivists like Addams) were extremely critical of the exclusive concern with the intellectual capacity of the student and of the "desiccated scholasticism" of the older education. He feared such knowledge could subvert education if it became a substitute for the child's reflective experience. On the other hand, he had a profound appreciation of the precious value of accumulated knowledge as mankind's intellectual capital. Dewey, whose own life and work as a philosopher, logician, and intellectual earned him international repute, could and did walk that tightrope, clearly maintaining his own balance. Apparently many of his followers were less up on their toes, intellectually speaking, and ended up in an antiintellectual position.[10]

A third limitation in the theory stems from one of its strengths, the manifold rather than the simplistic way in which Dewey viewed the "social." For him, it pertained not only to "primary" and "secondary" group relations, but also to formal and substantive aspects of social life. The word *social* referred not only to the activities and relationships between people, but also to social organizations and social institutions. He also recognized language and communication as inherently social phenomena (see Dewey, [1900] 1956b, pp. 43, 140-141). Perhaps Dewey's emphasis on cooperative aspects of human relations imparted a normative meaning. The absence of distinctions between the multiple meanings of *social* in Dewey's writings on education rendered the term unclear to his followers and other readers.

These three ambiguities contributed to the "progress" of progressive education theory in ways unanticipated as well as undesired by Dewey and Addams. Many progressive educators, Cremin (1964, p. 202) pointed out, literally or mechanically fixed on and "expanded one part of what progressive education had formally meant into its total meaning." Several aspects of that transformation are pertinent for subsequent preschool developments.

Dewey's general propositions, as carried out by successive generations of teachers—people with different backgrounds, commitments, and outlooks, living in periods less optimistic than the Progressive Era, eventually ended up as a vague, stale educational program. For example, later nursery school educators, it may be remembered, translated the Deweyan aim of developing "better habits" oriented to the future into an overemphasis, an authority cautioned, "on routine habit building" (Whipple, 1929, p. 230). Similarly, the phrase "free play" developed over the decades into one of the jargon phrases of early childhood education in the United States and other countries around the world.

Key terms derived from Froebel's principles, however,

apparently were the most problematic. Concepts like the "child's interests," "the whole child," or "creative self-expression," Cremin acknowledged, "in classroom practice . . . were not very good guides to positive action. At least the generation that invented them had an idea of what they meant. The generation that followed adopted them as a collection of ready-made clichés" (1964, p. 348). Wishy (1968, p. 139), for example, interpreted that educational aim, the self-realization of the child, the drawing out of his fullest potential, as a call for "the symmetrical development of all the powers of the individual." But in Dewey's writings on education the intellectual capacity of the individual was deemphasized and general, not exclusive, emphasis was placed on the social dimension. We may recall that later cohorts of progressive educators translated that deemphasis into a principled avoidance of instruction on or preparation for reading. Emphasis on the "social" was interpreted by succeeding progressive educators exclusively or primarily in terms of immediate and direct interpersonal relations. This resulted in dominant attention to the unfolding of the personality in terms of peer relations, in relation to the "social group," to the socioemotional dimension of the child. Instead of pursuing the aim of a "cooperative commonwealth" or the ideal of the adult worker as applied scientist, the progressive education movement produced a different image of the ideal personality. Progressive education, which under Dewey and Addams had set out to develop a socially cooperative individual conceived in relation to the larger society, led instead to a model personality seemingly autonomous of the school, other institutions, and of the social order. For want of a better title, that image may be called "the socially adjusted, flexible personality." Its major attributes are emphases on the social development of the child and on flexibility and freedom in the environment to facilitate the unfolding of the self.

These transformations of key concepts and propositions signify, in other words, that the progressive education movement had become routinized. (In his last published work on education, Dewey recognized this fact. We are told he "likened these progressive ideas gone stale to mustard plasters taken out of the medicine cabinet and applied externally as the need arose" [Cremin, 1964, p. 349].) The theory became transformed into a durable orthodoxy. In the late 1920s, that quality already was visible in "good" preschool programs. In 1929, an unexpected homogeneity in progressive kindergartens had been noted by a discomfited progressivist (Whipple, 1929, p. 270). Four decades later, a visitor to several "good" nursery schools was struck by the remarkable degree of similarity in the programs (Fishman, 1967).

The fate that befell progressivist theory displays the operation of social processes through different historical periods that sort and sift ideas, a process called *elective affinity*. The ideas selected then were redefined, losing their naturalist presuppositions and much of their original meaning. Moreover, Dewey could perhaps have recognized but not appreciated the irony that the progressive credo—the fullest development of the child's potential—was incorporated into the received wisdom. It was employed in a way that made knowledge in general suspect to Dewey, as a substitute for thought. As we shall see in later chapters, that credo loomed as one of the most frequently encountered rationales for favoring federally supported preschool programs in the 1960s. Individuals at the highest levels of national policy making and those with less influence unquestioningly invoked a tenet with little awareness of its debatable naturalist origin. Lacking specificity, it accommodated a range of different meanings and also covered over those differences. The philosophy and theory that had elevated an unclear conception of creativity to a high value thus provided a major "theorhetorical" image in the policy arena. Transformed into a banal phrase, the tenet was incorporated into federal statute.

Kindergartens and the Educational Establishment

The differential rate of growth of nursery school and kindergarten programs was noted in the chronological narrative. Several pertinent issues are implicated in that trend. We will indicate the terminological effect it had in the preschool field. Then we will present reasons for the postwar preference of public educators in general for kindergartens. That explanation will then be related to the stance taken by the educators as federal preschool policy unfolded in the mid-1960s.

It may be useful to first review some highlights of the respective growth of kindergartens and nursery schools. Having started about a half century before the nursery schools, the kindergartens had a considerable head start (see Appendix, Tables 3 and 5). Public sponsorship had helped impel the kindergartens into a commanding position by the time nursery schools began to spread. Thus by the year 1929 to 1930, the kindergartens enrolled about 150 children for each child in nursery school. In 1934, the stimulus of WPA funds for nursery schools, and an apparent decline in kindergartens decreased the lead in enrollment held by the latter to roughly eight to one. Despite its head start, however, by 1945 kindergartens enrolled only about one fourth of the five-year-olds in the country. During the postwar years, the nursery schools, without public funds to speak of, made slow progress, while kindergartens expanded rapidly. By the mid-1960s kindergartens enrolled slightly less than two thirds (62 percent) of the eligible five-year-old children (U.S. Department of Health, Education, and Welfare, 1967, p. 29).

In short, the two types of programs experienced differential rates of growth up to the first half of the 1960s. Overall the growth of kindergartens in number and in proportion to the "preschool" population far exceeded that of the nursery schools. This trend affected program terminology. During the century of preschool programs, 1860 to 1960, the program terms were hardly distinctive. Historically, most kindergartens operated classes for about half the regular school day. Prior to 1946, at times a sizable minority, at other times a majority of nursery schools, at least of the nonproprietary programs, apparently also conducted half-day programs. Until that time the program content, age groups served, and sponsorship, as well as program duration had been sufficiently overlapping as to preclude sharp differentiation between these two types of preschool programs.[11]

By the 1960s, with the increased number of children in

kindergartens within school systems, it became increasingly awkward and inappropriate to classify the kindergarten as a "preschool" program. Educators now distinguish these programs in terms of a model educational sequence. Kindergarten is defined as the preschool program that immediately precedes the primary grades, and nursery school is the educational program that precedes kindergarten. Current educational usage classifies both types as *preprimary* programs (Gore, 1965, pp. 4-5). Thus, after approximately a century of preschool programs, a distinctive program nomenclature has begun to emerge. That development reflects the growth of both types and the increased federal involvement. At last, it seems, preschool programs are of sufficient magnitude, and programatic and fiscal importance to be a matter of semantic consequence.

The preference for kindergartens, compared to nursery schools, on the part of public educators can be attributed to fiscal and programatic reasons. Incidentally, this attribution does not deny the possibility that precedent, the longer tradition of public kindergartens in the United States, affected educators' attitudes. Although both types of programs are costly, nursery schools apparently are considerably more expensive. A study early in the 1920s, it may be recalled, found an experimental nursery school program to be from four to six times greater than the unit cost in the public kindergarten. Although 'he fiscal differential between the two may have decreased, kindergartens seem to be less expensive for several reasons.

Kindergarten and nursery school programs are both labor intensive. According to professional standards they require higher teacher-student ratios than the elementary grades. However, standards of class size set for nursery schools exceed those established for kindergartens (Gore, 1965, pp. 27, 37). In the past, kindergartens have also been more economical in terms of classroom usage. Having been half-day programs historically, a kindergarten program can make use of one room for two groups of children each day. During those decades when many nursery school sessions lasted for a full day, they required more space per child. (This space problem is said to have been another reason that public school officials did not seek to retain the large-scale nursery school programs operated in their buildings or under their aegis when federal funds were withdrawn at the end of World War II [Moustakas and Berson, 1955, pp. 70-71].)

Physical facilities and staff represent the largest costs of education programs. Nursery school classes, having been more costly in both categories, were more expensive overall. Thus an opinion by preschool experts in 1955 suggested that nursery school would be "almost prohibitively" expensive within public schools.

Kindergartens apparently also presented fewer programatic problems to public school administrators. The incorporation of these programs into the public schools led to difficulties, at least after the kindergarten teachers adopted progressive education theories. Differences in education philosophy, theory, and curricula between the "preschool" progressivists and traditionalists in elementary education, on which Dewey had commented in 1899, continued for decades. Nevertheless, the inclusion of nursery schools within the public school systems, which had occurred in large numbers from 1933 to 1946, may have been even more problematic. Differences apparently arose over educational philosophy, goals, and curricula. Perhaps those differences were caused by tensions between the traditionalists and the progressivists. In addition, the literature also mentions difficulties over school regulations and discipline. (The differences may be simple, but basic. Preschool experts wondered whether or not principals who wanted their schools to be quiet would appreciate a noisy nursery school room [Moustakas and Berson, 1955, pp. 71-72].)

These fiscal and programatic reasons have been suggested to explain why public school administrators and school boards in the postwar years placed preschool priority on expansion of kindergartens. Thus in the 1960s, a federal commissioner advocated extension of kindergarten programs for all eligible preschool-age children, at the same time that the movement for nursery school programs began to gain momentum. When that momentum spurred federal legislative proposals the federal educational establishment was not in the avant-garde. Educators, the key personnel in conducting preschool programs, were seen by preschool policy makers as professionally hidebound and unsympathetic. Accordingly, federal policy makers tended, with a few exceptions, to circumscribe the role of the education profession and bureaucracy as preschool policy unfolded in the 1960s.

Notes

[1]Subtle but significant distinctions among "supporting," "supplementing," "supplanting," or "subverting" family functions vibrate throughout the day-care and child welfare literature and legislative enactments. For illustrations, see Kadushin (1967, pp. 23-25); professional child welfare reservations in the face of wartime pressures may be detected in Lundberg (1942); Catholic concern before 1962—when a glacial shift occurred—is expressed by the Bishops of the United States (1950); a recent orthopsychiatric example is Richmond's editorial, "How Long, Oh Lord, How Long: A Proposal for the Extension of Day Care Programs" (1967); and for the most pertinent day-care reference, with opinion data reflecting concerns over supplanting family functions, see Ruderman (1968). Yet there appears no central treatment of this issue in the literature. The professional and legislative agents of social parenthood appear unable or unwilling to recognize ambivalence toward familial parenthood.

[2]The literature describes still other matters for casework decision. When the mother stopped working, was the child to be dropped from the day nursery? Or, if the mother had a day off, should the child be permitted to attend? Setting of the fee to be charged—on the basis of the family's resources—was another task caseworkers apparently performed. And, with the advent of mothers' pensions, caseworkers could apply the eligibility rules and cost-benefit formulas to distinguish between cases to be admitted to day care, to allow the mother to work, and those mothers to be denied day-care admission, but publicly subsidized to stay home to rear the children. For illustrations of or references to such casework decision making see: Beer (1938, p. 182; 1957, p. 177); Mayer and Kahn (1965, p. 76); Whipple (1929, pp. 92-94); White House Conference (1930a, pp. 27-28).

[3]Establishment of the Lanham day nurseries led to another dilemma for caseworkers. Day care for hundreds of thousands, in the national defense, created a difficulty in defending casework technique. Because of "the wide demand for . . . the care of children which had no obvious relation to adequacy or inadequacy of the parent," the relevance of casework in day care was put into question. One answer to this question was to affirm new usages for casework, rather than to deny the charge of irrelevance or to stubbornly reassert the traditional screening function. The new usages were to prepare the child for entry into day care and to serve as a

liaison, to exchange information on the child between mother and day-care center (Lundberg, 1947, pp. 291-292). To some extent, this illustrates an unshakable hold of professional technique, the transmutation of methodology into fetish (Greenblatt and Katkin, 1972).

A different response to the expansion of day care during the war emphasized the neglected "conviction of the importance of truly universal services for children." The latter response focused on the goal of ecumenical service and simply transcended instrumental consideration of casework tasks (Lenroot, 1947, p. vi).

[4]This anecdote and several other previously cited fragments in the literature attest to the actual *use* of casework in day care. However, the literature devotes more space to prescriptions for use than to the facts of usage. As much evidence exists to dispute the extent of the use of casework in day care—at least in recent years—as to confirm its centrality: Mayer and Kahn report that casework is "more often ideology than practice" (1965, p. 148). A time and cost study of several day-care centers meeting professional standards revealed that 6 to 7 percent of total staff time was devoted to the casework tasks of admissions and counseling: At one center, most of the caseworker's time was devoted to setting fees with applicants (see Gurin and others, 1966, pp. 38, 77). A different study reached conclusions consistent with these comments (Prescott, 1965, p. 40; see also Kadushin, 1967, p. 342). Finally, on the basis of data from a survey in 1962 of 107 day-care centers, Ruderman concluded that "the social work component . . . is almost nonexistent" (1968, p. 103).

[5]Competitiveness between these sister agencies went back a long way, however. The commissioner of the U.S. Bureau of Education in 1912 had opposed establishment of the Children's Bureau. He assessed the purposes proposed for that agency as " 'with one possible exception . . . either direct or indirect problems of education with which the Bureau of Education now deals or should undertake' " (cited in Bremner, 1971, p. 770).

[6]A survey of WPA nursery schools reported the clientele approximating the socioeconomic composition of the general population " 'with some tendency [toward] greater proportions from the slightly skilled and laboring groups' " (cited in Campbell, Bair, and Harvey, 1939, p. 112). An indirect clue may be offered about the families using the Lanham centers. In contrast to prior periods when charitable day-care centers had ongoing, sometimes intricate, relations with social agencies, during the war upwards of three fourths of the families enrolled were not known to social agencies prior to day-care enrollment (Kadushin, 1967, p. 338).

[7]Explicit equations of the educational goal of nursery schools with a middle-class clientele appear more frequently in the postwar literature. Most of the statements contrary to the equation come from contemporaries during the twenties, the Depression, or the war. The last such reference found pertains to the year 1941 to 1942: It seems that when the predecessor WPA program was being phased out, before Lanham Act funds were extended to preschool programs, local school officials "left the double

impression that nursery schools were good things for the economically underprivileged but that they were a service which local schools could not undertake without Federal aid" (Goodykoontz, Davis, and Gabbard, 1947, p. 61).

[8]Before World War II, egalitarian conviction had been expressed intermittently by a handful of child welfare spokeswomen, but as a goal for the distant future. For example, one day-care luminary, projecting "Potentialities of [the] Day Nursery of [the] Future" in 1938, remarked wistfully, "Until the world realizes that every child ought to have the same chance to expand physically and mentally the Day Nursery will not fulfill its own potentiality [that is] to lead the way for the sane bringing up of children [to] set the pace for all child training" (Beer, 1938, p. 212). Egalitarian sentiments stimulated by World War II provided another justification for a universal perspective. That spirit was voiced in the recommendation of the 1940 White House Conference on Children in a Democracy that preschool programs be universally available, a recommendation reaffirmed by subsequent decennial White House Conferences on Children.

[9]That distinction has also been construed as entailing a basic effect on program quality. One school of social policy takes as a basic proposition that a program that selects a clientele of the poor inherently will be a poor program (see, for example, Schorr, 1974). Although we cannot pursue this issue at length here, we can point out that the history of preschool programs does not clearly and consistently support that basic proposition. The WPA-Lanham programs and postwar philanthropic day-care programs may be cited for the most part as examples to the contrary.

[10]An antiintellectual flavor has been found in Dewey's theory of education for a related, but different reason. Hofstadter pointed to the antiintellectualism implied in not defining cognition and knowledge as the goal of education, while stressing such other extrinsic objectives as an orientation to the social order or to "real life" (Hofstadter, cited in Lasch, 1967, p. 161). Lasch and Wishy subscribe to this criticism. Although it is tempting to pursue this matter in detail, only two points need be made here. First, even an educational objective defined purely in relation to knowledge may have a bearing, direct or indirect, on the social or political order, for only conceptually is the enterprise of education separate from the rest of society. Second, the implications of any theory of education—antiintellectual or otherwise—cannot be equated with the factual, day-to-day activities in the classroom. On this point, however, Dewey's theories apparently did have unfortunate consequences in fact, as will be shown shortly.

[11]Some changes have occurred more recently. Now both types are largely half-day programs. In the mid-1960s, they still overlapped in enrollment of four-year-olds, each getting about half of such children who are in preschool programs; almost all three-year-olds enrolled in school attend nursery schools; and almost all five-year-olds in preschool programs attend kindergartens. Thus despite the overlap with four-year-olds, the nursery school population is younger (see Schloss, 1967, p. 1).

FOUR

Development of State Child Care Policy

Until 1960, the federal government had gone without legislation *specifically* authorizing day-care programs. The only prior federal day-care programs had been established during national emergencies. (During World War I and the Korean War, however, such federal involvement had been successfully resisted.) Then in 1962, the first explicit federal authorization of day care was enacted, the "Public Welfare Amendments of 1962," Public Law 87-543, authorizing funds to the states for day-care services.

The questions naturally arise. Why at that time? How can that policy enactment be explained? What were the key features of the enacted policy? What was the policy process that led to

120

the legislation? What was the sequence of acts and who were the key actors? These questions are considered in this chapter.

In order to answer these questions, to make understandable the climax to the day-care "drama" in 1962, the stage and scene within which the policy action occurred must first be set. This calls first for a discussion of a number of day-care developments that came to a climax in 1962. Then significant developments in revision of the federal welfare program (ADC) are scrutinized, because of the close relationship to the day-care enactment. After that, the content and process of day-care policy formulation and enactment are examined in detail.

Public Purchase of Day Care

Purchase of day care became a crucial policy consideration in 1962. Accordingly, we examine this matter in some detail. It is useful to recognize public purchase of care from voluntary or proprietary agents as a procedure affecting the balance of day-care supply and demand. Therefore, we briefly discuss several mechanisms stimulated by or responsive to imbalances in the supply and demand of such services. Then attention turns to a critical incident in the purchase of day care that helps to clarify the subsequent importance of this matter in 1962.

These mechanisms consist of attempts to find combinations of "purely" economic, economically conditioned, and noneconomic factors in the provision of day-care services and its substitutes. In the course of affecting the ratio of supply and demand, they affect other arenas than the marketplace and may involve noneconomic techniques. Some balancing mechanisms have already been alluded to. Thus the limits reached by philanthropic funds, volunteer labor, and the charitable impulse in day care (that is, fear of encouraging maternal employment by the establishment of subsidized day nurseries) restricted the supply of such services as early as the Civil War period. This encouraged the emergence of that "mechanism" that historically in this country has greatly expanded the total day-care supply, namely commercial day care. The motivation for future profits took over at the limits set by philanthropy, which itself had derived from past profits and bequests.

Another, much less potent, mechanism is casework screening to dampen maternal employment in cases deemed not suitable for day-care admission. This mechanism for controlling the supply was itself limited by concerns over inefficiencies and increased costs from unused capacity within day-care centers. Thus when passage of mothers' pensions reduced the day-care demand from widows, admission criteria were revised to include two-parent families. The historic link which casework helped to forge between day care and the social work profession far overshadows the marketplace significance of casework as a balancing mechanism.

Mergers were another device that, by facilitating the rationalization of day-care operations, probably affected efficiency more than supply and demand. The merging of separate units into local associations, by increasing efficiency, may have kept more centers operating than might have been possible otherwise, especially when philanthropic funds grew scarce. Such mergers must not be confused with other types of day-care associations that performed functions more typical of business associations: self-regulation, standard setting, research, planning, and coordination. Such associations also lobbied for public inspection and regulation of day nurseries in order to prohibit abuses in commercial nurseries, which by design or not may reduce competition. Local, state, and regional associations of day nurseries go back to 1892, preceding by many years, as day-care enthusiasts have boasted, the formation of local councils of social agencies (White House Conference, 1930a, pp. 13-16). Coordination is not extensively recognized as usually limiting the establishment of new units and expansion of existing programs. One suspects that this aspect of coordination was fully appreciated and encouraged by those concerned with the limits of philanthropic funds and the inefficiencies in day-care operations. During World War II, the child welfare traditionalists who could not defer, even for the war, their concern about the deleterious effects of maternal employment also realized the meaning of coordination. They noted that "Day care is a serious venture . . . and should not be undertaken by sporadic groups whose activities are not related to a coordinated community plan" (Lundberg, 1942, p. 281).

One other balancing mechanism is the purchase of care by one organization or entity from another. Although this does not in the short run alter the total supply, in the long run it very well may. The operation of this mechanism will be examined in detail.

The pattern of public purchase of voluntary agency services that first developed in connection with foster homes and institutional care was applied to day care in 1962. Examining that pattern is necessary to help explain the importance of the purchase of care issue in 1962. The public purchase of care or service always involves more than just financial dealings. It also reflects and affects the social or institutional relationships between the purchaser and the vendor. Furthermore, when public institutions are one of the participating parties, the transaction must be sanctioned in the political arena.

Prior to the establishment of public child welfare services in the United States, social welfare programs and institutions existed under either religious or nonsectarian, eleemosynary auspices. In a number of cities and states public funds were expended, as lump sum grants or per capita payments, for child protection, "rescue," and custodial services provided by the private agencies. The public good, *bonum publicum*, was seen as served in that work was performed, whether by sectarian agencies or not, that otherwise would have required performance by public organizations. From the standpoint of public authority, purchase of voluntary care was an expedient arrangement by which responsibility for dependent children could be assumed without the costs of establishing large public bureaucracies. For sectarian agencies, the sale of custodial care not only permitted covering costs of their existing institutions, it also facilitated the "internal mission"—rearing and educating American children in the faith. When church monies were insufficient to construct additional facilities, public purchase of care made it possible to accommodate an expanded flock of children. The New York statute enacted in 1875, requiring commitment of dependent children to the custody of persons of the same religion as the parents ("wherever practicable") gave sanction and the force of law to the missionary function of sectarian custodial care.

As could have been anticipated, controversy and conflict

arose between public and private agencies—sectarian and non-sectarian. They disagreed on responsibility for admission to the voluntary programs and institutions, discharge from the institutions, state licensing, supervision, standard setting, and finances.[1] The classic controversy illuminates interinstitutional relations between the church as vendor and state as purchaser. Charges were levied by the New York City Commissioner of Public Charities in 1914 of scandalous and disgraceful conditions in private institutions receiving public funds for care of "charges of the City." The commissioner exercised the buyer's option, and the official's sense of responsibility, by suspending purchase of care from the offending institutions. One of a series in defense of Catholic institutions replied: " 'private charities may, in the opinion of modern sociologists, be permitted a temporary existence, provided they engage in work which, for the present, the State cannot conveniently assume, and provided further, that they act purely as agents of the State. . . . Modern sociology proposes to suppress legitimate individuality, by merging, as far as human nature will allow, all activities in the State' " (cited in Bremner, 1971, p. 404). To an organization that had begun establishing orphanages 1,600 years ago, the state appeared as an expedient, Johnny-come-lately.

In addition to the possible loss of funds, the threat endangered the existence of religious institutions and the socio-religious functions they performed. The nonfiscal aspect of the threat that an expanding state represented can be seen more clearly on an issue that would not directly affect church coffers, namely child labor. Some high Catholic clerics opposed the proposed Child Labor Amendment in the 1920s, stating that " 'For the parental control over children it would substitute the will of Congress and the dictate of a centralized bureaucracy, more in keeping with Soviet Russia than with the fundamental principles of American Government' " (cited in Bremner, 1971, p. 743). The church, which historically had acted as the parental surrogate of dependent children, viewed the state as an aspiring competitor for that social function.

As late as the 1920s, the church, along with such political conservatives as Nicholas Murray Butler, could hope to prevent dominance of the state in the interinstitutional balance of parental surrogation. By 1935, when public child welfare functions were authorized and funded by the Social Security Act, the balance shifted decisively in favor of the state: Now the voluntary agencies had to face direct competition from expanded state and local public agencies providing similar child welfare services.[2] Guidelines for regulating the competition were mutually agreed on by the interested organizations. Several of those guidelines outline the modus vivendi accepted by the public and private child welfare agencies. The parties agreed that the existence of each was legitimate; that the state had the supervisory obligation to determine which agencies were maintaining standards of good service; that in each case, purchase (and termination of sale) requires agreement between buyer and seller that the transaction would best meet the child's particular needs; that the purchaser should pay the vendor a fair price (maintenance costs); and that all parties " 'should collaborate in the development of comprehensive child-welfare programs [extending] child-welfare activities to uncovered areas' " (cited in Lundberg, 1947, pp. 313-315). (Rural areas generally had not been covered by the private agencies.)

The last-mentioned principle reflects contrasting "market" viewpoints held by the parties. Generally, the previously existing private agencies, hard hit by the Great Depression, hoped the newly available public funds would be used first to purchase their services rather than competing in their established territory; then the new or expanded state and county agencies could pay attention to opening up underdeveloped areas. The federal agency, however, feared the relatively small appropriation could easily be absorbed by purchase of care from existing (in part, substandard) agencies; the danger was that the new funds would simply take the place of vanishing private money to serve children already under care. In that eventuality, no expansion of child welfare services would occur.

The private vendor wished primarily to cover costs of existing child welfare operations, the federal investors to use the grants-in-aid as seed money to expand the scope of child welfare operations. These fiscal orientations have nothing per se to do with public versus voluntary, or sectarian versus nonsectarian considerations. That is, the same pressures would work on vendors of existing services and grantors seeking expansion of services, regardless of the agencies' auspices. The vendors and purchasers (or grantors) both may be voluntary, as may happen with a community fund organization facing a private agency with an opposing viewpoint on the service market. Or, a state agency unwilling for fiscal or political reasons to start or expand a program would be tempted to view federal seed money as a source of funds for existing operations. The impersonal market orientations reflect the amount of funds available in comparison to the costs of expanded services, the scale of existing service programs, plans and pressures for program expansion, and the financial relationships between the agencies.

The impersonality of the market does not, of course, automatically assure its use on behalf of antivoluntary or antisectarian sentiment, nor does it necessarily create a desire to expand the jurisdiction of public agencies. From the voluntary or sectarian agency viewpoint, however, all this may appear quite academic. Given a shrinking supply of philanthropic funds for welfare, a decision not to purchase service from existing voluntary agencies for any reason, but to allocate the funds to expand or create public agencies, would ensure the slow but sure extinction of the private agencies. Since 1935, therefore, purchase of care has served as a mechanism that public agencies can employ in several ways. This may range from simply establishing the presence of a public agency, to maintaining public dominance, or to applying the coup de grace to voluntary agencies. Taking drastic action, however, would normally incur high political and economic costs; instead, a state of tension obtains, ready to be unsettled when "reasons of state" cause a shift in the balance of services and payments.

Within the child welfare marketplace, application of that ambiguous standard in most states, which decides on the arrangement for the care of a dependent child best suited to the child's needs, results, in the majority of cases, in care provided under public auspices. But exceptions occur, especially where a mandatory sectarian standard exists or can be enacted. There

the voluntary sector gains a protected market or can even expand. New York State still retains the 1875 statute—Section
373 of the New York State Social Welfare Law—requiring foster
placement of a dependent child with persons of the same faith
as the parents. Consequently, to the present time, New York
City and State are the national exemplars of flourishing sectarianism in foster care.[3] Paradoxically, that city and state also
exemplify the highest flowering of antisectarianism in day care.
That attitude was displayed in a protracted, postwar struggle in
New York City involving Catholic, nonsectarian voluntary, and
public welfare interests in day care. (The account here relies on
a detailed description of that struggle that is unusual in the welfare literature for its candor [Mayer and Kahn, 1965, pp.
79-96].) In retrospect, that struggle could almost appear as a
rehearsal for what transpired in 1962, with some of the same
actors and issues, but which ended in an impasse. The New
York situation can serve as a case study in the nonresolution of
conflicting policies.

From 1933 on, while some public funds for day care
were available in New York City, Catholic programs received
none. The WPA program provided funds mainly through public
schools. During the war, public funds were barred for sectarian
day care by a ruling from the state attorney general that "no
state money could be used in the aid or maintenance of religious education, direct or indirect" (Mayer and Kahn, 1965, p.
87). After the war, the same ruling apparently applied. So, for
almost thirty years the Catholic sector, dependent on its own
funds, remained fixed. (In the 1920s, Catholic day-care programs constituted about 20 percent of the city's total [White
House Conference, 1930a, p. 13]. The *national* sectarian percentage in 1929 was 20 percent [White House Conference,
1930b, p. 158]. In 1965, the sectarian sector made up 19 percent of New York City's programs.)

During those decades the "public" sector increased, first
under the WPA, then during the war with tripartite funding.
The state and city each contributed one third shares, "voluntary" day-care agencies were responsible for the remainder,
supplementing parents' fees, if necessary. After the war, in

1947, the state terminated its aid. The city then picked up the bill, expanding public support of day care in a unique "public-private day-care" program.[4] (In a capsule summary, that arrangement involved: use of *public* funds to partially subsidize the programs; day care for poor and needy children selected by Welfare Department counselors; programs operated by *private* [voluntary] boards with directors responsible to them; coordination through a representative Day Care Council; and an elected Joint Policy Committee that set policy and met regularly with Welfare Department staff. Many of those features, especially the first three, were carried over from the tripartite, wartime program.)

The seeds of the New York struggle germinated during the decades of standstill in Catholic day care, while Catholic foster care grew substantially, and expansion of public day care was limited by the unavailability of state funds. In 1952, Catholics tried, with Welfare Department support, to enter the "public-private" day-care program. The Protestant and Jewish voluntary nonsectarians rebuffed this effort by citing the 1943 Attorney General's ruling, a ruling that derives from the prohibition against the use of public funds in education for religious instruction. Repulsed on "educational" grounds, Catholics supported numerous state legislative proposals for day care with a welfare label. The proposals called for administration by welfare departments, purchase of "group day care" from voluntary agencies at departmental options, and purchase of "family day care" for children under the age of three on the basis of the traditional "religious faith" standard used in foster care. However, an authoritative state welfare ruling, that the religious faith restriction in foster care was not mandatory in day care rendered even welfare auspices in New York of dubious utility to sectarian interests.

All legislative proposals supported by Catholics and by the City Welfare Department were consistently and effectively opposed by the Day Care Council and Joint Policy Committee of the "public-private" program. Among the philanthropic and civic-minded volunteers on the Council and Policy Committee are individuals who can "influence . . . local political authorities through . . . personal, social and political contacts" (Mayer and

Kahn, 1965, p. 45). Thus the public subsidy in New York City replaces the philanthropic bequest but permits continued exercise of charitable guardianship. The social position of the volunteers makes them too independent for simple cooptation; otherwise their sustained opposition to the Welfare Department on the sectarian issue could not have occurred.

The bills supported by the Joint Policy Committee proposed placing day care under educational auspices at first; then, when the educators declined, under the Youth Commission. Those bills were blocked in turn by Catholics and welfare officials. The legislative outcome of the conflict in New York was that "Not one bill—of literally hundreds—has passed" between 1947 and 1965 (Mayer and Kahn, 1965, p. 82). Yet, except for the administrative auspices proposed, the bills embodied ostensibly similar policies—formally common goals, care and protection of children made vulnerable by maternal employment, by paternal absence while in the armed forces, uniform cost-sharing features (equal state and local fiscal shares), and so on. The legislative impasse itself, however, is difficult evidence to refute that the conflicting interest groups were indeed pursuing different principal objectives.

Other groups and interests in New York, in addition to the principals, reportedly played a role in the stalemate: Upstate Republican legislators generally opposed, while downstate Democrats generally supported day care; Republican and Democratic governors were apparently equally disinterested in unnecessary controversy; and day-care proprietors opposed publicly subsidized competition. Sectarianism, however, Mayer and Kahn concluded (1965, p. 87), was "probably . . . the most serious single issue." More specifically, that issue means the conflict between Catholic groups and the voluntary, nonsectarian organizations. The representative leaders were, respectively, Charles Tobin, Secretary, New York State Welfare Conference, and Elinor Guggenheimer, President of the Day Care Council, 1948-1960, and later founding member and first President of the National Committee for Day Care of Children. The latter committee, as shall be seen later in this chapter, particularly played a stellar role in launching the 1962 federal legislation.

For Catholics, the New York struggle signified accelerated encroachment of public day care on sectarian programs. Public funds were being used to alter the interinstitutional balance of social parenthood. As one consequence, the church's "internal mission" was endangered: In 1965, about 41 percent of the children enrolled in the "public-private" programs were Catholic. The fiscal consequence, during a period of widely reported financial pressure on religious and philanthropic organizations, was probably no less dangerous to the church's internal revenue. Moreover, excluding Catholic day care from the public treasury carried premonitory meaning: If that could happen in New York City, the historic stronghold of Catholic child welfare, the prospects in states where Catholics were even more in the minority must have been chilling. For all these reasons, by 1962 Catholic groups would apparently have to respond to any federal day-care development as they did in New York, by insisting on a purchase-of-care proviso and by being prepared, if necessary, to oppose fiercely any offending day-care bill.

For the nonsectarians in New York, the conflict seemed to reflect an unyielding intent to prevent the introduction of subsidized sectarianism into another child welfare program. Whether resistance to simply sharing their influence in the "public-private" program merged with antisectarianism can only be subject to speculation. Eventually they came to recognize that staunch antisectarianism had led, perhaps unexpectedly, to an impasse without any hope of legislation. As a consequence, one of the nonsectarians' key aims, further expansion of the "public-private" program, remained stymied.

As a policy process the New York struggle is instructive. Both the sectarian and antisectarian principals, holding without compromising to positions compounded of material and ideal interests, may appear as tragic heroes. However, as we shall see later in this chapter, they may have learned, or rather lost their naiveté, as a result of the struggle during the postwar decades. Moreover, by 1960, when those searching for funds looked upward from city hall to state capitol and on to the national capitol, more experienced policy mechanics were at hand to shape and lubricate the legislation.

Other Postwar Day-Care Developments

Among the organizations deeply aware of the rush of women and mothers into the labor force during the postwar decades were child welfare, day-care, and nursery school associations. The daily activities of their members brought them into contact with women seeking day care or nursery schools and with children endangered by the scarcity of such programs. After an apparently fruitless effort to organize in 1948, a national committee was incorporated in June 1960. Elinor C. Guggenheimer, a leading figure in the Day Care Council of New York, was one of the founding members and principal organizers of the Committee, and became its first president. The National Committee for the Day Care of Children was established as a nonprofit, charitable organization, to publicize the need for day care, to promote adequate standards, to encourage local efforts toward developing day care, to stimulate research, and to serve as a clearinghouse on day-care information. Also, and most pertinent to the legislative developments in 1962, the committee lists among its activities, that it "mobilizes support at federal, state and local levels" (National Committee for the Day Care of Children, n.d.).

Postwar interest in day care had begun building up within the two federal agencies concerned with women and children, the Women's Bureau of the Department of Labor, and Children's Bureau of the Department of Health, Education, and Welfare. Their concern was expressed in several ways. Several surveys were conducted to examine the need for day care. During the Korean War industries producing war goods reported recruitment problems, while neglect of children of mothers working in such industries was noted in "defense communities." These reports led the interested federal agencies to undertake a study comparing different survey methods for determining community "need" for day care (Wiener, 1956).

Several years later, the Children's Bureau undertook another survey. Characteristically, the indices of day care "need" reflected that agency's traditional policy goal for day

care (preventing neglect of young children presumed vulnerable as a result of the mother's work outside the home). The
survey focused on the children of working mothers (Lajewski,
1959).

The later survey revealed a miniscule proportion of preschool children of the nation's working mothers (4 percent)
were enrolled in group day-care programs. Concern was also expressed in the survey report over the findings that children were
cared for by siblings or by the mother herself while on the job.
But the survey gave greatest emphasis to the "latch-key" children, because neglect was assumed prima facie.

Other data on the increased numbers of employed mothers and on the number of their children in the preschool ages,
the population "at risk," were also taken as evidence of an
increased "need" for day care. Still other data on the number
and capacity of licensed day-care centers served to confirm im-
pressions of a short supply of adequate day-care centers (Low,
1962). In 1960, the numbers of potentially vulnerable children
even by the most conservative comparison were by far larger
than during World War II. By contrast, between 1944 and 1960
the available day-care supply (capacity of day-care centers) increased by a bare 10 percent (see Appendix, Table 1).

That unfilled demand for day care drew the interest
usually attracted by a market vacuum, namely proprietors. By
1960, almost two thirds of the reported licensed day-care centers and 51 percent of licensed capacity in the United States
were under proprietary auspices (Low, 1962). Many states also
reported an increase in day-care programs under voluntary auspices. Day care under public auspices apparently showed the
smallest increase. The growth of the proprietary and voluntary
sectors, however, did increase public business. It placed a
greater burden on public agencies in licensing and supervising
day-care centers.

In addition to gathering and publishing data on employed
mothers, child-care arrangements, and day-care facilities, the
Children's Bureau and the Women's Bureau convened a national
conference in 1960 to call attention to day care.

The Kennedy Administration Overhauls Welfare

While these activities and interests were advancing, other more visible events were taking place: A Democratic administration had taken over after eight Republican years. One of President Kennedy's first domestic priorities was welfare reform.

Several different events occurred that put the spotlight on "welfare," that is, on the ADC program. In 1960, a well-publicized controversy flared up in Newburgh, New York over welfare restrictions proposed by its city manager. Those restrictions explicitly aimed at two targets, the high cost of the ADC program and the disproportionate number of blacks on the welfare rolls (Kadushin, 1967, pp. 166-167). The attention that controversy received nationally reflected a widespread concern over numerous problems in the ADC program. These were perceived differently by the public, recipients, and many welfare professionals. Since excellent analyses and summaries of the problems in the ADC program may be found in the literature (Kadushin, 1967, pp. 165-192; Schorr, 1968, pp. 17-76), only those aspects particularly pertinent to the 1962 welfare amendments will be dealt with here.

The changing goals of the ADC program, and the differential degree of their achievement eventually led to criticism of the program on policy grounds in addition to fiscal or racial grounds. The Social Security Act of 1935, which established the program, stated the original purpose as " 'enabling each State to furnish financial assistance, as far as practicable under the conditions in each State, to needy, dependent children' " (cited in Kadushin, 1967, p. 184). Such assistance provided to the dependent child's mother considerable degree of choice: " 'between staying at home to care for her children and taking a job away from home [and] as to what course of action she should follow with respect to seeking or continuing employment and to make a decision in consideration of her special circumstances, especially the extent to which the age or condition of her children may make her continuous presence at home desirable or necessary' " (cited in Schorr, 1968, p. 27).

In 1950, an amendment to the act added coverage of the adult taking care of the child. Usually this meant the mother. But the father in the home, even if ill or disabled, was not then eligible for assistance. High rates of unemployment between 1950 and 1960, especially during the recession at the end of that decade, led to a major change in ADC coverage. In 1961, children of unemployed fathers were made eligible for ADC, for one year. (The 1962 amendments, dealt with later in this chapter, proposed the continuation of that coverage.) In 1956, another significant addition was made to the aims of the program. An amendment that year established an explicit intent of the program of helping the child's parents (or relatives who served as caretakers) to " 'attain the maximum self-support and personal independence consistent with the maintenance of continuing parental care and protection' " (cited in Kadushin, 1967, p. 184). To the original intent of encouraging mothers to stay home and rear their children, the 1956 law joined the potentially contradictory aim of encouraging maternal self-support and independence, that is, employment. These aims were incorporated in the 1956 statute as part of the larger responsibility of helping to "maintain and strengthen family life." Besides providing financial assistance, the 1956 amendments called for the provision of services to facilitate the clients' attainment of self-supported independence. (Provision of services was included, a respondent reported, to obtain support from Monsignor John O'Grady, Secretary of the National Conference of Catholic Charities from 1920 to 1961, and to overcome fears on the part of social work staff that helping clients to become independent would mean forcing mothers to get jobs. In 1958, the amendment explicitly called for provision of casework services.) The 1956 revision, Kadushin observed, "exemplifies the continued ambivalence that plagues the program—the conflict between the desirability of permitting the mother to be available for the care of her children and the reluctance to support the family if the mother is, in any way, capable of . . . employment" (1967, p. 184). Schorr (1968, p. 31) saw the development of the ADC program moving in a direction that *"removes from the ADC mother effective choice about whether she will or will not work."*

Many states apparently did not provide much in the way of services. Trained social workers were in short supply, and adding such personnel to the staff would increase the states' personnel costs. But several states pursued the newer ADC goal in special, federally funded demonstration projects explicitly seeking to secure the employment of the female head of the household (Bell, 1962). A widely cited study of such a project, in Cook County, by Arthur Greenleigh, found the " 'primary purpose is to determine the effect of reduced caseloads and concentrated efforts on getting ADC mothers into self-supporting employment. . . . A firsthand evaluation of this project revealed cases closed by forcing the mother into employment against her will and *before she has been able to make adequate arrangements for the care of her child.* It also found cases closed where the arrangements for child care are not satisfactory or do not meet the State's standards for day care' " (cited in U.S., Congress, Senate, Committee on Finance, 1962, pp. 313-314, our emphasis). In the report, one of the answers to the question "What's wrong with ADC in Cook County?" is that "Day care for ADC children is almost impossible to get" (U.S., Congress, Senate, Committee on Finance, 1962, p. 320). The report explains that there are no public day-care centers in the county, the licensed nonprofit centers have a limited capacity and the other, presumably proprietary facilities are costly and not located conveniently to ADC families.

To recapitulate, the professional "policy" criticism of the ADC program pointed to the following: an internal inconsistency between the several goals; the differential achievement of separate aims; the use of coercion instead of choice in implementing these goals; and the shortage of adequate day care as a hindrance to implementation of the self-support objective. Two of the highlighted criticisms received wide resonance; ADC had failed to achieve client self-sufficiency, and the short supply of day care was an obstacle to that achievement. Both points came to the fore in the efforts by the new administration to revamp the widely criticized welfare program.

Even before the inauguration, the Kennedy Administration had launched what was to become a torrent of high-level examinations of the current welfare system. On January 10, 1961, the Task Force on Health and Social Security, chaired by Wilbur J. Cohen, reported to President-elect Kennedy. In testifying on the ADC program before the House Ways and Means Committee, in February 1961, the new Secretary of Health, Education, and Welfare (HEW), Abraham Ribicoff, seeking authorization during a prolonged recession to provide assistance to unemployed fathers and their dependent children, "assured the Committee of his intention to make a thorough study of the public welfare programs" (Cohen and Ball, 1962, p. 4).[5] He also promised to return to the committee with the recommendations from the study. The administration's welfare proposals were an outgrowth of this extensive, multifaceted review process. On February 1, 1962, President Kennedy sent to Congress what was the first presidential message exclusively on public welfare, and thus set a precedent that his successors were to follow. That same day the administration's specific proposals on public assistance and child welfare, in sections of the bill H. R. 10032, were introduced in the House by Wilbur Mills, Chairman of the Committee on Ways and Means.

Months later, after numerous twists and turns through the legislative process, the Public Welfare Amendments of 1962 were enacted. Controversy over the ADC program surrounded that measure. Some critics were opposed to the proposal to extend coverage of ADC-U, extending assistance "to a group of individuals (unemployed parents) who were, by definition, employable" (Cohen and Ball, 1962). By midsummer of 1961, the Newburgh proposals for work relief and other restrictive measures had brought public interest to "a boiling point" (Cohen and Ball, 1962). The program "was regularly attacked in the press for promoting immorality [subsidizing illegitimacy] and laxity [tolerating fraud]" (Schorr, 1968, p. 10). Many of the reports that Ribicoff had commissioned agreed with George Wyman's criticism of "cases of second and third generations receiving assistance" and with the call to make it clear that "the 'chain of dependency' is not the American Way of Life" (Wyman, 1962, pp. 118-119). The theme of the "endless cycle of dependency" was reiterated in the *Report of the Ad Hoc*

Committee on Public Welfare and in the testimony of the innumerable witnesses with professional standing before the respective House and Senate committees. This theme implicitly challenged the beneficence of the family in child rearing—at least the AFDC family. As such, it tacitly put into question the rationale of the ADC goal set in 1935. (A variant of this theme, stated in terms of black families, appeared later in the controversial Moynihan Report.)

To be sure, many of the attacks on the ADC program reflected taxpayer displeasure over its increasingly high cost. Some of these fiscal critics voiced their concern over the large proportion of black recipients, as in the Newburgh case, in stridently racist tones. Other observers stated this concern more neutrally in terms of dependency; and still others spoke sympathetically of the grim life on welfare in the ghetto.

The administration's initial proposals and the changes it subsequently agreed to, as well as the actions taken administratively by Ribicoff prior to enactment, were addressed to many of these criticisms. In response to these criticisms, together with the reexamination of ADC indicated by Secretary Ribicoff's thorough study, Congress finally approved the measure containing the major provisions sought by outside professionals and by the administration. " 'Its byword,' " said Ribicoff, " 'is prevention; where that is too late, rehabilitation—a fresh start' " (cited in Schorr, 1968, p. 10). The program, retitled Aid to Families of Dependent Children, encouraged states to extend social services to AFDC recipients and to train personnel for such work. These were considered the key provisions by which prevention of dependency and rehabilitation toward self-support were to be achieved. (Schorr [1968, p. 10] explained the difference between the service provisions of the 1956 and 1962 Amendments: "As the 1956 declarations of purpose had been notably ineffective, in 1962 Congress provided cash subsidies to states that would follow its lead.") This emphasis on service in revising the AFDC program, Kadushin observed, implied promise of a "considerable reduction in the recipient rate" (1967, p. 181).

The enacted amendments contained a provision for day care. Indeed, that day-care section, and its evolution, played a minor, but closely related part in the larger AFDC revision, described earlier. The process by which the obstacles to gaining legislative support for day care were overcome, and the means by which initial proposals evolved into the version finally enacted require close examination.

Day-Care Policy Views

One of the major methodological steps taken in conducting this policy analysis was to assess the various policy positions as means-ends schema. The intent was to sketch the various linkages between day care as an instrument and the ends to be achieved. Thus one of the major objectives in interviewing the respondents and reading the legislative records was to ascertain the rationales held by the opponents and proponents of the 1962 day-care bill. That information is presented in this section of our study.

Before presenting a summary of these policy views, several points must be made, in the interest of clarification. The data to be presented were not subjected to quantitative treatment for two main reasons. First, the respondent group essentially consists of an accidental sample; that is, it does not purport to be either a probability sample or a universe of policy influentials, so that a methodological basis for statistical generalization is absent. Second, the categories into which the responses fall do not neatly fit the technical requirements of a rigorous classification system.

The categories of response are not mutually exclusive. Equally important, respondents gave varying numbers of reasons for supporting or opposing the legislation and the several responses by a given individual often were inconsistent or contradictory. This is only to be expected in matters of social policy, which by definition involve complex axiologies of social interests and values. Stated differently, child rearing and family functioning are topics on which consistency between diverse values may be difficult to achieve. Additionally, to establish external validity, the relation between values and "reality," may be even more troublesome. In short, the subject matter of policy analysis, especially in a complex mass society, does not readily lend itself to neat classification or a simple typology.

These difficulties may be exemplified by illustrating a few anomalies found in day-care policy. For example, a minority, but considerable proportion of day-care advocates, some of whom gave effective advocacy service in 1962, volunteered their "personal" opposition or reservation to the employment of mothers with young children. Similarly, individuals with long career or avocational devotion to day-care selectivity, to admission for children of employed mothers or for children in "incomplete" families, declared day-care universality as an ideal. Day-care policy also makes strange bedfellows: Political liberals and conservative Catholics were both fearful of government *operation* of day care. Perhaps most paradoxical of all in the present context, is an informed report of legislative opposition to day care as enabling mothers to "live it up—play golf, drink martinis" when prior government preschool policy sought to facilitate maternal employment during war and depression, and, in 1962, aimed to get AFDC mothers off the relief rolls. Other paradoxes will be found later on. Our chronology of the policy process will be undertaken after the previously discussed policy rationales are summarized. That summary is intended to help clarify the later chronology.

Seven major grounds have been given for opposing day care. Since the midnineteenth century, opponents have objected to programs that they believed would violate *traditional conceptions of the family and of the maternal role*. That objection has been amply noted earlier, so that an extensive elaboration is not necessary here. However, it had particular salience in the 1962 legislative process. Speaking as a senator, in 1965, Ribicoff acknowledged this as one of three main objections mentioned by colleagues in cloakroom chats (U.S. Department of Health, Education, and Welfare, 1966b, p. 58). Federal legislators are far from being unrepresentative in this regard. In a large survey taken in 1961, many of the respondents—child welfare professionals, board members of voluntary social agencies, clergymen, labor officials, businessmen, and members of preschool associations and women's clubs—expressed approval of the normative conception of motherhood (Ruderman, 1968).

Many respondents, especially women, detected in the notion that day care encourages maternal employment an unawareness of contrary research evidence, as well as (in the words of a respondent) a telling "lack of reality as to what is happening out in the world of work." For example, Katherine B. Oettinger, as Chief of the Children's Bureau, countered that "the provision of day-care services no more causes mothers to work than carrying an umbrella causes rain" (U.S. Department of Health, Education, and Welfare, 1961, p. 46).

Issues in *labor economics* constitute the second major objection to day care. Some critics contend that the facilitation of maternal employment via day care increases the competition fathers face in the labor market. According to one respondent, organized labor rejects this contention; even during the depression, it was said, labor opposed a prohibition on employment of wives. But this objection, a legislator reported, contributed to senatorial resistance to supporting day care, especially during a period of recession. To this a female legislator (respondent) retorted, "not just males are unemployed." A variant objection, also heard in the past, is that government or philanthropic funding of day care serves as a hidden subsidy to employers. Several respondents found that ground for opposition curious in the face of numerous other more direct subsidies to employers. Still another variation links day care to the practice of paying unequal wages to women. One staunch opponent of such inequality, however, disclaimed any "principled objection to day care," but placed primary emphasis on paying mothers high enough wages to afford day care without subsidy.

Illustrations have been previously cited of objection taken to government support of day care as *welfare statism*; for example, Russell's and LaGuardia's concern over the state supplanting the mother. Only one expression of this concern was voiced in the 1962 situation; it will be cited in the chronology on the 1962 policy process.

A fourth objection, the *pejorative image of day care*

itself, is frequently cited as a hindrance to legislative support. Senator Ribicoff, among others, reports colleagues who view day care as "babysitting" (U.S. Department of Health, Education, and Welfare, 1966b, p. 58). Elinor Guggenheimer recognized as a major impediment the acceptance by *day care proponents* of the custodial reputation of day-care services and the justification of day care as appropriate for "inadequate," "incomplete," or "disturbed" families: "First and most devastating is the lack of conviction that we have in our selling. Even those of us who are imbued with a real fervor for day care tend to apologize for our product. We approach the whole matter negatively and feel impelled to explain it as a service to be used when all else fails" (U.S. Department of Health, Education, and Welfare, 1961, p. 11). This points to the dilemma faced by the traditional child welfare conception of day care: how to convince the public, legislators, and families that a supplemental program, only second-best to the family as a place for children, deserves more than second-best resources and repute? The solution found in the 1960s to this dilemma is discussed later.

Day-care selectivity is another facet of the negative image of day care. The opposite position, universally available day care, and its wider expression during World War II has been discussed in Chapter Three. Several advocates of selectivity among our respondents projected universal day care as a distant ideal. Only one respondent unambiguously asserted approval of day care for all children; that official also expressed preference for inclusion of a universal program within the public school system and "worries" about day care under welfare auspices.

A *confused professional identity* has been recognized as a major problem. Although day care has been explicitly considered a social service for decades by some social workers, social workers in other branches of the profession are "ashamed" or "surprised" at that affiliation (Beer, 1957, p. 22; Kadushin, 1967, p. 341). A day-care activist considered the inability of professionals to define day care clearly as perhaps the "greatest handicap" to gaining legislative support. (Fuzziness in definition, it was reported, resulted in having to "pull figures out of the air" in a "bourbon session" convened to plan for day care.) A federal official, commenting on the debated definition of day care over the decades, remarked that day care is "the most controversy-ridden area of child welfare."

Part of the confusion, of course, is reflected in disputes over day care as education or as care and custody and in the bureaucratic competition between the respective federal and state agencies. These threads have appeared and reappeared in several previous chapters. Still another facet of day care identity is its auspices, especially as between proprietary or nonprofit sponsorship. Only one of the individuals interviewed stated a readiness to accept proprietary centers as legitimate, as long as adequate standards were met.

The sixth, and perhaps most troublesome, hindrance to acceptance of day care is *sexism* or male chauvinism. Several of the preceding objections—such as belief that day care encourages maternal employment, or that it lends support to male unemployment, or alternatively, to wage inequality—were considered by female respondents as also indicating a male bias. But the most vigorous expression of that charge was tied to conceptions of motherhood. One woman (respondent) proclaimed, "the image of twenty-four-hour motherhood is one projected by damned male legislators . . . by upper-class men, such as bankers, businessmen, and legislators who never have been interested in young children and their problems." (This respondent, who resides in an upper-class neighborhood, went on to add that in the mid-1960s "the educational rationale has legitimated male concern with young children.") None of the other female respondents in our study criticized males so forcefully. However, about one third of the women interviewed on day care expressed feminist views that ranged from leveling charges of male chauvinism to supporting female equality (in employment opportunity, wages, and so on).

The seventh objection to legislative support for day care is its potential fiscal cost. Senator Ribicoff (U.S. Department of Health, Education, and Welfare, 1966b, p. 58) reported that colleagues asked, "Won't the program become so large and costly as to be economically nonfeasible?" Professionals and officials also suspect day care to be the potential "runaway" portion of child welfare costs. One authoritative national welfare estimate, in 1965-1966, of the probable day-care bill was $1,600,000,000 excluding capital costs. (According to one federal informant, this estimate and the back-up projections of children in need of day care were not to have been released outside the federal welfare administration. This is one tactic for concealing the "runaway." Another tactic, employed in a presidential task force, was fiscal camouflage: lumping day-care estimates in with the costs of other proposed programs.)

Five major reasons have been advanced for supporting day care. Historically the first rationale has been *preventing neglect* of children of mothers employed outside the home. This goal was previously discussed in Chapter Three.

A second goal of day care is to *help the child to achieve his maximum potential.* Of all the rationales heard or read in conducting the study, this is the reason most frequently encountered. The interviews were mainly conducted in 1965, when the hopes for Project Head Start created a heady mood; it may have prompted this type of response. Most declarations of this goal did not specify the content of the formal objective— that is, which of the wide range of human potentialities were to be furthered. When probed for greater specificity, one official responded, "potentiality for freedom and dignity."

Several individuals or groups, however, have indicated desired aims of human development. Religious doctrine, of which in the context of preschool programs Catholic views are most important, point in an other-worldly direction: "The child . . . belongs to this world surely, but his first and highest allegiance is to the kingdom of God" (Bishops of the United States, 1950, p. 1; for other sectarian illustrations, see Moustakas and Berson, 1955, pp. 181-184). Developing to its fullest the potential for Christian devotion constitutes the church's internal mission in day care. "Responsible" or "effective" citizenship in this world is a human potential articulated by clerical and lay respondents in the interviews. One legislator articulated two more specific roles, that of worker and taxpayer.

The third major objective held by day-care advocates rises from the level of the individual, goes beyond social roles, to

reach some *national benefit*. However, several respondents overlapped this objective and the preceding one. When asked, "How
does day care serve the national interest?" a number of individuals responded that it does so in terms of maximizing the child's
or human potential. The clearest case of conceptual indistinct-
ness in the categories is the response, "The benefits to the
nation are those accruing to children." The separation between
the two levels of the second and third objective was gauged by
the respondent who said it was in the national interest to "make
wise use of our resources," then exclaimed, "Isn't that awful!"
and added, "to provide maximum oppportunities in which people can develop their potential." Perhaps the most interesting
versions of this objective are those that explicitly link day care
and the nation. One statement in the literature made a linkage
with national reputation: "The United States is a wealthy country, supposedly a world leader. Other nations have their eyes
upon us, and some are always ready to magnify our faults. For
our own reputation and for the sake of humanity, we cannot
neglect a vital segment of our population, the children of working mothers" (Beer, 1957, pp. 188-189). But of all of the interview responses on the relation of day care to the national
interest, one stands out. The respondent (an upper-class woman
of lineage traceable back to Colonial times) said she had been
giving some thought to that question in regard to all federal preschool programs. She envisioned a succession of ends: (1) a first
step was toward citizenship training; (2) next was increasing
educational and cultural levels; (3) then mitigating or preventing
social pathologies, such as delinquency and school dropouts; (4)
perhaps preventing domestic "strife" or even "revolution"; (5)
gaining internal peace; and finally (6) showing other nations the
United States will not tolerate poverty.

Day care as a support for *freedom of role choice for
mothers* is a fourth objective. The women's liberation movement has articulated this aim most prominently. Although none
of the respondents explicitly proclaimed this aim, it was clearly
implied in the remarks of numerous female respondents. A variant of this objective is the rationale for providing day care to
AFDC children in order to allow their mothers to go to work
and thereby restore a positive self-image.

The preceding subgoal must be differentiated from a similar objective—providing day care to AFDC children so their mothers can become self-supporting and leave the relief rolls. The objective of *providing relief from relief* is the fifth major benefit anticipated as a consequence of providing day care. It obviously resembles the intent to break the "cycle of dependency" that underlay the welfare revision proposed by the Kennedy Administration.

With the range of policy views summarized, the narrative can now turn to the chronology of events leading to the enactment of the day-care measure in 1962.

The Process of Day-Care Policy Enactment

On August 3, 1961, when the heat of summer matched the boiling point reached over the Newburgh controversy, an important meeting took place. It was arranged that an officer of the National Committee for the Day Care of Children (NCDCC) would meet with Secretary of Labor Goldberg and Secretary of HEW Ribicoff. Welfare reform and Newburgh were on Ribicoff's mind (U.S. Department of Health, Education, and Welfare, 1966b, p. 49), day care on the officer's. A fervent, persuasive case for day care is said to have convinced Ribicoff to support a day-care measure. (Another respondent confirmed that the NCDCC "had worked imaginatively" on convincing Ribicoff. Still another provided a biographical explanation—Ribicoff's orphanhood as a poor, young boy was suggested as making him receptive to protecting dependent children.) The NCDCC was advised on how to proceed with preparing a legislative proposal. Guidance was not to be sought from the Children's Bureau. Perhaps that organization's historic, well-known ambivalence to day care was seen as a handicap. Assistance in policy formulation was to be obtained from several social welfare statesmen, Wayne Vasey of the National Association of Social Workers, Sanford Solender, and Joseph H. Reid of the Child Welfare League of America. Three weeks later, when a nonfederal expert's report was submitted, it included a recommendation for "a supplemental appropriation of $5,000,000 . . . to provide essential day care services for children" (Wyman, 1962, p. 87).

The administration's bill to reform welfare, H.R. 10032, which was submitted on February 1, 1962, contained a day-care provision as part of the proposal to expand and improve child welfare services. Three sections dealt with day care. One section earmarked part of child welfare service funds for day care. A maximum authorization of $10,000,000 was set for day care, but $5,000,000 would be provided in the first year. (One respondent described how that authorization figure was established. Past day-care bills submitted by Senator Jacob Javits and Congressman John V. Lindsay had ranged from $5,000,000 to $25,000,000. In 1962, "we sort of just split it down the middle." Day-care supporters could accept it and a higher amount would have led to opposition.) The second item called on state welfare agencies that used federal day-care funds to provide for "cooperative arrangements with the state health and education agencies to assure maximum utilization of them in the provision of health services and education for children receiving such day care" (U.S. Department of Health, Education, and Welfare, Children's Bureau, Social Security Administration, 1962, p. 2). Day care was mentioned a third time in the bill in the section that defined the term *child welfare services*. It provided an indication of the rationale for the day-care authorization. "The term *child welfare services* means public social services which supplement, or substitute for, parental care and supervision for the purpose of: (1) preventing or remedying, or assisting in the solution of problems which may result in the neglect, abuse, exploitation, or delinquency of children; (2) protecting and caring for homeless, dependent, or neglected children; (3) protecting and promoting the welfare of children of working mothers; and (4) otherwise protecting and promoting the welfare of children, including the strengthening of their own homes where possible, or, where needed, the provision of adequate care of children away from their homes in foster family homes or day care or other child-care facilities" (U.S. Department of Health, Education, and Welfare, Children's Bureau, Social Security Administration, 1962, Attachment, p. 3). Those three sections contained the only references to day care in the bill.

Hearings were held on H.R. 10032, by the House Ways

and Means Committee, one week after the bill was introduced. The Children's Bureau noted, "Of special interest is the fact that in addition to fifteen oral statements, there were fifty-two written submissions or letters endorsing the day-care provisions. No other provision of the bill received anywhere near that volume of support" (U.S. Department of Health, Education, and Welfare, Children's Bureau, Social Security Administration, 1962, p. 4). Such an outpouring of support, one week after the measure had been introduced, obviously indicated that a great deal of effective lobbying had been done prior to its introduction. One can begin to appreciate what the mobilizing of "support at federal, state, and local levels" by NCDCC meant; later, additional meaning will be given.

Those who appeared or wrote in support of the bill cited one or another, or combinations, of the five major objectives of day care, as well as counterpoints to the objections, discussed earlier. (In the interviews, respondents were asked about the seeming contradiction between the 1935 ADC goal, encouraging maternal child-rearing, and that in H.R. 10032, encouraging maternal self-support. Only one unconditionally acknowledged an inconsistency. Two responded in identical pragmatic terms— AFDC is a multibillion dollar program; day care is a "drop in the bucket." One legislator preferred to "think in terms of flexibility rather than inconsistency." Another believed a contradiction was obviated if the decision about working or not was made on an individual basis, with casework advice. And one official simply, but perhaps very wisely, said it was a complex matter in which one rule, working or staying home, would not do for all. Not noticed in the excitement felt by day-care advocates to get the 1962 bill passed was an historic irony: After a century-long effort to employ day-care staff also to keep mothers out of employment, which had even been attempted during a world war, the child welfare objective of day care was reversed.)

Historically most interesting, and most frequently cited, was the "relief from relief" objective. Many proponents sounded a minor chord, urging that day care not be used as a way to coerce AFDC mothers into employment. Joseph H. Reid also pointed to economies in comparison to foster or institutional care if children were neglected (see U.S., Congress, House, Committee on Ways and Means, 1962, pp. 444, 682, 688, 469-473).

Echoing of the major theme of relief from relief was not accidental: The policy formulators and lobbyists had agreed to link day care with that objective. That policy decision was orchestrated with the work of the HEW study groups, whose aim was reportedly to make AFDC "palatable."

Only three persons testified in opposition to the day-care provision in H.R. 10032. All three were Catholic spokesmen. The three were: Charles J. Tobin, Jr., Secretary of the New York State Catholic Welfare Council, who, it may be recalled, led the Catholic purchase of day-care effort in New York in opposition to the Day Care Council and Elinor Guggenheimer; Reverend Edward Head, of Catholic Charities in the Diocese of New York; and Monsignor Raymond J. Gallagher, Secretary of the National Conference of Catholic Charities. They made up for being overwhelmingly outnumbered by supporters of the provision by the sharpness of their criticism. Although the lay representative may perhaps be viewed as the staunchest critic,[6] a not unfamiliar phenomenon in Catholic circles, our discussion will follow the leading Catholic spokesman, Raymond Gallagher. Gallagher stated his objections: "We are alarmed by the assignment of millions of additional children to public day-care programs, as this bill proposes. We support day care for children of those mothers who must look for, or work at, a job as part of the program of self-rehabilitation. We believe that it is un-American to place such large numbers of children under governmental care in order to free so many mothers of young children to enter the labor market when there are so many able-bodied fathers being supported under other sections of this proposal" (cited in U.S. Congress, House, 1962, p. 578). (The last point refers to the proposal in the bill to extend, for five years, ADC coverage to unemployed fathers and their children. The following witness, Esther Peterson, Assistant Secretary of Labor, "roughly estimated ... between 10,000 to 15,000 children" could be provided day care under the full authorization of $10,000,000 [see U.S., Congress, House, Committee on Ways

and Means, 1962, p. 609].) Several Congressmen sought and obtained clarification.

One chief objection was that the provision did not explicitly limit day-care availability to mothers on relief to permit
achieving, in Edward Head's phrase, the "therapeutic objective"
of helping AFDC recipients to get work. A second objection
was that only public operation of day care was provided for; the
measure was silent on "purchasing day-care service from competent agencies now in existence." When one Congressman suggested that these represented differences over the extent, rather
than over the "existence" of day care, Gallagher concurred.
Then Congressman Alger (Texas) initiated a remarkable colloquy: "Do you feel any uncertainty at all in asking the Government to move into the area which traditionally has been church
and private [voluntary, sectarian, and nonsectarian]?" The
monsignor replied, somewhat agonizedly, "Mr. Alger, I appreciate the way you have expressed it. You said it far better than
I. That is my worry . . . I must tell you . . . I have a kind of feeling this is not really happening, I am sitting here listening to the
Catholic and Protestant churches indeed selling their services"
(U.S., Congress, House, Committee on Ways and Means, 1962,
p. 591).

Following the hearings, the House Ways and Means Committee held several executive sessions. The HEW staff worked
with the committee, in the words of a participant, "so as to end
up with something the Committee could live with . . . with language which would answer the objections . . . which would
neutralize the situation." On March 7, the committee "ordered
that a clean bill be introduced to supersede H.R. 10032.
. . . The clean bill [H.R. 10606] was introduced by Representative Mills on March 8" (U.S. Department of Health, Education,
and Welfare, Children's Bureau, Social Security Administration,
1962, p. 4).

The new measure made numerous changes pertaining to
other programs under the Social Security Act. With respect to
day care, three conditions were added:

> For an advisory committee, to advise the State pub-
> lic welfare agency on the general policy involved in the

provision of day care under the State plan, which shall include among its members representatives of other State
agencies concerned with day care or services related thereto
and persons representative of professional or civic or other
public or nonprofit private agencies, organizations or
groups concerned with the provision of day care;

For such safeguards as may be necessary to assure
provision of day care under the plan only in cases in which
it is in the best interest of the child and the mother and
only in cases in which it is determined, under criteria established by the State, that a need for such care exists; and

For giving priority, in determining the existence of
need for such day care, to members of low-income or other
groups in the population and to geographical areas which
have the greatest relative need for extension of such day
care. [U.S. Department of Health, Education, and Welfare,
Children's Bureau, Social Security Administration, 1962, p.
4]

Several interpretations and explanations are needed to
clarify the special language employed. It will be noted that no
explicit provision is made for purchase of care. Since 1958, the
device of an advisory committee has been employed in public
child welfare to tacitly recognize the legitimacy of voluntary
agencies—especially sectarian—and to assure those organizations
a voice in policy making. The advisory committee mechanism
assures that provision will be made for purchase of care.

The phrase "in the best interest of the child," incorporated in the second condition, is a resonant formula. It was intended to mollify Catholic fears that day care would develop
into a wedge, making wide the opening for mothers into the
labor market. The Children's Bureau found "the best interest of
the child" too restrictive and insisted on "the best interest of
the child and the mother."[7] The phrase implies a case-by-case
determination of need for day care rather than work or other
formal status of the mother as simply establishing eligibility. By
this formula, Catholics hoped to return to the day care objective of discouraging maternal employment, except for AFDC
cases.

The third condition also carries intricate, special meaning.
It should be noted that nowhere does that statement restrict
day-care eligibility to AFDC families. The Children's Bureau, a

respondent reported, had insisted on going beyond "low-income" and had added "other groups . . . and . . . geographical areas" in order to broaden that condition. One policy statesman reported he would have opposed the bill if it had limited day care to those on relief.

Containing those conditions on the day-care provision, H.R. 10606 passed the House and went to the Senate. The Committee on Finance of that body held hearings in mid-May. Only a few incidents need to be mentioned here. Senator Carl T. Curtis of Nebraska looked at the third condition in the clean bill and noted a stain. He remarked that "day care would be free to all . . . regardless of their economic condition" (U.S., Congress, Senate, Committee on Finance, 1962, p. 150). The bill did not explicitly require a fee payment, he pointed out, even if a mother could afford the full cost of care. Secretary Ribicoff agreed to remedy that seeming oversight. (As finally enacted, an addition was made to the third condition: "in cases in which the family is able to pay part or all of the costs of such care, for payment of such fees as may be reasonable in the light of such ability" [U.S. Department of Health, Education, and Welfare, Children's Bureau, Social Security Administration, 1962, Attachment, p. 2].)

Gallagher also testified before the Senate Committee. He endorsed the day-care provision in H.R. 10606 with "enthusiasm," but also expressed objection to the use of federal funds for day care for "an average family, where finances is not a problem" (U.S. Congress, Senate, Committee on Finance, 1962, p. 389).[8]

Some of the senators were reported as not convinced that the day-care measure in H.R. 10606 overcame their reservations. What the specific reservations were is not clear. At any rate, danger signals reached NCDCC. The chapter affiliate in Colorado, Senator Alcott's home state, was contacted. The affiliate obtained a statement of support for day care from the Denver Council of Churches, including the Catholic bishop. In addition, a parade of day-care children was organized in the senator's honor. "We boxed him in," reported the NCDCC official. Senator Cotton, of New Hampshire, which lacked an

NCDCC chapter, received an "avalanche of telegrams" within two days after word was passed by NCDCC to welfare "people" in that state.

All the enthusiastic endorsements and "grass roots" lobbying proved effective. With the single addition of the fee requirement, H.R. 10606 passed the Senate, was concurred in by House conferees, and was signed into law by President Kennedy on July 25, 1962.

Summary

Immediate answers can now be given to the questions posed at the outset of the chapter. A prospective and more long-term assessment of the policy process and the resulting legislation appears in the final chapter.

Day-care programs historically have been held by the general public and legislators as contrary to American mores. In past years, the exigencies of national depression and war overcame the traditional objections and led federal officials to establish such programs for the duration of those emergencies. In 1962, the desire to reduce welfare expenditures apparently made Congress receptive to a departure from norms regarding familial responsibility for the rearing of young children. Sensing that political climate, welfare statesmen touted day care as a means of getting AFDC mothers off the relief rolls. That combination of ends and means induced Congress to pass the first explicit piece of legislation providing federal support for pre-school programs.

Day-care advocates did not protest at or oppose the specific day-care policy adopted. Rather, the day-care supporters initiated, and participated in drafting the legislation. Employing such skills as social finesse and effective organizing at national, state, and local levels, they created an impressive lobby to gain the needed votes from the legislators.

The main features of that day-care policy warrant a careful appraisal. The final measure clearly contained three conditions reflecting the Catholic position, as stated by Gallagher. Those conditions, plus the fee requirement, produced a restrictive day-care measure, one hemmed in by explicit restraints and by a constricting legislative intent for day care to help achieve relief from relief. Conservative Catholic doctrine, it would therefore seem, had achieved an evident victory of a highly selective day-care provision. That, however, would be a facile assessment. Seeking to cut welfare costs by means of day care was a policy position taken by a liberal Democratic administration. It was also acceptable to, or at least acquiesced in by, day-care lobbyists and social welfare statesmen. The liberals may have accepted or acquiesced in that day-care objective out of conviction in its inherent validity. Tactical considerations were also involved. The relief-from-relief objective helped defuse the fiscal cost objection to day care. Day care, its supporters implied, would curb or even reduce burgeoning AFDC expenditures.

Aside from the major day-care goal posited in the administration's initial proposal (H.R. 10032), several subordinate features also call for notice. In H.R. 10032, the only rationale for day care was contained by implication in the definition of child welfare services. Even if H.R. 10032 had not been objected to by Catholic welfare leaders and had been adopted as proposed, it would have resulted in a day-care program within the traditional child welfare context. In comparison to the WPA or the Lanham day-care programs, the day-care provision in H.R. 10032 would have been much more narrow. The term *narrow* is used in the conceptual sense—in the fiscal sense, day care in H.R. 10032, and as enacted in H.R. 10606, was Lilliputian in contrast to the WPA or Lanham expenditures. In comparison to a universal conception of day care, the concept in the Kennedy Administration's proposal shrank to a crumb.

The contest in 1962 was between a narrow conception of day care accepted by liberals and a similar, restrictive conception of day care held by conservatives. That is the nature of the contest in which the day-care conservatives are said to have gained a statutory victory. In the midst of the contest, in 1961-1962, the day-care proponents opted for a likely sliver, rather than a highly improbable, pie-in-the-sky, universal provision. Several proponents acknowledged that strategy, one in which the sliver would hopefully turn into a wedge for broadening the provision of day care. However, even at that time, doubt gnawed at that prospective hope: During the House and Senate Committee hearings, use of day care in order to pressure AFDC mothers into the labor force was reported by some and cautioned against by other witnesses. Yet no amendment prohibiting such coercion was ever proposed.

Hindsight, it is said, has 20/20 vision. As a mental exercise, if it were possible to imagine being back in 1961-1962, one wonders what the day-care lobbyists would have made of a later complaint: "The purpose of day care is to focus on children; using it just to get people off welfare has twisted that purpose" (cited in Brozan, 1972, p. 54). Projecting that view from 1974 into the future, the conclusion seems unavoidable: The relief cast given to day care in 1962 reinforced a pejorative image of day care and magnified it for some time to come.

Furthermore, the scope of the program authorized, crumb-size in relation to the increasing number of employed mothers of preschool children, added to the unfilled market demand for day care. The 1962 Day Care Amendment, therefore, gave added impetus to the proprietary sector in day care, at least for women who could afford commercial day-care fees.

As a drama, the day-care enactment in 1962 was far "off Broadway" in comparison to a larger, major show that reached a climax in 1964-1965, during which years federal support for nursery education was enacted. The policy processes involved resemble in small part, and differ in larger part from the process just described. The discussion now moves to the developments in the mid-1960s.

Notes

[1] For documents on the classic controversy, see Bremner (1971, pp. 398-419). Knowledge of the charity scandals in New York City apparently was widespread even before the controversy erupted in 1914. A British welfare officer, writing around 1911, remarked on the "financially irresponsible" voluntary institutions in that city: Admission to the institutions "was entirely in the hands of [their] managers. They admitted; the city paid" ("Charity and Charities," p. 890).

[2] According to a respondent, Catholic efforts to impede expansion of state child welfare departments resulted in the 1935 requirement of more onerous matching of funds by states in the child welfare program than in contemporaneously enacted federal programs for crippled children and for maternal and child health. The same motive was imputed to Catholic opposition to removing the "rural limitation" in federal child welfare from 1945 to 1958, when, due to the "strategic role" played by the quondam Commissioner of Social Security, Charles Schottland, that removal was accomplished.

[3] In 1969, 44 percent of state and local *public* welfare payments for foster care went to voluntary child welfare agencies. That percentage varies tremendously among the states—from zero in four states to 75 percent in New York. New York and Pennsylvania historically have been atypical in this regard; without those two states, the national average in 1969 would have been around 30 percent. The national percentage has varied little during the 1960s, although the figures for individual states, such as Massachusetts, have changed considerably—from 11 percent in 1960 to 45 percent in 1969 (see U.S. Department of Health, Education, and Welfare, 1966a, 1969).

[4] One respondent, knowledgable about the situation in 1947, reported that the "Little Flower" (LaGuardia's nickname) had the city step in to avoid a financial burden on the city; it is not clear whether he had hoped to save public money by avoiding more costly institutionalization of neglected children, by preventing the buildup of a public day-care bureaucracy, or by tapping voluntary coffers. If he had hoped for the latter, he would have been disappointed. Postwar expansion depended mainly on public welfare funds, which increased from $1,500,000 in 1947 to $6,700,000 in 1965, while the voluntary agencies' share went from $120,000 to $190,000 (Mayer and Kahn, 1965, p. 48). In percentages, the city puts up 89 percent, parents' fees add up to 8.5 percent, and the voluntary agents provide 2.5 percent.

[5] The "study" involved a series of separate studies and reports by various groups internal and external to HEW. One group, the Ad Hoc Committee on Public Welfare, was expanded by Secretary Ribicoff, after meeting with representatives of the National Association of Social Workers, to include representatives of public and private welfare agencies, schools of social work, and others. Another consultant, George Wyman, was appointed to study possible changes in the public welfare program permissible under existing legislation. The Field Foundation provided funds for several of the study projects (see Cohen and Ball, 1962; U.S. Department of Health, Education, and Welfare, Children's Bureau, Social Security Administration, 1962).

[6] Tobin criticized the day-care measure as contrary to the "underlying philosophy of the ADC program" and urged that "studies be carried on to establish whether day care can be utilized to effectively help persons

who are recipients of public assistance" (U.S. Congress, House, Commitee on Ways and Means, 1962, p. 584).

[7]One legislator supported "the best interest of the child" in the desire to tie day care to the child and not to the working woman. This respondent gave primacy to adequate and equal wages for women. "Women's lib" advocates and Catholic clerics make especially strange bedfellows.

[8]Gallagher's shift from his earlier opposition was called by a knowledgable respondent an awakening to the "reality of the world" of day care as not causing maternal employment. On comparing the initial bill and the enacted measure, however, a simpler explanation appears: The changes satisfied the objections he had stated earlier in the House. At least in this case, one is inclined to agree with another assessment of Catholic lobbyists as "past masters of strategy [who] have learned those strategies over the centuries." Nor does this incident wholly confirm the belief of a respondent that the Catholic position on day care reflects its institutional nature to be more significant than its "philosophy." One is hesitant to disagree with proven experts at negotiating with Catholic spokesmen, yet the theological emphasis on the family seems to have been amply retained, except for AFDC families. Perhaps, however, Tobin would agree with the belief that institutional considerations won over concerns about ideals: Tobin did not endorse H.R. 10606, and, in testimony submitted on his behalf by Gallagher, instead of supporting funds for day care, he continued to urge the pilot studies he had earlier suggested in the hearings on H.R. 10032. His perservering consistency was in the stated interest of strengthening the religiously sanctioned, normative conception of the family. Apparently, to him the endangerment of the family outweighed the purchase of care and other gains in H.R. 10606, gains that had eluded Tobin, and Catholicism, in New York since 1947.

Another respondent suggested another possible "institutionalist" explanation. O'Grady, Gallagher's predecessor, was reputed to have been much more difficult to deal with. Perhaps, it was suggested, Gallagher's relative cooperativeness may have reflected "a changing hierarchy," one that did not want to always appear in a "negative light" as an intransigent opposition.

FIVE

Development of State
Nursery School Policy

As we have indicated in Chapter Two, preschool programs—
infant schools, kindergartens, and nursery schools—had existed
since the 1830s almost entirely without federal involvement
until 1964.[1] In 1964, the Economic Opportunity Act, Public
Law 88-452 (hereafter cited as EOA), authorized federal educational assistance under which Project Headstart was initiated.
That initiative was followed by funds and explicit authority for
preschool programs under the Elementary and Secondary Education Act of 1965, Public Law 89-10 (hereafter referred to as
ESEA).

In this chapter, we attempt to explain why federal policy
changed during a nonemergency period. The main features of

157

the policy adopted, and the acts and actors in the process leading to enactment, are the main topics to be dealt with in this
chapter.

As with the enactment of day-care legislation, federal authorization of an appropriation for preschool programs became
carried along with—and added momentum to—broader developments of historic, national significance. It is necessary to understand the unfolding of two issues, themselves intricately interrelated, in order to comprehend the policy outcome. They were
the impasse over federal aid for elementary and secondary education and the church-state controversy in the field of education. A summary of those two matters will set the stage for the
policy breakthrough in 1964 and 1965.

State, Church, and Education

During the colonial period and up until about the first
third of the nineteenth century, education was almost universally deemed to be primarily the responsibility of family and
church. (The discussion here relies on U.S. Library of Congress,
1961, prepared by Charles Quattlebaum.) Constitutional silence
on education is attributed to aristocratic notions held by some
of the founders that education was mainly for persons of wealth
and influence, to the need to avoid an "unresolvable issue"
(Which church should control education?) and to absorption
with weightier matters in establishing a new state. Education,
therefore, fell under the Tenth Amendment clause reserving to
the states powers not delegated to the national government.

The federal government, however, was not neutral toward
education. By word and deed, it sought to assist and encourage
the territories and states to promote education—in 1785, the
Continental Congress initiated the practice of aiding territories
and, later, states, by endowment of public land for schools. In
1787, land for public institutions of higher education was en-
dowed pursuant to the declaration in the Northwest Ordinance:
"Religion, morality, and knowledge, being necessary to good
government and the happiness of mankind, schools, and the
means of education shall forever be encouraged" (cited in U.S.

Library of Congress, 1961, p. 13). A series of other educational aids to the states were enacted during the nineteenth century, of which the first Morrill Act (1862), making land grants for colleges, may be best known.

Less well-known are other, direct federal activities in the field of education undertaken under the authority to govern the seat of the federal government—for example, providing for education in the District of Columbia, in 1804, under implied powers pertaining to United States territories and possessions, and under various powers connected with the national defense. The last includes a long series of measures on military education: an educational program initiated in 1777, under direct federal administration, to instruct military personnel; the establishment in 1802 of the Military Academy at West Point, the first in a series of federal institutions of higher education—the Naval Academy (1845), the Army Medical School (1893), the Army War College (1901), the Coast Guard Academy (1915), and the Air Force Academy (1954); and a number of other defense-related educational programs and services, such as R.O.T.C. and G.I. bills for veterans' education.

In the nineteenth century, federal policy supporting education in the states had one outstanding feature—funds and land were provided but the curriculum was not specified. That is, the federal aid did not attempt to influence the kind of education for the states to develop. The federal aid had several historically profound consequences—it provided the "first stable support for free public education in more than half of the States" (U.S. Library of Congress, 1961, p. 14). The federal grants lent great fiscal weight to philosophic and political considerations favoring public over private and, especially private religious, education.

Federal policy changed in 1917 in regard to levels of education to be categorically supported. Prior to that year, federal aid to the states either did not specify the level of education, or only pertained to higher education. In that year, the Smith-Hughes Act authorized federal funds for vocational education below college level. The Great Depression heightened federal involvement in public elementary and secondary education (as well as in higher education). Specifically, the WPA established

preschool programs and conducted other programs to employ
unemployed teachers, the National Youth Administration provided work training for unemployed youth and part-time employment for needy students, and the WPA made grants and
loans to the states for public school construction. The World
War II Lanham Act, under which day care and nursery schools
received federal support, also made federal funds available for
construction or improvement of school buildings in defense-
impacted areas. Postwar provision of funds for operating and
constructing public schools in federally impacted areas was
made on a limited basis, under special appropriations. In 1950,
the lack of uniformity in the special provisions led to enactment
of a general program of federal aid to public schools in impacted areas: Public Law 815 provided construction funds and
Public Law 874, operation funds. In 1958, as an immediate
effect of the embittered educational reappraisal following Russia's successful launching of Sputnik in October 1957, the National Defense Education Act established new federal policies
emphasizing the sciences, mathematics, and foreign language at
all levels of education except preschool. All of these direct and
indirect educational interventions of the federal government are
based on constitutional provisions related to the national defense, to jurisdiction over the District of Columbia, territories
and possessions, and to the general welfare.

Quattlebaum (U.S. Library of Congress, 1961, p. 52)
reached three important conclusions in his review of the federal
role in education: "Most of the educational programs of the
Federal Government are not aimed at educational goals as their
ultimate purpose . . . . The educational programs are usually a
means to an end—such as the promotion of agriculture or commerce. This does not detract from the educational significance
of the programs . . . . The Federal Government has no program
of general aid to elementary and secondary schools. The extensive educational activities directly administered by the Federal
Government consist principally of education for the national
defense. Furthermore, the majority of Federal funds expended
for educational purposes are used for defense-connected programs."

The last conclusion bears on events in 1964-1965 to be related later. Absence of a federal program of general aid to elementary and secondary education was due to several related reasons, of which the controversy over public aid to parochial schools proved to be the most significant.[2] A brief review of that controversy is necessary to explain how that hurdle was overcome in 1964-1965.

The controversy—which derives from the First Amendment prohibition on Congress to "make no law respecting an establishment of religion, or prohibiting the free exercise thereof"—for a century or more made Federal aid unavailable to parochial schools. (Many states also incorporated clauses establishing "a wall of separation between church and state"; some state walls even exceed the height of federal barriers [see Steinhilber, Will, Sokolowski, and Murray, in U.S., Congress, Senate, Subcommittee on Education of the Committee on Labor and Public Welfare, 1965, pp. 185-230].)[3] Slowly, however, during the twentieth century, by federal legislation and judicial decision, various forms of aid, direct and indirect, were made available to church-related schools—at all levels—and/or to their students. For example, the National School Lunch Act of 1946, which authorized federal grants-in-aid to the states, explicitly permits participation by nonprofit private schools. (Strict constitutional or statutory prohibitions prevented twenty-eight of the fifty states, in 1962, from administering the federally-aided school lunch program in parochial schools within their borders. This led to an unusual expedient—a unit of the U.S. Department of Agriculture administers the school lunch programs in the affected states [Kreisberg, 1965, pp. 419-444].) More well-known is the Supreme Court decision *Everson v. Board of Education* (330 U.S. 1 [1947]) holding constitutional a New Jersey law that provided for reimbursement from public funds to parents for money expended by them for transportation of their children to parochial schools. That decision, and the earlier decision in the *Cochran* case (Louisiana, 1930), which held constitutional the use of state funds to provide secular textbooks for all school children, in parochial or public schools, exemplify what has come to be known as the *child-benefit doctrine*. That doctrine holds that the Louisiana and New Jersey laws primarily aimed to benefit the school child and that any benefit to the parochial school was merely incidental to the primary aim.

The assertion of that doctrine after World War II appeared at a period of transition and change within the whole institution of education. The President's Commission on Higher Education in 1946 had noted "educational deficiencies and inequalities" that wartime priorities had doubtlessly exacerbated (U.S. Library of Congress, 1961, p. 35). Increased numbers of children from the postwar baby boom had to be accommodated in school; parochial school enrollment was increasing at an accelerated rate. School systems, especially in the private sector, faced increasing financial strains. This pressure brought about an historic change of Catholic policy. Between the two world wars, the National Catholic Welfare Conference had opposed federal aid to education out of fear of federal control. In 1945, support of such aid was implied in a statement indicating opposition to a program of federal aid that excluded parochial schools (Meranto, 1967, p. 52). A decade later the Bishops of the United States (1955, p. 5) felt compelled to speak out for political consideration to parochial schools: "They have . . . full right to be considered and dealt with as components of the American educational system. They protest against the kind of thinking that would reduce them to a secondary level, and against unfair and discriminatory treatment which would, in effect, write them off as less wholly dedicated to the public welfare than the state-supported schools. The students of these schools have the right to benefit from those measures, grants, or aids, which are manifestly designed for the health, safety, and welfare of American youth, irrespective of the school attended."

That public statement signaled an intention to press for inclusion of sectarian schools in the legislation of aid to education. The National Defense Education Act of 1958—a spinoff from Sputnik—did indeed expressly provide funds to enable private, nonprofit—as well as public—colleges and universities to make low-interest loans to their students. That act also authorized loans to elementary and secondary schools for science, math, and language equipment and for renovations necessary for such equipment; moreover, 12 percent of each appropriation for such equipment is *required* to be allotted for loans to private, nonprofit schools (U.S., Congress, Senate, Subcommittee on Education of the Committee on Labor and Public Welfare, 1965, p. 146). (It would be a fair guess that approximately 12 percent of all elementary and secondary pupils in 1958 attended parochial schools; in 1961 the percentage was "around 13" percent [National Catholic Welfare Conference, 1961].) In the interest of national defense, aid was granted parochial schools that otherwise would have been hotly contested. But that federal aid could not be used to reduce the pressure from the two highest educational costs, for salaries and construction. By the end of the 1950s, the absence of general aid for primary and secondary schools left Catholic education in an economic, political, and institutional crisis. Without access to funds from the public treasury, the Catholic school system could not expand to enroll the increasing number of Catholic children. Even if that system maintained a stable school population, it would lose children of the faith to the public schools; and if rising costs and an increased resistance by Catholic parents to double school taxation forced a reduction in school operations, the loss would be even greater. Continued denial of access to public funds for general education foreshadowed a prospect infinitely more chilling than that of the day-care problem with which Catholicism had had to contend in New York City from 1946 to 1962: The established balance between parochial and public schools on a national scale was becoming upset. The freeze-out of Catholic day-care centers from the "public-private" day-care arrangement in New York, discussed in Chapter Four, was minor in comparison to the membership and fiscal stakes in the restricted availability of federal aid to education to parochial schools.

Thus, in 1961, when the first Catholic president of the United States proposed legislation for general aid to primary and secondary schools, in the form of funds for construction and salaries, when he indicated that parochial schools would be walled off by the First Amendment from the approximately

$800,000,000 a year under the proposal, the leadership of the Catholic hierarchy had a crucial decision to make.[4] The choice was whether or not to create a political fight on the issue. This would mean employing all the political influence the Church could wield, at the risk of not only losing the hoped for educational aid, but also possibly antagonizing the non-Catholic majority. Caught between these risks or the possible glacial decline of Catholic education, the leadership decided to fight. That decision produced a public-sectarian confrontation in the legislative arena.

The hierarchy stated its position explicitly. It suggested the proposed federal aid program be amended to include provision of long-term, low-interest loans to parochial schools, and added: " 'In the event that a Federal aid bill is enacted which excludes children in private schools, these children will be victims of discriminatory legislation. There will be no alternative but to oppose such discrimination' " (cited in Meranto, 1967, p. 61; the discussion of events in 1961 relies considerably on Meranto). Although some consideration was given to such an amendment, a legal brief suggested a general loan provision to sectarian schools would be constitutionally invalid (U.S., Congress, Senate, Subcommittee on Education of the Committee on Labor and Public Welfare, 1965, p. 115). The administration's bill passed the Senate after eight days of voting on amendments and then went to the House, "which had passed only one general school-aid bill since 1870" (Meranto, 1967, p. 64). Although the bill fared well in the Committee on Education and Labor, it became stuck in the Rules Committee: To the coalition between southern Democrats and conservative Republicans was added a crucial tie-breaking vote by a Catholic legislator, Congressman James J. Delaney of New York. Delaney had called for "nondiscriminatory legislation making federal grants available to parents of children in public or parochial schools" (Meranto, 1967, p. 62). (Delaney's district was located in the Diocese of Cardinal Spellman, who had stated publicly his opposition to any bill that would "penalize" children for attending parochial school rather than public school.) The result was the tabling of the administration's general education bill, another to extend provisions of the National Defense Education Act, and a bill to aid higher education. No education legislation was enacted in 1961.

Three conclusions may be drawn from the 1961 stalemate. The majority of legislators had been largely unwilling and some perhaps unable to reach an accommodation or compromise with the Catholic forces. Some believed they could command the votes necessary to win. The Catholic forces, in turn, demonstrated the will and ability to block passage of educational aid to public primary and secondary schools. The Catholics had shown a willingness to compromise, that is, to accept less than equal treatment for parochial schools. This is not to deny that loans represent a "grant of credit." Yet grants of funds to the states do not have to be repaid and so represent a greater financial advantage to the recipient. Before the year 1961 had ended, the National Catholic Welfare Conference (1961) indicated a continued readiness to compromise. Their legal review had concluded that "Practicalities, not slogans, should govern."

The third conclusion deals not with the magnitudes of political influence, the will to wield it, or readiness to compromise, but with the absence of a symbolic formula expressing the rationale for and rhetoric of a compromise policy: "The 1961 action pointed out the absolute necessity of resolving the church-state issue if the proponents of federal aid for education were to realize their objective. For the supporters of school aid in 1965, the devising of an acceptable formula to deal with this issue was a prerequisite for any earnest attempt to pass aid legislation" (Meranto, 1967, p. 66). In addition to the development of such a rationale, resolution of differences would require discussion, negotiation, and accommodation of substantive differences on school aid policy.

Preschool Policy Views

In assessing the various preschool policy positions as means-ends schema, it is necessary to repeat some prefatory cautions mentioned in Chapter Four. The answers from respondents were not treated quantitatively, to avoid an impression of precision that is unwarranted for reasons of sampling and of classification. Other problems of goal analysis, mentioned in Chapter Three, also deserve repetition. They include problems in delineation, transformation, and agglutination of goals, and discrepancies between stated and enacted goals as they appear and reappear in the course of history.

A special difficulty arises with regard to preschool goals in the context of legislative enactment in 1964-1965. The two pertinent pieces of legislation barely mentioned preschool education. The EOA of 1964 does not employ the terms *preschool, kindergarten, nursery school, Head Start,* or any other word pertaining specifically to such programs. The word *preschool* appears twice in the ESEA, which nevertheless provided more explicit statutory legitimacy to expenditures for such programs under that act; however, no definition, description, condition, or other stipulations is made regarding preschool programs. (The reasons for this statutory invisibility in EOA and low profile in ESEA are elucidated later in this chapter, and also in Chapter Six.) Finally, the legislative peculiarities surrounding these two laws may be appreciated from the fact that the $150,000,000 for preschool programs authorized under the ESEA were openly designated, by President Lyndon Johnson, to be spent as part of the Community Action Program of the *EOA* (see "Johnson's Message to Congress," 1965).

As a result of the virtual statutory silence regarding preschool programs many goal statements relating specifically to such programs were obtained "privately" in interviews rather than from the public legislative record. Many of the preschool goal positions discussed hereafter were expressed in regard to elementary and secondary education in general. Another complication of the statutory vagueness on preschool policy is that many of the main programatic features that one would expect to appear in legislation were worked out after the passage of the legislation, in the process of developing program plans. As a result, many of the policy positions examined were taken in the course of the early planning and implementation of Project Head Start, not prior to or in the process of enactment of the

EOA. Such oddities in the policy process lay behind one respondent's answer to a question on the source of the idea for a preschool program under the EOA and on the policy considerations involved. The respondent, an official in the Office of Economic Opportunity (OEO) retorted: "Is policy [really] made?"

The review of the policy rationales is intended to provide a roundup of preschool viewpoints and a basis for clarifying the chronology of the policy process that follows later. First the objections and reservations to nursery school programs are considered. The rationales for favoring such programs follow. Selective illustrations of the pros and cons from interviews, legislative hearings, or from the literature are cited.

Nine major grounds are found in opposition to preschool programs and/or to federal funding of such programs. As with other levels of education, federal support for preschool programs also became entangled in the two historic obstacles to federal aid to education, *the separation between church and state* and *the traditional pattern of state and local responsibility* for public education. These have been previously discussed. The pertinence of the first in 1964-1965 is examined later.

Educational priorities contain the third objection. Many educators, especially at the top of the public education hierarchy, and particularly in the U.S. Office of Education (OE) placed priority on universally available kindergarten programs. Officials in that office apparently "saw the War on Poverty as more the concern of the Labor Department. . . . They were more concerned with extending kindergarten to all, since this is a far-from-realized goal" (Mayer and Kahn, 1965, p. 126). It may be recalled that, even by the early 1960s, existing kindergartens could only accommodate less than two thirds of the eligible five-year-olds. Prior to President Johnson's Education Message on January 13, 1965, Commissioner of Education Francis Keppel had advocated in the OE journal, *American Education*, universal, public kindergarten programs, but public preschool programs only for children whose parents could not afford to pay. (A federal respondent offered his opinion that Keppel was stating his personal view, not administration policy.)

A fourth objection, the *questionable effectiveness* of nursery school programs, did enter into the legislative arena. Senator Robert Kennedy questioned the claim by "representatives of the school system" that the educational and cultural deprivation of children from "deprived neighborhoods" results from improper early education at ages two, three, or four. Kennedy's questions were apparently satisfied by plans for research and evaluation revealed by his brother-in-law, Sargent Shriver, Director of OEO (U.S., Congress, Senate, Subcommittee on Education of the Committee on Labor and Public Welfare, 1965, p. 2635).

Professionals, of course, had more knowledge of the state of evidence on the effects of preschool programs, nursery school and experimental kindergarten programs. Earlier studies had not found IQ gains attributable to nursery schools. In the early 1960s, however, Deutsch (1962) had reported positive effects in later grades of children who had attended his special compensatory preschool program. Two other studies,[5] which indicated a fadeout of preschool gains in kindergarten and first grade when considered together with the earlier evidence, however, tended to neutralize Deutsch's results. Several respondents mentioned the absence of conclusive evidence as to the effectiveness of nursery schools. One gave it as the reason the Office of Education had not pushed for preschool programs; the other anticipated it as a criticism with which Head Start planners and administrators would have to contend.

Particularly crucial were the doubts that a one-shot program in one summer—the initial Head Start plan—would prove effective. These doubts were so widespread and serious that "had a vote been taken" at a consultative meeting of preschool experts at OEO, "it might have gone against starting Head Start."[6]

Several educators expressed a variant of the criticism on effectiveness in relation to the quality of the preschool programs to be established. This, in turn, was stated in terms of the class size and other standards to be adopted by Head Start. They thought that only with adequate standards, including appropriately trained staff, would an effective program result.

A fifth reservation held by some legislators and professionals is that nursery schools *inculcate stereotyped middle-class goals*. Many opinions along this line are expressed in terms of the disinterest or inability of many or most teachers in teaching slum children ("Children Under Six," 1964). (This reservation, of course, also extends to programs at other levels of education.) Concern with this issue was implied in an amendment to ESEA, for an American Teachers Corps of bright, idealistic teachers, proposed by Senators Edward Kennedy (Massachusetts) and Gaylord Nelson (Wisconsin). (See U.S., Congress, Senate, Subcommittee on Education of the Committee on Labor and Public Welfare, 1965, pp. 2964-2973.)[7]

Lack of clarity of goals in nursery schools is a sixth reason for questioning nursery schools. Whether preschool programs should prepare for school entry by teaching children reading and other cognitive and communication skills or train for sociability, it may be remembered, was a dispute from the 1900s on between the progressivists and traditionalists in education. Uncertainty and disagreement over those alternatives plus others, such as whether to focus on mental health and ego development or on physical health, were voiced by a number of respondents or were recounted as topics of preschool policy discussion at the OEO consultative meeting and at several presidential advisory committee meetings. (For example, one respondent, a member of a presidential task force, reported that, in the early 1960s, when the group was asked what a program for infant day care should consist of, "We had to say we didn't know. We could say what a program for care of infants in Israel or Russia does . . . but we don't know what to do with babies in the U.S.") In 1965, one federal official—a respondent—echoed the concern expressed in the nineteenth century by Horace Mann and by progressivists in the 1920s in asking, "Are we pushing children too early into school readiness activities?"

Participants at a multiprofessional conference phrased this goal problem in terms of choosing an ideal adult type— "What kind of person do we want the child to become?" Another participant remarked, somewhat impatiently, "Why is it that we say we don't know what we are educating children for? That is an amazing statement. I can go almost any place else in the world and they will tell me exactly what children are to grow up to be and what kind of qualities they ought to have. Why is it that we are so confused in our society? I am not sure but that the confusion is in the minds of the social scientists" ("Children Under Six," 1964, pp. 5-7).

A variant of confusion regarding goals was the sense of uncertainty over the distinction between kindergarten and nursery school. One influential senator, it was reported by a professional staff member of a senatorial committee, was not clear about that distinction. Another respondent, a federal official, acknowledged uncertainty among educators whether training for kindergarten should be different than for the primary grades.

The seventh impediment to support of nursery schools consisted of a host of *administrative problems* seen by educators and other preschool policy makers. Included were such perennials as space shortages in schools and a lack of trained teachers.

Both the EOA and ESEA explicitly aimed to combat poverty. That aim was reflected in the statutory formulas for allocating funds and designating eligible EOA project applicants and recipient school districts under ESEA. The formulae were such, however, that not all children eligible for the programs were required to meet the poverty distinctions. After the first summer when a large number of middle-class parents had enrolled their children, OEO established the figure of 85 percent from impoverished families as its requirement. No specific proportion of impoverished children was set under ESEA for any given school or preschool program. Poverty as a criterion for eligibility again raises the issue of selectivity or universality in preschool policy, which is dealt with later. This allocative complexity was another anticipated administrative problem. One federal administrator, a respondent, feared that the funds might be expended on nonpoverty groups or in nonpoverty areas. So did several Republican senators who submitted a dissenting opinion (see U.S., Congress, Senate, Committee on Labor and Public Welfare, 1965, pp. 87-88). Reports years later proved these early fears were not foolish.

A related *potential* administrative difficulty concerned inequitable allocations, within a school district, between two school systems explicitly entitled to federal funds for specified educational activities under the ESEA, public and private, including parochial, schools. A federal administrator worried about what would transpire in areas with large Catholic populations. "God knows," he wondered, "what [the Catholic-dominated school boards] may do." (Subsequently, disputes over the allocation of federal funds did arise between public and parochial schools; see Farber, 1966a and 1966b.)

Of all the administrative problems anticipated in the EOA and ESEA, one of the most controversial specifically concerned coordination of preschool programs conducted under each statute. The EOA was enacted in 1964 and the preschool funds proposed to be spent in 1965 under the ESEA were to be administered not by OE, but by the OEO. Overlap between OEO and OE bothered even Shriver's brother-in-law, Senator Robert Kennedy. Shriver tried to assure the senators that coordination would be achieved through a Joint Education Staff of representatives from both agencies and as a result of his harmonious personal relations with Commissioner of Education Keppel and Secretary of HEW Anthony Celebreeze. Senator Jacob Javits pointed out that coordination of overlapping government functions cannot be left to relations between personalities, who may come and go, but calls for statutory delineation (U.S., Congress, Senate, Committee on Education of the Committee on Labor and Public Welfare, 1965, pp. 2622-2624).

The report on ESEA by the Committee on Labor and Public Welfare, which in addition to the proposed legislative bill itself and the debates published in the *Congressional Record* are the principal documents for establishing legislative intent, also devoted several pages to the problem of coordination. But a contention in those pages revealed that concern over the need for preschool programs weighed more heavily than administrative neatness: "Testimony before the Education Subcommittee has demonstrated that the educational needs of children of low-income backgrounds outstrip the available resources of local communities and require assistance both under Title I of [ESEA] and from the Office of Economic Opportunity" (U.S.,

Congress, Senate, Committee on Labor and Public Welfare, 1965, p. 12).[8]

The eighth argument against nursery school programs as a means of overcoming educational deprivation challenged that means-ends scheme on grounds almost as discomfiting as the doubts about preschool effectiveness. This argument charged *professional and bureaucratic rigidities* on the part of educators. It was widely and authoritatively alleged. For example, one educational expert asked: "Can the standards of today's school be taken safely as the model for the transformation of the culturally-deprived child? . . . or should not some thought be given . . . to the transformation of the school itself?" (Getzels, 1965, p. 113). Similarly, a black educator reported the conclusion by a "White House Panel on Educational Research and Development [that] 'by all known criteria the majority of urban . . . slum schools are failures.' But, [he added] , it is not a lost cause. Good slum schools do exist" (Cuban, 1965, p. 2975). A few legislators shared this critical view, such as Senator Robert Kennedy. During the hearings on ESEA he asked the Commissioner of Education whether educational deprivation stemmed not merely from deprived family backgrounds. Would the commissioner agree that in his "experience of studying the school systems around the United States, that the school system itself has created an educationally deprived system?" Keppel replied, "I am sorry to say that is true." Kennedy went on to protest that to put federal money into such school systems would be "wasting the money." The Commissioner then questioned his assumption that "school systems are not prepared to change" (U.S., Congress, Senate, Committee on Education of the Committee on Labor and Public Welfare, 1965, p. 511).[9]

That critical assessment of urban, public "lower" education in general and of teachers as professionals was also a dominant feeling tone expressed behind the scenes in the early Head Start deliberations and planning. A number of interviewees reported negative opinions of teachers and schools in the Head Start Planning Committee. (The committee, established in December 1964, consisted of nationally known experts in preschool and related disciplines appointed by Shriver. Recommendations of the committee—which met twice a week for three months early in 1965—reportedly were accorded the de facto status of final decisions.) Many committee members were said by an informed respondent to have held "the conviction that schools had failed kids in poor families and that schools are rigid bureaucracies."

That antieducator tone was expressed in several ways. It reinforced an early suggestion made to Sargent Shriver that volunteers be used in a preschool program. The story, reported by several respondents, is that the idea of a preschool program was first suggested to Shriver at a cocktail party by Mary Bunting, then President of Radcliffe College. As recounted, she informed Shriver of many undereducated poor kids and of many unoccupied middle-class women and suggested preschool programs to meet the needs of both groups. (Although the report may have some validity, one may be skeptical of that as the original notion of a preschool program under EOA, for reasons to be stated later.) At any rate, the preschool expert-consultants who met on November 23, 1964, to advise OEO are said to have discussed the desirability and efficacy of using middle- and upper-class volunteers. The "Summary Findings" (U.S. Office of Economic Opportunity, 1964) on that meeting provides supportive evidence of a circumstantial nature.

Antipathy towards educators was also reflected in a vigorous dispute (described as a "battle") over key terms to be employed in publications on Head Start; the avoidance of education-linked words will be dealt with later. Finally, the antieducator sentiment also reflected a deeper antagonism against professionalism. Shriver himself was said to be wary of professionals who he believed had a trained incapacity that leads to seeing the world only from within their disciplinary perspective. Before Head Start had even been planned, OEO, it was reported by a knowledgable source, had committed itself to educational ventures modeled on the Ford Foundation's Great Cities Projects. (Yarmolinsky [1969] corroborates early consideration was given to preschool programs within OEO.) The Planning Committee, made up of a majority of physicians and child development specialists, saw educational deprivation broadly and insisted on a multidisciplined approach, adding medical and social components onto the educational programs.

The ninth and most traditional, albeit often undeclared, ground for opposing nursery schools has been the *high cost* of a quality program. Curiously, almost no reference to that resource requirement appears publicly in the policy context of the mid-1960s. Considerations in private were more curious. An early request by Shriver for a budgetary estimate for a compensatory education program produced a figure of $20,000,000. At that time it was said, presumably by Shriver, to be too high. Only months later, President Johnson proposed $150,000,000. The fiscal and planning climate was depicted by one respondent, a statesman in his profession, in reply to a question about the major policy considerations for the Head Start Planning Committee. "There was only one consideration, but I don't know if you can report it—it would probably be denied. Can $150 million be spent on a preschool program between January and July 1965?"

Reasons advanced for favoring preschool programs and/or federal support fall into four (somewhat overlapping) categories. The most venerable is that basic tenet of philosophical naturalism, *facilitating fulfillment of the individual's creative potential.* This goal of early childhood education, it may be recalled, was a culture value whose diffusion owes much to Dewey and the progressive education movement and reflects original statements by Rousseau. That goal formulation proved to be not only durable, but also one of the most frequently encountered normative aims of education proposals, preschool or otherwise, encountered in this study. That same ideal, it may be remembered was also held by advocates of day-care legislation. The breadth of its diffusion was only exceeded by its prominence in the policy arena. President Kennedy invoked that aim in his education message of 1963: " 'We must give special attention to increasing the opportunities and incentives for all Americans to develop their talents to the utmost' " (cited in National Education Association, 1965, p. 757). A version of that formulation was stated as a national goal in the Declaration of Purpose of the Economic Opportunity Act: "The United States can achieve its full economic and social potential as a nation only if every individual has the opportunity to contribute to the full extent of his capabilities" (U.S. Public Law 89-10, 79 Stat. 27. 1965, p. 1). Perhaps only one additional illustration need be quoted because of its specific linkage to preschool programs. The report of the Head Start Planning Committee to Shriver listed, as first among the points deserving "special emphasis," "the overriding goal of each [preschool] program [for children of the poor] should be to create an environment in which every child has the maximum opportunity and support in developing his full potential" (U.S. Office of Economic Opportunity, 1965a, p. 1). Policy makers resoundingly articulated this goal in the mid-1960s. In his message to Congress on poverty, President Johnson referred to fulfillment of every citizen's capacities as the American goal (U.S., Congress, House, 1964). The same theme echoed and reechoed in the House and Senate chambers during the debates on the floor on the EOA and ESEA. Because all these formulations are essentially similar they need not be quoted, but merely cited from U.S. Congress, *Congressional Record*: Senator Wayne Morse (1964b), p. 16142; Senator Ralph Yarborough (1964e), p. 18420; Congressman Philip Philbin (1965c), p. 6148; and Congressman Richard White (1965c), p. 6149.

Senator Morse provided a refreshing variation by specifying a particular talent to be maximized—"intellectual brainpower" (U.S., Congress, Senate, Subcommittee on Education of the Committee on Labor and Public Welfare, 1964, p. 114). President Johnson later placed this idea at the apogee of the policy orbit. A message to Congress listed several aspirations for America: to be the "richest, the mightiest, the most productive nation in the world," and asked, "Which of our pursuits is most worthy of our devotion? If we were required to choose, I believe we would place one item at the top of the list: fulfillment of the individual" (Excerpts from President's Special Message, 1967, p. 26).

Widespread agreement on a goal within the policy arena might be conceived as evidence of that apex of "intellectual" success, sought by Dewey, among others, of seeing one's ideas put to practical use. On the other hand, the ironic alternative appears more appropriate: The wide incorporation of the naturalist goal into conventional wisdom illustrates the hazard Dewey also appreciated, namely knowledge passed on serving as a substitute for thought. A formulation advocating expression of creativity became transformed into a conventional cliché. Creativity became the cliché to which many policy makers conformed.

Beginning in the late 1950s, preschool programs became identified as a means of *improving the school readiness* of "culturally" or "educationally" deprived children. Grant funds from the Ford Foundation truly became venture capital, starting and stimulating a host of programs for the "deprived" or "disadvantaged." By early 1965—prior to Head Start—compensatory preschool programs were in operation in seventy cities; over half of the programs had been established within the preceding year or two (Getzels, 1965, pp. 110-111; see also Bertolaet, 1965; Marris and Rein, 1969).

That trend toward special educational programs also reflected the growing awareness among some educators of the joint effects on the inner cities of the postwar migration North by blacks from the South and the flight to the suburbs by whites. The special programs represented efforts by a vanguard group of educators to be responsive to the host of special social problems of the slums, such as school dropouts, delinquency, and so on. As educators, they tended to look for or accept educational approaches to the "problems of the disadvantaged." Some did so naively; that is, they assumed education to be a panacea for a wide variety of social ills. Others "merely" assumed preschool programs would be efficacious in helping unprepared children of the slums to catch up with middle-class children and not fall behind in school achievement. (The more ambitious goal of renewing cities and overcoming broader social problems is dealt with later.)

The Ford Foundation's Great Cities programs took cognizance of the educational problems of lower-class children by altering the grade school and junior high curriculum to take into account the differential abilities of those children, and by "enriching" their education. Some projects went beyond this approach. Reflecting research findings on the normative and cognitive impact of early childhood experience, they aimed for prevention in addition to remediation. Programs initiated before elementary school, preschool programs, would compensate for the deprivation in early rearing by equipping the young, lower-class child with the requisite values, communication skills, and information. So equipped by means of compensatory education, the young child from the slums would not experience school as discontinuous with his past (Getzels, 1965, p. 106). Improving school readiness of children from the slums, or—in the educational and policy jargon of the mid-1960s—compensatory education, was one of the two goals of preschool programs most frequently posited by respondents in this study. (Most interviews were conducted a month after passage of the ESEA in April, 1965.) This goal was incorporated into the "Declaration of Policy," Section 201, of the ESEA: "In recognition of the special educational needs of children of low-income families . . . the Congress hereby declares it to be the policy of the United States to provide financial assistance (as set forth in this title) . . . to expand and improve . . . educational programs by various means (including preschool programs) which contribute particularly to meeting the special educational needs of educationally deprived children."

An implication of compensatory education for the institution of the family must be noted. The concept of cultural deprivation of poor children implies a critique of the rearing received from their parents. That criticism was itself attacked in harsh, stark terms by a participant at a professional conference: "The ultimate in antiparent attitude [sic] is coming out in our new antipoverty programs. In these programs, the parent is the enemy. The parent is the representative of the culture which must be destroyed if his children are to be saved" (cited in "Who Should Teach Young Children?" 1965, p. 15). More often, the shortcomings of parents in the ghettos were stated less sharply, although candidly, as in the words of one respondent, a nationally prominent expert on children: "For the overwhelming number of lower-class children the mother is neither accessible or competent." However, if the parent was seen as "the enemy," the various compensatory programs sought to involve, not exclude, low-income parents. Many of the Great Cities and similar projects that predated Head Start included "organized visits to the homes by teachers and social workers" (National Education Association, 1965, p. 755). The OEO was advised by its Planning Committee on Head Start that "parents should be involved both for their own and their children's benefit" (U.S. Office of Economic Opportunity, 1965b, p. 5). The Planning Committee proposed numerous forms of parent involvement: in "nonprofessional, subprofessional, and semiprofessional roles" as program staff members, a conception reflecting the "anti-professional" attitude in that committee, in OEO generally, and in planning the program (U.S. Office of Economic Opportunity, 1965b, p. 5).[10]

Given that orientation, respondents generally were not inclined to see Head Start as weakening the family or the maternal role. Thus another professional expert anticipated no diminution of family responsibility if the preschool programs were properly conducted—that is, involved the parents. Another, however, wondered whether the popularity and greater availability of preschool programs would encourage mothers who were accessible to and competent with their children to leave their children for others to rear, that is encourage middle-class mothers to enroll their children in the programs. A third nationally known expert believed every home needs to supplement the activities of children approximately three years of age and on with some sort of group experience.

A start toward *breaking the cycle of poverty* was the third goal projected for preschool programs. This goal formulation encompasses the preceding one, but extends a perspective beyond childhood and adolescence to activities of youth and adults. Two respondents, both members of the Head Start Planning Committee, who had also served on President Kennedy's Committee on Mental Retardation, independently attributed to the deliberations of the latter committee the genesis of the core idea: interrupting the cycle of poverty for one generation through programs for children *under* three. The nursery school years of three to five years were seen as too late for effective intervention. (Initially, day care had been the mechanism decided on. Given a realization that knowledge about such early child-care programs was lacking, a series of conferences and research and demonstration projects were undertaken. The accumulated theoretical, evidential, and programatic knowledge is presented in Chandler, Lourie, and Peters [1968]. By 1967, at least one of these experts no longer believed the cycle of poverty could be interrupted in one generation without disrupting the family as an institution. He cited the Israeli experience with programs for children of Middle Eastern immigrants as evidence that a "pressure cooker" approach alienates children from their families.)

During the Washington spring of 1965, when Head Start was starting up and the landmark ESEA had been enacted, this was the prime goal held for preschool programs for the poor. It represented the diffusion of ideas from the fields of child development, education, and orthopsychiatry into the political sphere.[11] From the perspective of these specialists, intervention in the early childhood years offered the best hope of breaking the poverty cycle. For example, Bronfenbrenner, invited to testify by Republican congressmen during hearings to consider the Economic Opportunity bill, said that the Job Corps also proposed in that measure "does not hit at the heart of the matter." Quoting President Johnson's intent, "to strike at poverty at its source," Bronfenbrenner stated, "to me, this means striking at poverty where it hits first and most damagingly—in early childhood" (cited in U.S., Congress, House, Committee on Education and Labor, 1964, pp. 3018-3019).

Several versions of this goal emphasized different ideological viewpoints on poverty. A "conservative" implication was imparted by one politically influential respondent who cited President Johnson's goal phrase of producing taxpayers, not tax users. Replacing "taxeaters" (welfare clients) with taxpayers also was defined as the main purpose of the EOA by one of the Congressmen who cosponsored the bill in the House, Landrum of Georgia (U.S., Congress, *Congressional Record*, 1964c, p. 17624). "Liberal" formulations put the emphasis on equalizing

opportunities or on egalitarianism, "leveling class distinctions."

From the standpoint of ideology, the Johnson Administration's War on Poverty raised a number of issues. Interest-
ingly, some conservatives and liberals both attacked the measure
for its inattention to that basic economic opportunity, jobs. In
the floor debate on the Economic Opportunity bill, Senator
Gruening called the measure a "bandaid program" and cited the
recommendation by Leon Keyserling and Gunnar Myrdal that
to eliminate unemployment and effectively fight poverty, the
United States needs a large-scale public works program (U.S.,
Congress, *Congressional Record*, 1964a, p. 16078). (Gruening
also inserted into the record an article by Myrdal that carried a
prophetic warning: " 'I am convinced that discrimination in
reverse, that is, to the advantage of the Negroes is misdirected.
Nothing would with more certainty create hatred for Negroes
among other poor groups in America. . . . Moreover, special welfare policies for Negroes are not very practical . . . the same is
true of education,' " cited on p. 16090.) A legislative aide to a
liberal senator agreed, calling the EOA "a most superficial
attack on poverty," which would fail because the main cause of
the problem is inadequate employment. Conservative Republicans in the Senate, such as Senator Tower (U.S., Congress, *Congressional Record*, 1964a, p. 16057), and in the House, Congressmen Frelinghuysen, Griffin, Ashbrook, and others (U.S.,
Congress, House, Committee on Education and Labor, 1964, p.
3016), called an unfettered free enterprise system the best
weapon against poverty.

The neglect of employment measures in the EOA apparently was not an oversight; yet, incongruously, that piece of
legislation was developed, with President Johnson's approval, by
his Council of Economic Advisors (Sundquist, 1969, p. 21).

Radical proposals for dealing with poverty by the redistribution of wealth did not enter the policy arena in 1964. One
authoritative interpretation of the EOA noted that "The philosophy behind the [EOA] is not that existing wealth should be
redistributed but that poor people can and must be provided
with opportunities to earn a decent living and maintain their

families on a comfortable living standard" (U.S., Congress, House, Committee on Education and Labor, 1964, p. 2955).

Compensatory education as the start to the solution of poverty may, in some formulations, imply a causal theory of poverty. Specialists on early childhood understandably tended to perceive the problem solely from their specialized perspectives. Many educators and some politicians viewed education as a panacea for a range of problems reaching from the schoolroom, across the community, on to the social order. For example, Senator Pat McNamara, who had introduced the EOA in the Senate (as S. 2642), disclaimed a pretense "that this legislation [ESEA] will fully solve the problem of poverty." Its aims were more modest: "Programs receiving Federal support must not treat the poverty condition symptomatically, but must attack the root of the problem in a way that promises a final solution" (U.S., Congress, *Congressional Record*, 1964a, pp. 16055-16056). Some specialists could not accept the implied theory of causation. They experienced cognitive dissonance, for example, at a conference on educational deprivation when "Over and over, participants stuck on the question of whether the school alone can make the necessary impact without society's opening up really equal opportunities in employment, in housing, in civic affairs" (Passow, 1963, p. 351). One black educator, despairing of substantial progress in jobs and housing, placed the burden of combating poverty and discrimination on the schools "by default." Yet, citing the experience of past immigrant groups, and discounting instant achievement, he argued that urban schools can, if properly staffed and funded, serve as "regenerative agents for both the individual and the community" (Cuban, 1965, p. 2974).

Another ideological issue raised by the policy of compensatory preschool education to help combat poverty concerned the possibility that special programs for the poor might result in economically segregated preschool systems. Only one respondent, a legislator, unequivocally suggested that to be a real possibility and indicated favoring measures to not visibly stigmatize the poor; however, that respondent also opposed federal funding of universally available preschool programs. Several respon-

dents partially evaded the issue and in part hinted at the likelihood of preschool programs along class lines in the immediate
future, but expressed the vague hope that programs like Head
Start would eventually raise the quality of all education programs. Another respondent, an officer of a national voluntary
organization, believed that class-segregated programs would
follow as a consequence only if the poverty-linked policy in
ESEA became permanent, rather than being a temporary expedient. A federal official readily assented to the proposition
that Head Start was an economically segregated program, but
was biased "in favor of the poor." Shriver also had expressed
this view (U.S., Congress, Senate, Select Committee on Poverty
of Committee on Labor and Public Welfare, 1964, pp. 68-74).

A few respondents believed that the absence of a means
test in the program assured that the federally funded preschool
programs would not be segregated along class lines. (This raises
a difficulty that this study could not clarify. The poverty designation called for in the ESEA applies to the school district, not
to the individual child. Yet OEO also stipulates a 15 percent
quota of nonpoor as eligible. How eligibility for that quota was
to be established without application of an income test to the
individual applicant is not clear.)

Several respondents indicated with different degrees of
tartness that the question concerning the possibility of class
segregated education was impractical or unrealistic. An official
in a national organization, after responding in the negative as to
the possibility of programs becoming segregated along class
lines, added that the EOA addressed itself to the "realities of
poverty"; there would be cause for concern only if the gap between the poor and nonpoor increased as a result of the legislation. A professional expert on children stated that criticism
implied by the question is "artificial" and "misses the point—we
must start with children where they are." A legislative aide
found the question has "little relation to reality, for we don't
live in an ideal world"; this respondent later described the EOA
as a "most superficial attack on poverty."

Another officer of a national organization also responded
in the negative, but went on to cite findings of inequalities

between schools in poor neighborhoods and those in middle- and upper-class neighborhoods. Another response challenged the question as making a false assumption. The question, a congressional staff member stated, "presumes an economically integrated school system now exists," and she added a personal opinion to the contrary.

Another facet of this issue is the desirability of preschool programs based on universal rather than selective standards. A number of respondents viewed universally available programs as a distant ideal, but indicated that practicality called for supporting federal aid for a selective program (ESEA) as a temporary expedient. Many who took this position added as additional justification the difficulty over past decades in gaining federal legislation for general aid to education. One respondent, an expert on preschool programs, expressed a clear and elaborated rationale in favor of universally available preschool programs. Following Head Start, many educators also came to advocate preschool programs not only for poor, disadvantaged children. "The pampered also are disadvantaged; so are those whose parents are obsessed with the need to impress and achieve; so are those . . . whose parents show them little love" (Hechinger, 1966b, p. 1).

The fourth, and last, value attributed to compensatory education programs related to the *national defense*. By no means were all, or even the most influential statements of this ideal uttered by conservatives; unusual ideological alliances were formed over educational policy. Liberals expressed an unusually conservative concern with national defense. Some, such as Senator Morse, stated the concern in abstract terms: "The school system of this country is one of the three greatest defense weapons we have. The economy is another. Our Defense Establishment is the third" (U.S., Congress, Senate, Subcommittee on Education of the Committee on Labor and Public Welfare, 1964, p. 96). Along the same lines, a legislative respondent reported having said to the Foreign Relations Committee that "the first and foremost critical foreign policy problem was the educational crisis, and that if we don't face up to the educational crisis, we sacrifice one of the greatest weapons for our security." Others, including President Johnson, put the issue in terms of literacy, intellect or "brainpower" as critical national resources.

Policy makers across a wide ideological spectrum placed the accent on education as a weapon in defending the social order against internal disorder. Congressman Landrum defended the EOA bill he had introduced as a mechanism for defusing the social dynamite in the slums. (U.S., Congress, *Congressional Record*, 1964c, pp. 17623-17624). Ghetto riots after 1965 (when some of the interviews were conducted) heightened this concern. One respondent, who had played a behind-the-scene role in the fashioning of ESEA, had riots not far in back of his mind when answering how the legislation he had helped shape served the public interest. At first responding blandly that it was in the public interest to reach the educationally and eco-nomically deprived, he then spoke with feeling of "the poor Negroes driven out of the South to live a ghetto life in the North. . . . When you think of the recent riots, Jesus, what the hell can we do if not educate them—train the National Guard to more effectively suppress riots? There is one problem with edu-cation to deal with riots and poverty—the results are not demonstrable for generations."

A linkage between riots and education was also drawn after 1965 by political and professional policy makers. Senator Morse attributed the unrest to "the educational starvation which the Negroes have suffered." More impatient with urban schools than he had been in 1965, Senator Robert Kennedy gave the "ghetto school . . . a flunking grade" (Morse and Ken-nedy cited in Hunter, 1967b, p. 14).

The urban riots were reported to have reinforced the rec-ommendation made by a White House panel on education in 1967. At a time when the NEA and the Republican leadership in Congress had shifted in favor of general—noncategorical—fed-eral aid to education, the riots underscored the panel's conclu-sion that "the important thing now is a major effort to reach the disadvantaged" (Hunter, 1967a, pp. 1, 21).

John McCone, former Director, Central Intelligence Agency, and head of a California commission that had investigated the Watts riots in 1965, two years later stressed preschool programs in a report he filed with the National Advisory Commission on Civil Disorders. Warning that racial strife might " 'split our society irretrievably and destroy our country,' " he made two basic, long-range recommendations: begin "permanent Head Start programs" for ghetto children three or four years of age and reduce the size of such preschool classes (cited in Herbers, 1967b, pp. 1, 30).

But Fred M. Hechinger, education editor of the *New York Times*, had become far less optimistic about preschool programs in 1967 than he had been a year earlier (Hechinger, 1966c). Writing about the utility of such programs for achieving internal order, he noted somberly, "It is doubtful whether either the national mood or the educational expertise is prepared to face the fact at which Head Start merely hinted: That masses of children of the slums may have to be 'taken over' by a new education process—not the old-line schools—at two or three years of age, and that they may have to stay in the program from early morning to evening, and perhaps through the night. Unless education can assume the responsibility for otherwise lost children, the pilot projects, crash programs, and integration gimmicks will be aspirin against an epidemic of the plague" (Hechinger, 1967b, p. E7).

One other variation of defending the social order as a goal of preschool programs was encountered. It involves the national repute or concern for social justice. Preschool programs were seen by one federal official as serving the national interest by showing a concern for the poor. Such programs, he said, "show somebody cares for the poor." Another official saw Head Start as an early attempt to deal with human suffering, and with delinquency and relief. An advisor to OEO recounted an anecdote from a Head Start program. One father, who had learned to speak English from his child in a Head Start program, was said to have proclaimed: "This is the first time America shows it cares for me." Finally, the respondent mentioned in Chapter Four may be recalled. A succession of ends was envisioned: citizenship training, improving cultural levels, reducing or preventing social pathology, strife, or even revolution, and a manifestation to the world of our national concern for social justice.

In a study of British history at the turn of the century, Semmel termed the relationship between a declared concern for social justice and defense of the social order *social imperialism*. The term refers to explicit political and legislative efforts "designed to draw all classes together in defense of the nation and empire and aimed to prove to the least well-to-do class that its interests were inseparable from those of the nation" (Semmel, 1968, p. 12). Such an explicit linkage between social justice and national defense was not drawn by respondents in this study. It also did not appear to have been implied by liberals who had urged federal aid to education in the name of national defense. On the other hand, a conservative legislator found an ideological flaw in a federal program to aid the poor, such as the EOA: It implied an admission of widespread poverty, which might make it appear to foreigners that capitalism is "less enriching" to the masses than communism (see the remarks by Congressman Albert Watson [U.S., Congress, *Congressional Record*, 1964c, p. 17616]).

The Process of Preschool Policy Enactment

The 1961 stalemate of federal aid to elementary and secondary education over the church-state issue had occurred at a time when other forces were at play, namely economics and politics. These two forces had combined in a way to point to a promising lead in the search for federal support to general education. The recession in 1960-1961 had merely accelerated a process that had been underway at least since 1953, the slowdown in the share of income to those at the bottom and an increased flow of income up to the affluent (Macdonald, 1963). Not until Harrington's *The Other America: Poverty in the United States* was published, in 1962, however, did the results of the distributive processes come to the forefront of public awareness. Poverty became recognized as a problem in the political arena, symbolized by President Kennedy's creation of a Cabinet Task Force on Poverty, chaired by Attorney General Robert Kennedy.

After President Kennedy was assassinated, the opportunity to launch a major attack on poverty fell to Lyndon Johnson, who assumed the presidency only one year before a presidential election. In January, 1964, President Johnson announced he would propose legislation to launch a billion-dollar "all-out war on human poverty and unemployment. . . . It can be done by this summer." Johnson went on to proclaim that his administration "today here and now declares unconditional war on poverty in America. . . . Our chief weapons . . . will be better schools, and better health, and better homes, and better training, and better job opportunities" (cited in U.S., Congress, Senate, Committee on Labor and Public Welfare, 1964, pp. 223-224; for additional declarations of that war, see pp. 225-226 and 228).

Before that legislative proposal, the EOA, was submitted to Congress on March 16, 1964, an educational bill had been introduced on February 10 that contained a novel feature. It consisted of a rationale to justify federal support for education on the basis of the impact of federal activity relating to unemployment and welfare, that is, to poverty. That feature was to reappear with some revision in the EOA. Senator Morse had introduced it in his educational bill, S. 2528, which proposed to amend Public Law 8.74, the law authorizing funds for elementary and secondary education "in areas affected by Federal activity," the aid to federally impacted areas enacted in 1950.

That educational bill represented the outcome of "long and hard" legislative planning by the following members of the Subcommittee on Education of the Committee on Labor and Public Welfare, U.S. Senate: Jack Forsythe, General Counsel; Charles Lee, Professional Staff Member; and Senator Wayne Morse, Chairman.[12] A lesson had been learned from the frustrating stalemate in 1961 over general aid to education. Because educational aid on a general basis could not be passed, some other basis was required. The legislative planners went back to the books to do their homework. One of the readings was the Quattlebaum report, which had pointed in its conclusion to the national defense justification for much of the federal role and funding in education. That conclusion suggested a way out, caused by political necessity, of avoiding a general basis for legislative aid. Later, Senator Morse proudly remarked, "I suppose I can best describe what happened by saying that we had a brainstorm as we worked on impacted area legislation" (U.S., Congress, Senate, Subcommittee on Education of the Committee on Labor and Public Welfare, 1965, p. 99). The brainstorm was in finding a connection between aid to "lower" education and a rationale for federal involvement that could justify expanded federal funding beyond that already permitted under the 1950 defense-impact legislation.

The federal connection was literally to follow with educational funds the federal dollars expended for noneducational social welfare programs. The basis proposed under S. 2528 for authorizing federal funds for public education involved proportions of school children on AFDC or whose parents, living in federally designated areas of "substantial unemployment," receive unemployment compensation. In other words, areas with specified proportions of AFDC children, or "areas of substantial umemployment with unemployed parents" were to be designated as "areas affected by federal activity," just as defense-impacted areas had been since 1950 (U.S., Congress, Senate, Subcommittee on Education of the Committee on Labor and Public Welfare, 1964, p. 3). In short, a categorical (that is, not general) federal connection was drawn between "lower" education and localities penetrated by federal unemployment and welfare policy.

Before introducing that measure, Morse had taken some steps toward gaining support for the federal categorical connection he hoped could get through Congress. Earlier in February, he met with officials of the not unimportant National Education Association (NEA), a union then of some 900,000 members, to convince them to support his bill. "I told them that as a result of the study we had made that we could get legislation that we all wanted, provided we cast it correctly in a form familiar to Congress, which meant as an amendment to an existing law, and in a form which would have political sex appeal to as wide a spectrum of Congressmen as we could possibly get Administrative approval for from a budgetary standpoint. I told them that while I was just as strong for a general aid bill as ever, it probably couldn't be enacted yet. While keeping to this as a long-range objective, I suggested that we should try to unite on legislation which would approach what we wanted on a categorical basis" (1965, p. 2).

Morse did obtain NEA support (U.S., Congress, Senate, Subcommittee on Education of the Committee on Labor and Public Welfare, 1965, p. 99), but not that of the Johnson Administration. By July 29, 1964, when the Subcommittee on Education began its hearings on S. 2528, the House hearings on the EOA had been held weeks earlier and the Senate had just passed that bill. Secretary Celebrezze wrote on July 29, in response to a request on March 2 for an HEW response on S. 2528, that "The objectives of the bill are highly commendable" but that "the administration's proposed Economic Opportunity Act of 1964 . . . is the most appropriate vehicle for the accomplishment of those objectives" (U.S., Congress, Senate, Subcommittee on Education of the Committee on Labor and Public Welfare, 1964, p. 7).

On July 30, Commissioner Keppel testified; although he referred to the EOA, the main reservations he had about the Morse proposal were "troublesome administrative questions" about factors in the allocative formula and doubts about Morse's estimated cost of the bill, $218,000,000. He added that the administration continued to support their previously submitted omnibus, general aid to education bill, S. 580. Keppel's testimony drew a lengthy dressing-down from Morse. Placing the responsibility on President Johnson, Morse accused the administration of "stalling on needed legislation"; charged unconcern over the "sad, sad plight" of "one of the three greatest defense weapons we have," education; implied oversight of the difficulties in overcoming the "major emotional blockade" preventing passage of a general aid bill; and bluntly attacked the "undeclared war in South Vietnam" and the "wasteful" foreign aid program. The administration, he added, had "lost" him not only on educational legislation, but on other issues as well. "I cannot support the policy of the administration to give away in effect hundreds of millions of dollars [for] the foreign aid program . . . being negotiated now" (U.S., Congress, Senate, Subcommittee on Education of the Committee on Labor and Public Welfare, 1964, pp. 96-99).

Almost a year later, Morse, former law professor and dean, described those hearings in less heated, academic terms: "Now I conduct my hearings in the form of a seminar, with term papers assigned to the Administration witnesses. So I told the Commissioner, more in sorrow than in anger, that in my judgment he had flunked the course. And I made him my emissary to the Administration to tell it, all the way to the top, that they had failed it, too. But I held out hope. I told the Commissioner that he could repeat the course for make-up credit" (1965, p. 3). More than the passage of time had occurred between the tongue-lashing in July 1964 and the light-hearted metaphor in May 1965. In October 1964, while in the East Room of the White House to witness the signing of a bill amending the National Defense Education Act (NDEA), Morse was "asked" to meet with Keppel, Wilbur Cohen, and Celebrezze. At that meeting, according to a later report by Morse, "Keppel . . . said, 'We are rejoining your seminar next year. We are going to support the principle of your bill.' And in all my years of teaching, I have never felt so good about a student passing a course as I did that day. I finally got the instruction through" (U.S., Congress, Senate, Subcommittee on Education of the Committee on Labor and Public Welfare, 1965, p. 100).

The metaphor deserves a brief analysis. The lesson learned and who the student was need to be made explicit. The lesson refers to the formula for a federal connection that Morse and his staff had devised. It consisted of casting a new, controversial legislative proposal as an amendment onto an existing, widely accepted statute—in legislative jargon, a piece of "boiler-plate." Specifically, it welded the new notion of welfare- and unemployment-affected areas to a well-established idea of defense-impacted areas in the NDEA. Secondly, by choosing a categorical basis for aid, for example, welfare and unemployment, a "general" aid approach appeared to be bypassed. In actuality, combining categories of conditions that are widely distributed in the country with a low cutoff point, made approximately as many parts of the country eligible to coverage as would a general aid measure. (S. 2528 proposed to make eligible for federal education funds any school district with ten or more

AFDC children or children of parents receiving unemployment compensation in the designated unemployment areas, or 3 or more percent of such children among the total number in daily average attendance in the district's public schools.) Parts of this "lesson" were incorporated into the two pertinent pieces of legislation, the EOA and the ESEA.

Returning to Morse's metaphor, the word *seminar* probably alludes to the background explanation given by Morse to the NEA officials in February 1964. But it is doubtful that the word *student* refers, as seems implied, to Keppel. The latter had, in the July 1964 hearings, stated administrative support for a pending general aid bill (S. 580). A switch from a general aid approach to a categorical approach (which the ESEA was subsequently to embody), that is, a shift in so highly and traditionally controversial a legislative area as federal aid to "lower" education, very likely would not be made by the commissioner or secretary alone. (Some circumstantial evidence supports the conjecture about Keppel's legislative positions. Bailey [1966] attributes Keppel's failure to support the earlier Morse measure, S. 2528, as caused by his having been "under Executive discipline.") White House involvement would be called for on such a matter in any administration. With a president known to desire an historical reputation as the "Education President," the policy decision was most likely approved by Johnson (Hunter, 1965; see also U.S. Congress, Senate, Committee on Labor and Public Welfare, 1964, pp. 236-239). (Johnson, who had been a teacher before entering politics, held deeply to educationalist beliefs: "There is something very quiet and moving about the President when he talks [about education] . . . . He sees education as the ultimate hope of race and poverty, and he looks to modern communications and Federal aid as the means of achieving equality of opportunity" (Reston, 1967, p. 46). That approval, it is conjectured here, followed informal communication between the President and the Senator, such as is reported to have occurred when the cattleman, L. B. J., visited Morse's cattle farm in Maryland.

In other words, the student who made Morse feel so pleased by passing the course was probably President Johnson.

However, the lesson the instructor was so proud of contained at least one serious flaw. Because S. 2528 authorized funds only to public schools, had the administration supported the measure, a repeat of the 1961 stalemate may well have reoccurred. That possibility was implied in the written statement that Right Reverend Monsignor Frederick G. Hochwalt, the education spokesman for the National Catholic Welfare Conference, submitted in lieu of an appearance at the hearings. Hochwalt commented on Morse's brainchild as follows: "A thorough review of the entire impacted aid program would appear to be in order. . . . We are growing increasingly apprehensive that this form of Federal assistance may be assuming proportions approaching general programs of assistance without adequate appreciation of implications" (U.S., Congress, Senate, Subcommittee on Education of the Committee on Labor and Public Welfare, 1964, p. 126). The Catholic spokesman saw clearly past the form to the substance of the matter. Although Morse and his staff had very ingeniously devised a federal connection to justify "categorical" aid to elementary and secondary education, they had not found a politically useful resolution of the church-state dilemma. A crude, but emerging, "solution" to that dilemma was being constructed in the legislative course of the EOA.

The war on poverty was declared, it may be recalled, in January 1964, several weeks after the assassination of John F. Kennedy, with a president expecting substantial legislative and/ or programatic results by summer, when the election campaign would formally begin. An event occurring the day following the introduction of the initial EOA bills (S. 2642 and H.R. 10440) suggests a political dimension to the timing. On March 17, "the Democratic National Committee delivered to the office of every Democratic Congressman a so-called 'poverty kit,' complete with prewritten speeches, canned press releases . . . to be used in all the hustings" (U.S. Congress, House, 1964b, p. 3037). Partisan politics, then, had an important bearing on the contents of the antipoverty proposal and the process by which the legislation proceeded. In this regard, the overall rationale for federal intervention merits notice. The EOA built on AFDC rolls and unemployment levels to establish the bases for a federal connection, and expanded that connection to provide an issue with its own "political sex appeal," namely poverty.

Two particular educational issues in the context of the EOA are especially relevant to us: first, the broader issue of separation of church and state in relation to education; and second, policy on preschool programs.

Hearings were held in the House Committee on Education and Labor for fifteen days in March and April, 1964. The bill listed educational activities as one of the functions that could be included under a local community action program. When testifying during the hearings, Attorney General Robert Kennedy was asked whether parochial school children would be eligible to participate in those educational activities and, an OEO official reported, himself answered no. This was one of a series of controversial questions relating to the separation of church and state in regard to the Community Action Program (CAP). Some of the questions apparently arose in conjunction with changing versions of the bill in regard to educational activities. (One version prohibited aid for educational activities under a CAP, unless approved by the local public school authority; another would permit participation by parochial school students if the funds were administered by public officials [see U.S. Congress, *Congressional Record*, 1964d, p. 17674].) All the early versions apparently raised danger signals. One such danger, authoritatively reported by the Republican minority on the House Committee, is that those versions "aroused the opposition of those desiring equal aid for private schools" (U.S., Congress, House, Committee on Education and Labor, 1964, p. 3023). Congressman Carey (New York), a member of the committee, who was said by a federal official to be a "major spokesman for Catholic views, especially those of Cardinal Spellman," was reported to have strongly objected to a provision that would exclude parochial school students.

On the other hand, Congressman Phil Landrum (Georgia), cosponsor of the bill with Adam Clayton Powell (New York), was said to be opposed to the use of federal funds for parochial school students. The resulting controversy created dissension between Southern and Northern Democrats. Furthermore, it endangered any educational activity within the CAP and perhaps Title II in its entirety.

After the hearings were concluded, "abruptly, with vital witnesses still unheard," according to the Republican members, the Democratic members of the committee apparently went into an extended period of caucus meetings. To the Republicans, it was a "lockout period of ten days during which [they] were excluded from committee chairs. As a consequence, the executive sessions were bereft of meaningful debate and deliberation. Worthwhile amendments were turned aside by a straight line party vote. The party word had gone out, the product had to be delivered" (U.S., Congress, House, Committee on Education and Labor, 1964, p. 3037).

The product was a "clean bill," H. R. 11377, which contained an unusual phrase in regard to education. Only "special remedial and other noncurricular educational assistance" is stipulated as being eligible for support, and "general aid to elementary and secondary education" is prohibited under Section 205(a) and (b) of the bill. That phrase, in conjunction with explicit eligibility of "private nonprofit agencies" to CAP grants or contracts, represents the compromise formula on the church-state controversy. (Formulation of the compromise phrase is attributed by a federal respondent to Congressman O'Hara, Michigan, a "liberal Catholic.") For the most part, the phrase defied clear explication, except for preschool and day-care programs as illustrations of such "assistance."

Asked by legislators to clarify the phrase, federal officials found it "wicked"—difficult to interpret in a way not vulnerable to criticism as permitting aid to parochial schools. The Republican minority on the House Committee also complained that they "were unable to obtain an intelligible explanation of the meaning of this new language." More slyly, they wrote that "it presents an interesting study of obfuscation which would never be chronicled in any 'Profile of Courage'" (U.S. Congress, House, 1964b, p. 3023. For other colloquies on the phrase, see remarks by Congressmen Hugh Carey, Charles Goodell, and James Roosevelt [U.S., Congress, *Congressional Record*, 1964d, pp. 17674-17675, 17679].)

As a compromise, the "wicked" formulation sufficed, for the EOA was enacted. The process, however, produced its own irony. Conservative legislators came to cite objections from the American Civil Liberties Union. In the interest of fighting poverty and of party unity, liberals, along with nonliberal, Catholic allies, tended either to accept the compromise tacitly or to defend it as consistent with the "child benefit" doctrine, as benefiting the individual child in the parochial school, but not the institution. (An exception among Democratic legislators was Senator Samuel Ervin who proposed, unsuccessfully, to amend the EOA to prohibit grants to church-controlled schools. Nonlegislative opposition, of course, also could be found [see "Project Head Start," 1965].) In addition, the compromise left other residues. After Project Head Start had been decided on, the compromise formula contributed to measures to minimize its identification as an educational program. But even during the legislative passage, controversy over separation of church and state and the resulting compromise may have suggested the wisdom of ambiguity and unspecificity about preschool programs.

Preschool education as a recommended or possible program under the EOA played an interesting, but anomalous part in the legislative process. As has been stated earlier, the act did not make explicit reference to preschool education. Yet testimony in favor of such programs was presented during the earliest hearings, held by the House Committee in March and April. However, not the majority Democrats, but the Republican minority had invited testimony from such experts on child development and early childhood education as Urie Bronfenbrenner and O. K. Moore. Bronfenbrenner testified that "We now have research evidence indicating that the environ of poverty has its most debilitating effect on the very young children in the first few years of life . . . [the result of improper early training] is a child so retarded in his development that when he gets to school he is unable to profit from the experience. What is more, the effect is cumulative, the longer he remains in school, the further behind he gets" (cited by Congressman Goodell—see U.S., Congress, *Congressional Record*, 1965a, p. 5770). Numerous other witnesses reportedly testified to the necessity of preschool programs during the hearings on EOA by the Select Subcommittee on Poverty of the Senate Committee on Labor and Public Welfare.

Perhaps most unexpected was the advocacy of preschool programs by Republican legislators who opposed the EOA. Congressman Albert Quie (Minnesota) was the most ardent advocate of preschool programs. As a member of the House Committee on Education and Labor and on the floor of the House he scored the EOA for its omission of programs to deal with "the root of the trouble . . . found in early childhood." His extensive remarks during the debate on EOA on the floor of the House revealed detailed knowledge of findings and explanations from the work of Deutsch, Havighurst, MacIver, and of Bronfenbrenner's views on compensatory education and his recommendation of preschool training (see Congressman's Quie's remarks, U.S., Congress, *Congressional Record*, 1964d, pp. 17706-17708. Quie also recognized the need of a "special corps . . . of teachers . . . free of prejudices and preconceptions" of deprived children, a proposal that placed him in the company of Democratic liberals—Senators Robert and Edward Kennedy, Morse, and Nelson.)

Perhaps the Democratic tactic had been to maintain a low profile on preschool programs in order to minimize a controversy over federal aid to education during the legislative process. If so, Quie's criticism and advocacy of preschool programs was at worst a nuisance, at best a joke the tacticians enjoyed. On the other hand, it is not impossible that the Republican critic may have stimulated thoughts in the direction of Project Head Start. The possibility that a Republican Congressman served as the policy godfather of Head Start cannot be completely rejected.[13]

Given the statutory invisibility of preschool programs in the EOA, the authority for and content of Project Head Start was unclear for some months after the legislation was enacted. But, as was mentioned earlier, by late fall several consultant groups had been convened by OEO. The Head Start Planning Committee, mentioned earlier, functioned as a de facto group for *program* policy making and implementation.[14]

The crucial policy decisions were not left for outsiders to

make. Reference we have made previously indicated the "resistance" of the consultative experts to proceed (see note 6). Their doubts about the possible effectiveness of a preschool program over one summer were described as sufficiently serious that, had a vote been taken by that group, the verdict might have been against recommending that OEO proceed to develop Head Start. But professional doubts did not restrain President Johnson and Sargent Shriver, who apparently felt it was too late to turn back. Thus the question to the Planning Committee whether $150,000,000 could be spent for a preschool program between January and July 1965 seems to have been largely moot. One respondent believed there was a commitment by OEO prior to Head Start to educational ventures similar to those developed by the Ford Foundation. A federal official put it clearly: By the time the Planning Committee was established, the question was not whether, but how to develop Head Start.

The Planning Committee shaped Head Start, imparting a multidisciplinary focus consisting of social and medical as well as educational components, an emphasis on participation by parents as well as children, and a stance that was antiprofessional-educator. The latter attitude reflected the personal views of many committee members. But it also reflected an impersonal political consideration. This was stated explicitly in the reply by a respondent, who held an influential position in connection with Head Start, to a question as to the reason for choice of a pediatrician as the Director of Project Head Start: "That choice was not exactly due to the narrow focus of educators. There were political issues involved. Remember now, a large-scale Federal program involving education was being developed. That would arouse opposition, so I suggested they choose a physician to head it up. They quickly saw the advantages."[15] (Another respondent, an educator, said if Keppel had known that by the summer of 1965 Head Start would involve one half million children, mainly in school buildings, he would have been "very interested" in who directed Head Start. Another educator confirmed the point that the educators had not realized the magnitude of the project that was developing.)

Similar considerations led to the dispute over a term used

in an early Head Start publication. In that publication, the word
teacher had been used and this term evoked all the hostility that
noneducators have concerning the narrow specialization and
professional jargon of "educators." The resulting dispute—
"battle" was the term used by one respondent—led to a policy
decision to avoid the use of the term *teacher* and instead to employ *group leader*. (Public relations considerations presumably
underlay another semantic decision—selection of the project
name. "Project Success" was considered but dropped. "Kiddy
Corps" was discussed by staff, but they were told they would
be fired if that title were used. "Head Start" was suggested at a
staff meeting.)

The offending document is believed to be OEO's "Concept of a Child Development Center," dated March 18, 1965. It
is of tangential interest at this point, for reasons suggested by
the subtitle: "Relationship to Preschool and Day Care." That is,
the document dealt with the traditional distinction between
nursery school and day care. Reference is made in the document to a "Memorandum of Agreement Regarding Day Care
Services and Preschool Education," signed by the Commissioners of Education and Welfare, January 6, 1965: "The essential function and purpose of preschool education is the training,
education, and development of the child. By contrast, the primary function and purpose of a day care service is the care and
protection of children" (U.S. Office of Economic Opportunity,
1965a, p. 2). The agreement is reminiscent of a similar con-
cordat signed twenty years earlier (Lundberg, 1947, p. 295).
This agreement reached by the Welfare Administration and
Office of Education, both units within HEW, indicates more
than an attempt to regulate interorganizational rivalry. Much
more significant is the incorporation into a high-level federal
compact of questionable distinctions between the presumed
clientele and "social" purpose of day care and nursery school
programs. Those distinctions overlook past similarities and reflect the social class biases analyzed in Chapters Two and Three.
Expression of such distinctions in federal policy could contribute to their becoming more congealed in the future.

The discussion of preschool programs within a federal

antipoverty framework in the OEO document could not avoid the social class issue. The pamphlet essentially bypassed the anomalous and antiquated distinction in the 1965 Agreement. OEO called for essentially similar programs and standards for the two kinds of preschool programs except for "administrative considerations" of the daily schedule and associated effects on meals and naps. However, the document reveals the basic inherent and unavoidable tension between the view that the "developmental tasks of all children" are similar and the perspective that children of the poor have special needs.

Political considerations of a partisan nature and the non-partisan issue of the separation of church and state converged and influenced the process and content of preschool policy within the context of the federal war on poverty. The salient church-state controversy had been deflected sufficiently as to gain passage of the EOA. But even adherents of aid to parochial schools would have had to agree that the formula employed was far too ambiguous to serve as boilerplate for subsequent legislation.

Future legislation, especially the ESEA, was being worked out during the summer and fall of 1964, that is, during the presidential election campaign. Several presidential task forces had been appointed in anticipation of an election victory, including one dealing with education, chaired by John Gardner, then of the Carnegie Corporation. The first draft of the ESEA reflected the recommendations of Gardner's task force (Bailey, 1966, p. 5). President Johnson's landslide victory in that election made possible a transformation from intent and reports into an actual legislative proposal by a governing Administration. On January 12, 1965, President Johnson sent his Education Message to the Congress, and the ESEA proposal was introduced (as S. 370 and H.R. 2362).

The ESEA was also cast in the form of an amendment to that familiar piece of prior legislation, Public Law 874 ("Financial Assistance for Local Educational Agencies in Areas Affected by Federal Activity"). Again, as in the brainstorm bill S. 2528 and EOA, low income and AFDC served to designate areas according to the degree they were "affected by federal activity." (Of course, use of the tie-in between education and poverty was not accidental. Although Commissioner Keppel had not supported Senator Morse's earlier proposal containing that connection, S. 2528, Keppel's staff "was stimulated to pursue the implications of Morse's suggestion" [see Bailey, 1966, p. 7]. Staff reports from the Office of Education had been provided to the Gardner task force and they influenced the task force's recommendations.) Through the provision of federal financial aid, the legislation aimed to "contribute particularly to meeting the special educational needs of educationally deprived children" in the designated areas (U.S. Public Law 89-10, 79 Stat 27, Elementary and Secondary Education Act of 1965, 1965, p. 1).[16]

Several titles of the ESEA provided for aid to children in private schools. In developing programs and projects under Title I, local school agencies would be required to make provision for including educationally deprived children enrolled in private schools in "special educational arrangements (such as dual enrollment, educational radio and television," and so on). Title II authorized grants for library resources, textbooks, and other printed instructional materials "for the use of children and teachers in public and private elementary and secondary schools." Such materials would be limited to those approved by public educational authorities or those in use in the local public school, a limitation apparently intended to preclude materials for sectarian instruction or religious worship. If state law or constitution did not authorize, or forbade, a state educational agency to distribute such materials to parochial schools, the federal commissioner of education would be required to arrange for provision of the material and to pay the costs out of the state's allotment. Students in parochial as well as public schools were also eligible for the supplementary educational centers and services to be funded under Title III grants. Such supplementary activities included comprehensive guidance and counseling, vocational guidance, specialized instruction in science and in foreign languages, and so on. Legal title of centers constructed under this provision would be required to be held by public agencies.

The provisions relating to private schools and their students were carefully shaped. The bill did not propose to furnish direct funds or loans to private and parochial schools for salaries or construction. But it did mandate participation by such schools in developing some of the programs—for example, Title III—and a share of the educational materials and services to students in those nonpublic schools. Care had also been taken to include a broad prohibition of any payment under ESEA "for religious worship or instruction." (That injunction appears in Section 605, the very last part of the bill.) That combination of limitations and entitlements was put together through a series of meetings between the major interested parties, the National Catholic Welfare Conference, National Educational Association, and the Johnson Administration. Apparently even before Senator Morse was told, in October 1964, that the administration was going to support the federal connection he had devised, Commissioner Keppel had arranged his own "seminar" meetings to plan for a bill that, in the words of a respondent who was one of the interested parties, "could gain the consensus of the various interests." (That respondent reported he and Keppel had a mutual friend and that this facilitated development of a good working relationship.)

Several studies corroborate this report of Keppel's restless pursuit of an educational bill that could gain the support of a broad coalition of forces. Keppel was said to have held discussions and meetings with "hundreds of people in all sorts of places" to help "sell the proposal" once it had been put together (Meranto, 1967, p. 70). Another report of his "brokerage role" with influential organizations and individuals credits Keppel with "seminal and pervasive influence" in the initiation and drafting of ESEA and the building of a political consensus to gain its passage (see Bailey, 1966, p. 5-9). Republicans apparently heard of Keppel's activities seeking to plan for and organize support for the bill, and queried, " 'Where did this bill come from?' " (Congressman Hugh Carey, in U.S., Congress, *Congressional Record*, 1965a, p. 5758). One legislative respondent said, in response to this query, during an interview, "The educators weren't involved. . . . The National Catholic Welfare

Conference, Christopher Jencks, Paul Goodman, and Marcus Raskin [of the Institute of Policy Studies] were involved." (If true, a combination of official Catholic spokesmen, a self-defined socialist—Jencks, and an anarchist—Goodman, would indeed make up a strange alliance. Another respondent, however, denied involvement of the Institute of Policy Studies.)

This time the administration had done its homework, and met with success. During the hearings by the House Education and Labor Committee, support for H.R. 2362 was voiced by almost all of the major religious and educator groups. The NEA spokesman called the bill a "realistic" proposal that "in no way violates the principle of separation of church and state" (cited in Meranto, 1967, pp. 69-71).

Meranto points out that although NEA policy approves only federal aid for purposes permissible by state laws and constitutions, Title II of the ESEA violates this principle. But Congressman Powell defended the Title II provision of books to parochial school pupils by the Commissioner of Education if state law or constitution constrains a state educational authority: "Those who would argue that this is a violation of states' rights need only to be reminded that this is the current practice in the operation of a hot lunch program. I wonder if the opponents would 'feed the body but not the mind' " (U.S., Congress, *Congressional Record*, 1965a, p. 5734).

General approval was stated by Arthur Flemming, former secretary of HEW, representing the National Council of Churches of Christ. He found the proposal "basically sound" and welcomed the "dual school enrollment" or "shared time" provision in Title I.[17] Whereas the National Council favors federal aid to help public schools extend some facilities and other resources to private school students, Flemming indicated continued opposition to grants of tax funds to nonpublic schools. Therefore, although approving the intent in Titles II and III of assisting students rather than assisting the private schools, he recommended revisions to ensure administration by public authorities and that the educational materials be loaned, not granted, to the private schools, and that ownership of the materials clearly reside with public authority. Baptist, Lutheran,

Methodist, Episcopalian, and Presbyterian spokesmen also testified generally in support of the bill. The Presbyterian representative commended both the deflection of the church-state impasse and the connection between education and poverty: " 'First, I am glad to see for the first time in many years a very real prospect for the enactment of a significant program of Federal aid to public schools. H.R. 2362 represents a fantastically skillful break in the stalemate occasioned by the church-state dilemma in previous legislative efforts. . . . Second, the use of the poverty-impacted area concept is a highly commendable device by which to match resources with need' " (cited in Meranto, 1967, p. 75). Support by these Protestant groups was qualified, however, by concern over who would retain title to the library materials authorized under Title II and who would control the centers called for under Title III.

The Catholic spokesman on education, Monsignor Hochwalt expressed " 'reserved approval and cautious optimism' " of the bill as a " 'workable compromise.' " He clearly indicated his reservations as psychological and tactical, rather than logical and substantive: " 'We reserve our cautions, however, since the legislative road ahead may be a long and difficult one with the provisions subject to change and amendments' " (cited in Meranto, 1967, p. 76).

Opposition to the bill was expressed by the Council of Chief State School Officials, the American Jewish Congress, and the American Civil Liberties Union, on grounds beyond those that the Protestant groups supporting the measure had also questioned. The ACLU, fearing the dual enrollment provisions of Title I might encourage a proliferation of private schools to avoid racial integration, proposed a prohibition against segregated shared time programs under Title I. Most objections, however, focused on the provisions in Titles II and III on ownership of the educational materials and administrative control of the supplementary centers.

These objections were taken up by the House General Subcommittee on Education, chaired by Representative Carl Perkins of Kentucky. (Amending a carefully devised, controversial measure is dangerous. It opens up the possibility of unfriendly amendments, a danger implied in Hochwalt's cautious remarks. But the House Subcommittee and parent Committee on Education and Labor, dominated by Democrats, were safe groups to consider amending H.R. 2362.) Amendments along the lines suggested by Arthur Flemming were adopted. Title I was amended to provide "assurance that the control of funds . . . and title to property derived therefrom, shall be in a public agency . . . and that a public agency will administer and control such funds and property" (Section 205 (a), 3). Provisions were added to Title II giving title and administrative control to public authorities over the library materials for parochial school pupils; such materials could only be loaned, not granted, to private school teachers and pupils. Title III was amended to permit only public agencies to manage the supplementary centers.

These amendments embody several "principles": first, the analogy of the application of public school services to part-time students, that is, to students also enrolled in parochial schools; the lending principle and the related retention of titular ownership by public authority; and the reservation of administrative responsibility for public funds to public agencies. These devices, a legislative craftsman reported, were selected as tactical solutions to making permeable the wall separating church and state without providing a clear target to those seeking to keep the church-state separation watertight.

After cleaning up the bill with amendments related to the church-state issue, the committee passed it and sent it on to the House. The minority reportedly criticized the bill, among numerous other reasons, for "omitting preschool training . . . the most important educational period in one's life" (U.S. Congress, *Congressional Record*, 1965a, p. 5739). Committee Chairman Perkins submitted a rebuttal, pointing out that the bill twice employs the phrase "preschool programs" (U.S., Congress, *Congressional Record*, 1965a, p. 5739). Perkins attributed the minority's great emphasis on preschool training simply "to cast doubt on H.R. 2362." Congressmen Goodell and Quie carried their criticism to the House floor. Said Goodell: "Any bill designed to upgrade and modernize American education which does not focus on preschool training is antiquated before it is even enacted" (U.S., Congress, *Congressional Record*, 1965a, p. 5770). Quie, who had so strongly recommended including preschool programs in the EOA, continued to cite research and program evidence in support of the need for such programs in the ESEA. Not satisfied by the two brief references in the bill, he proposed an amendment calling for the expenditure of $300,000,000—double the allocation proposed earlier by President Johnson—"to reach the culturally or socially deprived children of preschool age" (U.S., Congress, *Congressional Record*, 1965a, p. 6018). Efforts to amend H.R. 2362 beyond the changes made in committee failed, and the measure was adopted by the House on March 26.

In the Senate, hearings on S. 370, an identical version of H.R. 2362 prior to amendment by the House committee, were also held during late January and early February, 1965. At those hearings the same "alignment of the major interest groups" was shown as had occurred in the House hearings. Missing from the opposition in 1965, Meranto (1967, pp. 80-81) noted, were the "nonreligious organizations which traditionally have opposed federal school aid on the basis of fiscal considerations, federal control, and need. Such organizations as the U.S. Chamber of Commerce . . . the National Association of Manufacturers, the American Legion, the D.A.R., and the American Farm Bureau did not take their usual active parts in opposing the school aid bill." Two reasons are cited for the lack of opposition by the conservative nonreligious groups. Some suggest the landslide Democratic victory in 1964 was taken as an indication by such groups as the Chamber of Commerce that opposition could not effectively block a bill in face of an "overwhelmingly liberal Congress." Others have also suggested increasing concern on the part of the Chamber of Commerce and other business groups with the economic consequences attributed to educational deprivation. Existence of a Chamber Task Force on Economic Growth and Opportunity and its book-length report (Chamber of Commerce, 1966),[18] add some weight in support of this second explanation.

Several additional developments of interest took place during the Senate processing of ESEA. On March 30, the Senate

Committee "laid aside" S. 370 in favor of H.R. 2362 as passed by the House, that is, with its "solution" to the church-state conflict. This step illustrates what Morse meant in stating that he and Congressman Perkins had "agreed upon our strategy and instructed our staffs to work in closest harmony as the two versions of the bill moved through subcommittee" (1965, p. 4). Morse went on to explain: "Had Carl [Perkins] run into insuperable difficulties on the House side, then instead of H.R. 2362, we would have pushed ahead with S. 370 and reconciled differences in conference. But our previous experience with conference action where formulas and where church-state issues were involved made us want to avoid this course, if at all possible" (1965, p. 4).

In adopting H.R. 2362, the Democrats in the Senate could offer a measure that had already proved passable. Furthermore, any amendments in the Senate would require a House-Senate conference committee. For these reasons, a second tactic employed within the Senate was to avoid amendments at all costs. Even friendly amendments, such as the Kennedy-Nelson proposals for a national Teacher Corps, were not welcomed. Nor, of course, was Senator Ervin's suggestion of an amendment to provide for judicial review appreciated (U.S., Congress, Senate, Subcommittee on Education of the Committee on Labor and Public Welfare, 1965, pp. 3135-3137). Adopting H.R. 2362 and rejecting any and all amendments were two tactics apparently decided on by President Johnson. He was also said to have insisted on speedy action, calling on the committee chairmen to hold hearings on Saturdays. Opponents viewed these executive pressures as railroading the legislative measure and as transforming the legislature into a rubber stamp (Meranto, 1967, p. 105).[19] Nonpartisan corroboration of the minority's charge, that President Johnson pressured for immediate action and that his supporters in Congress acquiesced, is provided by Selover (1969, pp. 160-163).

The bill passed the Senate on April 9, and on April 11, President Johnson signed the ESEA into law. Having returned for the ceremonial signing to the Texas schoolhouse he had attended as a boy, Johnson said, " 'As President ... I believe deeply that no law I have signed or will ever sign means more to the future of our nation' " (cited in Buder, 1967a, p. E9).

Summary

The explanation for the shift in federal policy exemplified by support of preschool programs, the main features of that policy, and short-term aspects of the policy process can now be summarized. However, provision for preschool programs was absent in the EOA and minimal in the ESEA and both those pieces of legislation, so central to this study, contained many other features. Therefore, the conclusions must touch on several issues in addition to those directly pertaining to preschool programs. In the next chapter, we present an assessment, from a more long-run perspective, of preschool policy, the policy process, and possible developments in the future.

Looked at retrospectively, ESEA stands as a major departure in federal education policy. Meranto (1967, p. 6) suggests it may, "in the long run, represent the most important change in national domestic policy since the New Deal period." Given other enactments between 1945 and 1965, such as Medicare and the Civil Rights Acts, that assessment seems exaggerated.

One dimension of the significance of ESEA consists of the factors that made possible such a major shift in federal educational policy. That is the problem Meranto (1967) addressed and analyzed in depth. The major situational factors he credits arc, first, a set of circumstantial conditions: the rediscovery of poverty, postwar "metropolitan" trends, and the civil rights movement. Indeed, we must add, the widespread desire to pacify poverty, restlessness, and discontent in the black ghettos can easily be underestimated as an important influence in gaining passage of the EOA and ESEA. Second, developments among "major demand articulators" were important. Of these, one was a spirit of compromise among constituent and interest groups following the lesson learned in 1961—that substantial federal aid to education could not pass over Catholic opposition. Meranto cites one religious spokesman who spoke candidly: "No one wanted another eyeball-to-eyeball episode like '61—a repeat of that would have meant the end of Federal aid for a long time. Since neither side wanted to be responsible for such a development both sides were willing to look for ways to compromise" (1967, p. 82). Another favorable group, the Democratic party, had gained a landslide victory, providing a better than 2-to-1 majority in Congress. Furthermore, the Eighty-Ninth Congress contained the largest number (ninety-four) of Catholic legislators to date. In that Congress, Catholics for the first time outnumbered any other specific religious denomination, although Protestants as a group outnumbered the Catholic legislators (Hunter, 1965). President Johnson, according to Clinton Rossiter, possessed greater initiative in policy making than any chief executive in recent times, but also enjoyed a popular mandate and the will and determination to exert "every available resource" to get federal aid to education enacted (Meranto, 1967, p. 105).

All of these situational conditions and factors at play among the important policy makers probably would not have sufficed without prior alterations of committee arrangements in Congress. In 1959, the party ratio in the House Committee on Education and Labor was revised in favor of the majority party, which in 1965 redounded to benefit the Democrats. The voluntary retirement in 1961 of Congressman Graham Barden, North Carolina, a man widely held to be a bottleneck in obstructing school aid, resulted in his replacement by a proeducation Northerner, Adam Clayton Powell. The expansion of the House Rules Committee in 1964 permitted reform by addition of several liberal members who could tip the balance, thus assuring clearance by that crucial committee of a school aid bill to the floor for consideration.

All the foregoing, however, may be viewed as preconditions of the policy process without which the legislative innovations, the tie-in between education and poverty initiated by Morse and his associates, and the church-state compromise devised by Keppel, the NEA, the National Catholic Welfare Conference (NCWC), and Perkins, would not have been enacted. These novel legislative features, in the EOA and especially the

ESEA, represent the symbolic formulas or policy rationales employed to counter and overcome the traditional reasons for objecting to extensive federal aid to education and for opposing public funds for private schools. The perseverance of proeducation policy makers, especially a senator and a president, the availability of an insightful, historical analysis of federal aid to education, and recognition of the need for extensive efforts to coalesce a consensus of influence groups around an acceptable compromise, we believe were the decisive elements of the process that produced the crucial innovations. Inclusion of virtually all the relevant influence groups in the planning of ESEA assured testimony at the hearings from a large number of favorable witnesses.

We now assess the main attributes of the preschool policy developed within the framework of the EOA and ESEA. First of all, it must be repeated, both pieces of legislation barely provided for preschool programs. The EOA of 1964, constructed to give maximum feasible latitude to its administrative chief, was silent on preschool programs. The ESEA set preschool policy by merely invoking a "plebiscitarian" phrase and not otherwise addressing the main constituents of a preschool policy. Both laws left preschool policy articulation and elaboration completely to the executive branch. The preschool program under EOA and ESEA may constitute an important precedent as a public activity barely legitimatized by legislative enactment. It also illustrates how executive aggrandizement can be encouraged in part by legislators' surrender of their legislative responsibilities.

The need for the legislative innovations mentioned earlier reveals another meaning of ESEA. That law may be compared with the National Defense Education Act of 1958, which authorized loans to parochial school for science, math, and language equipment, and mandated a proportionate allocation of funds to those schools. But the differences between the two laws highlight the normative gradients in the United States between national defense, poverty, education, and constitutional requirements. The proclaimed interest in national defense legitimated aid otherwise available to deprived grade and high school pupils or to parochial schools only under highly complex conditions. Despite efforts by Morse, Johnson, and other liberals, education hardly rates as a valued institution comparable to the military and the economy. Rather, education seems to receive a low national priority unless other reasons, such as strengthening the national defense or maintaining internal order, lend it greater importance. Similarly, the preschool programs were supported not for intrinsic reasons of their possible contribution to child development, but for other, instrumental considerations, such as combating poverty. But these instrumental reasons, embodied in the innovative formulas, helped gain passage of the legislation.

Both the EOA and Title I of ESEA purportedly represent programs for dealing with poverty and associated conditions, especially among blacks in urban slums. The meaning of such legislation as antipoverty measures may be suggested by comparison to other proposed solutions. None of the alternative solutions were as indirect or as noncontroversial in the 1960s as education, especially preschool education. The main alternatives would include: the radical call for redistribution of wealth; liberal economic proposals for the government to serve as the employer of last resort; the conservative answer of employment created by free enterprise; and the reactionary recipe for controlling poverty and achieving internal order by armed force, for example, by the National Guard.

The preschool program established by the EOA and ESEA may be examined as an antipoverty measure. The program aimed to combat poverty principally by educating the younger members of impoverished families. Although children three to five years of age received prime attention in the Head Start program, the older generation, the children's parents, were not simply written off. National policy, at least in the early years of OEO, required parental involvement in a range of activities in the local preschool programs, including policy making. As is widely known, "maximum feasible participation" of the poor was proclaimed initially as a major tenet of the EOA's Community Action Program.

Still, within Project Head Start, the major thrust was to

interrupt the cycle of poverty at the lower age level. This means that even the staunchest proponent of such a preschool program could not hope for success in overcoming poverty until the young generation matured to adulthood. Chronologically, Head Start policy was a long shot. In the short run, that policy, at least initially, simply overlooked the host of influences beyond the preschool years or assumed they would reinforce the head-start. Even in the short run, research proved the assumption, or oversight, to have been misguided. Typically, many gains made by children in Head Start programs dissipated quickly as the children proceeded into the elementary school grades.

Another meaning of preschool programs as a means of overcoming poverty can be discerned by comparison to an alternative proposal in the educational sphere. Preschool education as a strategy for dealing with poverty rested on a theory in the field of child development, the theory of cultural deprivation. That theory gained dominance in the policy arena over a competing explanation of the educational deficits of poor children, especially urban blacks. A minority of social science theorists and policy makers held to the belief that those deficits are primarily caused by inferior public schools. They predicted ephemeral results from preschool programs unless the public schools underwent a transformation. However, the theory of cultural deprivation obviously proved ideologically more acceptable to most policy makers.

No assessment of the ESEA can pass over the "solution" it represents to the church-state problem. As legalistic formulas, the various provisions skirted the First Amendment and extended the applicability of other precedents, such as school lunch program and rulings on shared-time programs. As was anticipated by strict constructionist opponents, however, the legal fictions immediately gave way to several hard realities. In the absence of precise federal guidelines, delegation of major enforcement duties to state and local officials resulted in the operation of sectarian politics at the local level (see, for example, "Church and State in the Schools," 1966; Ervin, 1966; Perkins, 1966). The issue of where dual enrollment programs would be located proved to be as critical as had been expected.

A study of the implementation of ESEA reported three major effects of parochial school location: hiring or veto over hiring by parochial school officials of the "public" teacher; hiring with public funds, by parochial schools, of coordinators or secretaries needed for the federally aided programs; and conversion of publicly purchased equipment lent to parochial schools into "indefinite" or "permanent" loan because it was impractical for the teacher to carry the equipment back and forth (LaNoue, 1967). Perhaps the publicity and concern over these difficulties, resulting from the ESEA, contributed to the Supreme Court's later veering away from the child-benefit doctrine (Graham, 1971).

The dual enrollment provision, however, may have stimulated later developments pointing to both expansion of private schools and to novel "solutions" of the church-state controversy. Civil libertarians had feared use of that provision as a means of circumventing court decisions on school integration. Impressionistically, private, church-related schools seem to be expanding in the South. Allocation of public funds to each parent, or the proposed voucher system, may appear attractive to parents interested in enrolling their children in such schools. If these possibilities were to be realized, the long history of the church-state controversy may take a unique turn. This would occur if nonminority, Protestant parents, find parochial schools more desirable than public schools.

Substantively, the preschool policy initially developed under ESEA authority was simply the Head Start policy. That policy explicitly reflected a selective, poverty orientation. Curiously, however, at the outset that orientation did not result in a socially negative reputation of the Head Start program. Several respondents reported that, in the early years, middle-class parents enrolled their children in Head Start in large numbers. Resulting criticism of the program as deviating from the stated poverty focus led to more restrictive admission requirements. Subsequent administrative enforcement as a poverty-focused program and publicity surrounding "maximum feasible participation" by the poor, not the poverty focus per se, produced a negative social definition.

Nor did the selective orientation automatically result in

programs with inferior content. Rather, in bypassing the conventional distinction between day-care and nursery school programs, and in linking program content to the developmental needs of children, rather than to presumed clientele and "social" purpose, OEO policy represented a progressive development reminiscent of the WPA program. In applying essentially similar program standards to both full-day and half-day programs for children of poor families, Head Start made a significant social advance. These progressive views were incorporated in the *Federal Interagency Day Care Requirements* promulgated in 1968 (see U.S. Department of Health, Education, and Welfare, U.S. Office of Economic Opportunity, and U.S. Department of Labor, 1968b).

In summation, it may be said beyond any doubt that ESEA had great significance for preschool education. It contributed markedly to an "explosive growth" in nursery school enrollments between 1965 and 1970 (see Appendix, Table 3). That growth continued: Nursery school enrollments in 1974 were double what they had been in 1964 (1,300,000 and 500,000 children, respectively), despite a 17 percent decline during the same decade in the number of preschool-age children ("Nursery School Enrollment," 1974; Rosenthal, 1971). The contributions were direct, by providing funds for deprived children to attend such schools, and indirect, by publicizing the benefits claimed for such programs. Not only parents came to have an appreciation for preschool programs. Some educators also moved to increase preschool classes, even when it resulted in holding down kindergarten enrollment (Kihss, 1967). And education policy makers recommended extension of preschool education beyond deprived groups to all children whose parents want it (Hechinger, 1967a).

Notes

[1]The Great Depression programs (WPA, Farm Security Agency) and World War II (Lanham) programs constitute the main exceptions. Three other programs involving smaller numbers of children round out all known federal preschool activities prior to the mid-1960s: (1) kinder-

gartens in federal schools for Indians; (2) in schools on federal installations; and (3) day-care centers on Army posts. The first two programs enrolled 4,333 and 2,462 children, respectively, in 1963 (see U.S. Department of Health, Education, and Welfare, 1967, p. 2, Table 2). In 1966,
approximately 20,000 children attended day-care centers on Army posts
(see Chapter Two, p. 65).

[2]Other impediments that served over the years to bar general aid to
"lower" education were the absence of an acceptable rationale for federal
involvement in an area reserved to the states, the traditional pattern of
state financing and control of education, fear of federal control of education—especially after the 1954 Supreme Court decision regarding racial
desegregation of schools, and the drain on federal revenue. These impediments had led to the proliferation of piecemeal federal provisions in special categories of aid. Numerous national commissions and advisory groups
had scored the resulting uncoordinated, fragmented nature of federal "policy" on education. Specialized, piecemeal provisions also contributed to
uneven, inequitable educational programs in the several states. During the
depression, this stimulated the National Resources Planning Board to recommend equal access for all children to elementary and secondary education, which universal tenor resounded right after World War II, in the
recommendations of a presidential commission, with an accent on domestic defense. The successful search for the rationale in the mid-1960s will be
discussed shortly.
      Another among these impediments had been removed or greatly
diminished in 1964 as a factor complicating enactment of general aid to
education; the Civil Rights Act of 1964 had outlawed the use of federal
funds in segregated school programs (see Meranto, 1967, p. 132).
      Except for the racial issue, and the church-state difficulty, the at-
traction to the financially hard-pressed states of federal funds apparently
overcame most lingering fears of "Federal control of education." One
legislator interviewed in 1965 reported no witnesses before his committee
taking up his challenge to cite specifics on any mention of ostensible federal encroachments. A high government official confirmed the evaporation
of most such fears, except possibly on the part of right-wing extremists
(for example, Birchites); another respondent, a member of OEO's Planning
Committee on Project Head Start, also attributed the one report of such a
fear to a "probable Bircher." Several respondents pointed to the voluntary
nature of state and local participation in the federal programs as allaying
this fear.

[3]The depth of antiparochial sentiment in some states may be
gauged by an Oregon statute, in the mid-1920s, making education in public school mandatory. The statute aimed to "Americanize" all children in
the "public school melting pot." The U.S. Supreme Court ruled the law
unconstitutional (*Pierce v. Society of Sisters*, 268, U.S. 510 [1925]), saying a legislature could not grant a monopoly on education to a state, that a
state is not at liberty to homogenize its children: " 'The fundamental
theory of liberty upon which all governments in the Union repose excludes

any general power of the state to standardize its children by forcing them to accept instruction from public school teachers only. The child is not the mere creature of the state' " (cited in National Catholic Welfare Conference, 1961, p. 8).

[4]Kennedy's position is widely attributed to a commitment implied in a campaign speech in which he—the second Catholic presidential candidate in U.S. history—sought to allay non-Catholic fears. In a speech in 1960 to Protestant ministers in Houston, Texas, he had enunciated his policy on the church and state: "I believe in an America where the separation of church and state is absolute . . . where no church or church school is granted any public funds" (cited by Meranto, 1967, p. 59). A coreligionist interviewed for this study concurred in the attribution.

[5]One study gave a blunt, premonitory warning that was to reecho in later comments and research " 'the most useful conclusion which may be drawn from these data is that one-shot compensatory programs would seem to be a waste of time and money. . . . If these implications are supported by future research it would seem that curricular revision over the entire twelve-year school curriculum is a necessary part of any lasting solution to the basic problem of urban public school education' " (Larson and Olson, cited by Getzels, 1965, p. 111). The second study was performed in New York by Max Wolff, of Yeshiva University. He found that the advantages of Head Start programs "rapidly dissipated" in the early school grades. He concluded that " 'Head Start cannot substitute for the long overdue improvement in the elementary schools which have failed the Negro and Puerto Rican children' " (cited in Semple, 1966, p. 1).

[6]This assertion, quoting one of several respondents to the same effect, is substantially confirmed by the content and tone of an internal document. The meeting, convened by OEO and held on November 23, 1964, included such experts as Benjamin Bloom, James Hymes, Carl Marburger, Evelyn Omwake, and John Silber. A memorandum, dated December 1, 1964, on the "Summary Findings" of that meeting, regarding "Summer School Entry Program," reported:

> 1. *Resistance.* Prior to, and during Mr. Boone's [Shriver's deputy] attendance, doubts were expressed about launching such a program. A few weeks will not make up for experiences children may not have had in their previous four or five years of life. Unwise to confuse the public about the relationship of a "bargain counter" last-minute educational exposure, and the opportunities provided by year-round schools for children at least from ages three through five years. Impossible to predict that the positive values to some children of the summer-only program would be visible in the classroom. Alternative advised: focus on full-year, organized preschool education, or set up one, or a few, "massive model" school entry programs, and learn what can be learned for future efforts.

2. *Acceptance.* On the assumption that the program
will be launched, summer of 1965, and on the assumption
that vast sums of money may be available in the near future
for the group education of children below present school
age, locate the school-entry groups within Indian Reservations, migrant work camps, and within urban and rural
school systems.

Head Start, of course, was launched on a different basis. At a White
House Conference that summer, Getzels (1965, p. 112) questioned the
long-term consequences: "May not long-term mischief be done to the idea
of compensatory preschool education if the possible lack of positive educational effects from this type of 'one-shot' program are immediately attributed to what some like to think is the inevitable failure of lower-class
parents to cooperate, the immutability of the abilities of the children, or
to the conception of compensatory education itself, rather than to possible shortcomings in the operation of the specific programs?"

[7] A forceful rejoinder to the objection of inculcating middle-class
values was made in an article by a black educator submitted for the record
by Senator Nelson as the inspiration for and supplement to his and Kennedy's amendment. "To question, as some do, whether urban youth
should adjust to middle-class values," Larry Cuban wrote, "is irrelevant.
The overriding concern of the deprived is to get in—meaning the barbecue
pit, the powermower, the dishwasher. To condemn this desire as crass
materialism or shoddy conformity is a more pernicious form of paternal-
ism than that practiced by a white Southerner speaking about his
'Nigras' " (Cuban, 1965, p. 2975).

[8] For the most part, however, testimony on ESEA did not pertain
to preschool programs. In the Senate committee hearings on legislation
that, in an historic shift, explicitly authorized federal funds for preschool
programs, at a level far from immodest, mention of preschool programs in
the 3,300 pages of testimony, and testimony by nationally known experts
on preschool programs or on child development, is as sparse as several
needles in a haystack (U.S., Congress, Senate, Subcommittee on Education
of the Committee on Labor and Public Welfare, 1965, p. 515; and pp.
2615, 2620-2621). (Perhaps preschool programs received more attention
in the House Committee hearings.) Reasons for the absence of professional
expert testimony on preschool programs under ESEA are not known. Perhaps the experts who had testified in favor of the EOA had been sufficiently persuasive.

[9] That colloquy took place as a result of Kennedy's effort to have
the commissioner define "educationally deprived children" (an undefined
term in the ESEA). His effort was of little avail. The commissioner submitted for the record an article that lists among the characteristics of culturally disadvantaged children: "Newcomers to the city who have had
limited opportunities for intellectual, social, esthetic, and physical development. Not-so-new residents . . . who are oblivious to the opportunities

which surround them. Residents of the city who have rejected those opportunities because of feelings of insecurity, an inadequate or distorted
sense of values, lack of familial encouragement, or limited aspirations"
(Bertolaet, 1965, p. 502).

That sketch is only somewhat more reticent than others, contained
in reports on the educationally deprived submitted for the record by Commissioner Keppel, which acknowledge that most such children are from
"minority groups" in the "inner city"—that is, black, Puerto Rican, Mexi-
can American, and American Indian (see U.S. Department of Health, Education, and Welfare, 1963b, and National Education Association, 1965).

[10]Antagonism towards professionals—more accurately, towards
educators—was consistent with the well-known general orientation in OEO
stressing significant participation of the indigent to the "maximum extent
feasible." Within the Head Start programs, as in the community action
programs more generally, this orientation was to become the source of
controversy with educators over how to manage preschool programs (see,
for example, Hoffman, 1966; "Project Head Start Revises Guidelines,"
1967; Loftus, 1968a).

[11]The various theories and their role in the policy arena only can
be touched on here. Numerous developments in education circles followed
from the Great Cities and similar projects. Professional interest, experience, and concern among educators was expressed in publications, conferences, and resolutions by professional associations. For relevant bibliog-
raphies, see Bertolaet (1965, pp. 508-509), and National Education
Association (1965, pp. 812-813). Of the publications, Frank Reissman
(1962) was quite influential.

The OE sponsored a conference in 1962 (U.S. Department of
Health, Education and Welfare, 1963b); in that same year, the Ford Foundation funded a conference at Teachers' College (see Passow, 1963).
Deutsch (1962) presented his early findings to still a different conference
that year. Still another was held at the Arden House in December 1962
(Arden House Conference, 1964). For resolutions by the NEA, the American Association of School Administrators, and the Council of Chief State
School Officers (all adopted in 1962) claiming or implying educational
efficacy and responsibility in enriching the deprived, see National Education Association (1965, p. 752).

[12]The account presented here of the events surrounding S. 2528 is
based in part on remarks by Senator Morse during the later hearings on
ESEA (U.S., Congress, Senate, Subcommittee on Education of the Committee on Labor and Public Welfare, 1965, pp. 99-101); in part on an
address by Morse (1965), and in part on interview comments by Senator
Morse, Charles Lee, and other respondents. To assure anonymity, confi-
dentiality, and the obligation to critical objectivity, the public record will
be relied on whenever possible.

[13]Nor can the possibility be dismissed outright that Quie and other

Republicans were simply trying to embarrass the majority party with their critique that preschool programs were not called for in the EOA. However, the extensiveness and tone of Quie's remarks are not readily consistent with that suspicion. His actions in regard to the ESEA, to be mentioned later, also lend some counterweight to that suspicion. Additional weight is given by his effort, in 1965, to make explicit statutory provision for preschool programs.

It may be well at this point to complete the discussion of Head Start's parentage. Doubt was indicated earlier for not *fully* accepting the repeatedly mentioned attribution of parenthood to Bunting. Aside from Quie's conjectured influence, some doubt seems indicated for a separate reason. Resemblances can be traced between the CAP's and the Ford Foundation's antipoverty projects, which often contained a preschool component. The linkage consists of independent informed reports that Title II of the EOA, the CAP, was modeled on the Ford projects. A commitment to the educational type of program in those projects was reported to have been made before Head Start had been planned. In part, of course, time differentials may be involved; Bunting's suggestion may have led to the early commitment to preschool programs. In larger part, the notion of early training as preventive compensatory education was a "doctrinal current" that had spread to several disciplines and to a not inconsiderable number of "avant garde" professionals.

[14]Members of the committee were: Robert E. Cooke (Chairman), George B. Brain, Urie Bronfenbrenner, Mamie Phipps Clark, Edward Perry Crump, Edward Davens, Mitchell I. Ginsberg, James Hymes, Sister Jacqueline, Mary Kind Kneedler, Reginald Lourie, John Niemeyer, Myron E. Wegman, and Edward Zigler. The chairman was reported to have been the pediatrician to the children of President and Mrs. Kennedy.

[15]One side effect of designating a pediatrician as director of Head Start was reported later by the director. Some physicians' complaints suggest "they regarded the program predominantly as a medical one" (Richmond, 1966). The director served part-time. One knowledgable respondent believed that the Chief Administrative Officer, Jule Sugarman, deserved the title Mr. Head Start for his outstanding performance. Sugarman and his secretary were reported by another official as the only full-time employees in Project Head Start during the feverish spring of 1965, when applications and inquiries were flooding in. An OEO staffing pattern that relied on numerous consultants, rather than on permanent civil service employees, was attributed to Shriver's desire to report a low permanent staff size, so as to counter personal criticism, during the EOA hearings, of Shriver as the "poverty Czar" interested in building a bureaucratic empire. Not only were permanent positions kept to a minimum, but it was said that before dates for reporting on personnel, consultants would be "dropped" and "added" immediately afterwards. Another explanation offered for the skimpy staff size was the desire to repeat Shriver's Peace Corps experience of getting a great deal of work from an enthusiastic staff. These arrangements also reflect the deliberate drafting of the EOA "to grant the broadest possible discretion" to the OEO director (Sundquist, 1969, p. 27).

[16]Title I, "Financial Assistance to Local Educational Agencies for the Education of Children of Low-Income Families," authorized grants to school districts where 3 percent of the school-age children, or a minimum of one hundred children were from poor families. The criteria and minimums were such that 94 percent of the counties in the United States would be eligible for some funds, a point criticized by Republicans as indicating a more general than categorical approach (U.S., Congress, Senate, Committee on Labor and Public Welfare, 1965, p. 87). The formula for allocating also drew Republican criticism for ostensible discrimination against areas in the South and West, and favoritism of "a few Eastern States." In actuality, the formula for distributing the more than one billion dollars under Title I was such that approximately 40 percent of that sum would go to twelve Southern states. That distribution in particular, and formulas allocating funds in general, of course, reflect political considerations.

[17]The term *dual enrollment* refers to the practice of enrolling parochial school pupils in special educational programs conducted by public school authorities. Ambiguities surrounding dual enrollment operations, such as the locale and the organizational status of the teachers involved, were probed by Republican opponents. Representative Goodell tried but failed to pin down his colleagues (Carey, Perkins, and Powell):

> *Goodell:* "Now I understand. In other words we may have a public school program in a private school. . . . If the public school authority is providing one of these programs in a private school on private school property, then you conceive that this may be a public school program under your definition?"
>
> *Carey:* "It remains a public school program because it is initiated as a public school program and it is a public school program wherever it is held."
>
> *Goodell:* "All right then, under this bill then you feel these services can be provided by public school authorities in the private schools?"
>
> *Carey:* "No."

[U.S., Congress, *Congressional Record*, 1965a, p. 5755]

[18]Several of the recommendations in that report are of interest. Recommendation 5 states that "every community with large numbers of children from economically and culturally deprived families should institute preschool age educational programs as integral parts of its public school system. . . . The Head Start Program, now under the Office of Economic Opportunity, should be transferred to the U.S. Office of Education" (Chamber of Commerce, 1966, pp. 1, 38). Recommendation 11 calls for federal revenue sharing and tax credits to help finance improved public education; states and localities are asked to recognize the need for proportionately more educational funds per pupil in disadvantaged than in well-off districts, in order to close the "quality gap in education" (pp. 3, 59). Recommendation 14 endorses the fostering of competition with existing public school systems: "If all parents, at every income level, could choose

between sending their children to public schools and sending their children to approved private schools at public expense, both public and private education would improve" (pp. 4, 68).

[19]Pressure by the administration and acquiescence by the majority drew a bitter protest from the Republican minority on the Senate subcommittee. Their remarks make interesting reading almost a decade later.

This important and complex piece of legislation—on which your committee heard more than ninety witnesses whose testimony filled six volumes and more than 3,200 pages—is to pass this body without a dot or comma changed; this by fiat from the Chief Executive. . . .

We are told that this embargo on amendments—even technical amendments to correct drafting ambiguities—is a one-shot proposition. We are assured that on this bill and on this bill only will the Senate yield its legislative powers. Yet the majority speaks these words uneasily, for it knows from long tradition and experience that the branch of Congress that gives up its independence to an aggrandizing Executive not only lays the basis for new and greater demands of passive compliance but also begins to lose the confidence of the people whose votes have given it life. . . .

There is no doubt that the administration can muster the votes to accept any version of its choice. Yet, feigning great concern for the allegedly uncertain fate of this bill, the administration commands the Senate to speed it through with every flaw intact. This is not statesmanship. . . . This is a fetish—a fetish of the unwise and unrestrained use of power, which cannot in the long run or the short, serve the interests of the Nation. [U.S., Congress, Senate, Committee on Labor and Public Welfare, 1965, pp. 81-82]

One of the Republican signatories of the minority views, Senator Winston Prouty (Vermont), made a very similar speech on the Senate floor during consideration of the bill by that house (Meranto, 1967, pp. 105-106).

SIX

Preschool
Policy Makers
and Processes

In the previous chapters, we have presented a descriptive historical narrative of preschool development in the United States;
analyzed several problems and perspectives emerging from the
history of preschool programs with bearing on the legislation of
the 1960s; and described enactment of the three key pieces of
legislation germane to this study. The descriptive chapters present the data collected from interviews and the documentary
and other pertinent literature. Here the conclusions that rest on
the descriptions of the legislative process and products are presented.

The conclusions fall into three categories. The first two

221

deal with policy makers and the policy process. They represent
serendipitous findings relevant to the making of social policy. In
these two parts, patterns noted in the detailed narratives on
legislative policy formation are highlighted, and conclusions
they suggest are offered. Discussion of these generalizations in
relation to various theoretical propositions reflects an attempt
to explore their more general meaning, not to test those propositions, nor to offer our conclusions as a developed theory.

The final part of this concluding chapter concerns the
four dilemmas noted at the outset as implicated in national preschool policy. Specifically, we will assess the preschool legislation as efforts to resolve the dilemmas that had confronted the
policy makers. That assessment will entail reaching short-run
and longer-term conclusions.

Policy Makers

At the outset, a brief sketch of preschool policy making
at the beginning of its century-long history in the United States
is compared to policy making in the twentieth century in order
to highlight our topic. The comparison is not necessary to identify the key groups that participated in making the policy enacted in the 1960s. Who the participants were is an empirical
question previously answered, insofar as the data permitted an
answer, in the detailed "legislative history." The comparison,
however, will help us present in sharper focus some features of
the groups pertinent here—status circles, professions, bureaucracies, and politicians. Even more important, it opens up the
central issue concerning those who participated in setting policy: In a modern, mass society of manifold groups of varying
complexity, who aligned the diverse groups so as to effect passage of the first legislated preschool policy in our history?

The social setting a century ago consisted of the following components: a continent-wide, uncrowded, and heretofore
agrarian-commercial society; expanding industrialization in the
form of relatively small, freely competing economic units; a
maternal work force in factories developing in the cities simul-
taneously alongside upper-class, conscience-guided philan-

thropic women of leisure; the extended family system already dispersing under centrifugal pressures of moving frontier and industry; and relatively cohesive local communities, self-governed through voluntary associations and rudimentary political structures, reflecting a comprehensible social order and a relatively broad social consensus, but weak state and national governments.

In that social context, preschool policy was made in either of two ways. Philanthropic ladies acting as private individuals, or in concert with voluntary associations, fashioned social policy within a community here or there by directly setting up an infant school or day-care center. Guided by social and humanitarian ideals, ladies in a few cities acted similarly, but independently, in volunteering their untrained service and personal beneficence. Such preschool policy making was constrained by the limited supply of upper-class ladies with commitment, energy, and funds. Probably competing perspectives on philanthropic ends and means held by the few preexisting benevolent societies or church groups hindered charitable day-care venture.

Or policy was made by a neighborhood mother through the simple act of deciding to go into the preschool business. Only marketplace factors of demand and supply operated to constrain such enterprise.

Whether philanthropist or proprietress, the policy maker did not need or seek legislation, but simply established a program. Nor did the policy maker have to contend with legal code, state or federal regulation, organizational or professional opposition (except, perhaps, for church groups), program standards or requirements, or political influence.

These modes of policy making reflect the social setting. Midnineteenth-century American preschool policy making displays social thought at the level of "invention" or "establishment," patterns Mannheim related to the liberal social order of early, developing capitalism (Mannheim, 1940). Within one century, the social order in which such modes of preschool policy making occurred was fundamentally transformed. The relevant components of the transformed social order include: a continent essentially divided into large agribusiness farms interspersed with clusters of dense megapoli; a highly advanced industrial service economy based on administered competition between multinational firms, corporate conglomerates, and enfranchised chains; a developed maternal work force of lower- and middle-class women in offices and factories; families further nucleated into uni- and biparental forms, but displaying vestiges of extendedness; social space of high density resulting from the proliferation of formal organizations, including philanthropic foundations, professions, and other organized interest groups; in relative terms, a fragmented social consensus and opaque social order; and a superpowerful national government with an effective radius of control down to the local level. The multiplicity and density of organized interest groups and magnification of central governmental power highlight the comparison of social contexts in which preschool policy was made in nineteenth- and twentieth-century America (Lippmann, 1946, pp. 14-15; Mannheim, 1940, p. 335).

The twentieth-century preschool policy makers did not directly establish and operate preschool programs; rather, they affected legislation. These policy makers did not make policy as private individuals. They acted in the main as members of a number of more or less formally organized groups involved in complex chains of events over extended periods of time. To effectuate a policy in this context required a coordinating structure or groups; the "planning" level of thought is the requisite cognitive orientation. Mannheim (1940) identified this orientation as characteristic of the bureaucratically organized mass society of high developed industrial capitalism. At this level of policy making, the core question regarding the policy makers is: Who plans the policy planning?

We will pursue the answer to this question by examining the various groups participating in the policy enactments of the 1960s. By implication from the sketch of the social order in the twentieth century, as well as from the description of federal policy enactment in the 1960s, it is clear that "the legislature is not the only group enacting legislation" (Lasswell and Kaplan, 1950, p. 196). Several groups constituted the principal participants: status elites, professionals, bureaucrats, and politicians. Membership in these variably organized groupings is not mutually exclusive. (Although omitted from these groups, philanthropic foundations played a significant part in preschool affairs. In Chapters Two, Four, and Five, a number of foundations were mentioned: the Carnegie Foundation, Field Foundation, Ford Foundation, and Laura S. Rockefeller Foundation. Their support stimulated research and theory development in the field of child development; training of researchers and teachers in that field and in early childhood education; program innovation, experimentation, and evaluation; and professional and policy conferences. For an analysis of the social and economic functions that foundations perform, see Bensman and Vidich [1971, Chap. Ten].)

At the outset it may be well to point out several parties to the preschool system who did not participate in making policy in the mid-1960s. (Noninvolvement of the unorganized proprietors in policy making in the 1960s has been discussed in Chapter Three). The absence of the presumptive beneficiaries, children and families, has been a feature in common to preschool policy in the nineteenth and twentieth centuries. (Two exceptions may be noted. In various communities, women banded together, especially after World War II, and established cooperative nursery schools [Moustakas and Berson, 1955]. Also, as a result of pressure from student-mothers in several periods of history, colleges and universities succumbed and established preschool programs. For an example in the 1920s, see Whipple, [1929, pp. 217-223]; for a survey covering campus day-care centers in the 1960s, see Greenblatt and Eberhard [1973].) Within the policy arena, preschool-age children stand mute—unable to express their interests, families silent—unaware of possible claims or unwilling to articulate them, and neither organized in their own right. Representation, if any, has been provided by surrogates, either established by tradition (kin, ecclesiastic spokesmen), by law (family court, judges, social workers, and so forth), or by self-election (volunteers, philanthropists). Representation by self-designated surrogates has occurred at many points in the history of American preschool policy.

Upper-class women assumed civic, social, and moral obligations for dependent children and lower-class mothers working in factories, thereby making nineteenth-century policy in the United States,[1] as elsewhere. (In the United States, aside from the nameless benefactresses of infant schools and day-care centers, we again cite the pioneer mothers of the kindergarten and other preschool programs: Margarethe Schurz, Mary Peabody Mann, Elizabeth Peabody, Anna Bryan, and Patty S. Hill. And, as we suggested previously, Jane Addams may well deserve to be recognized as the godmother of progressive education.) In the twentieth century, females from the higher social strata continued to represent working mothers and children in the policy arena. A well-to-do woman, an officer of a national day-care organization, took the initiative in 1961, it may be recalled, which eventually led to the 1962 Day Care Amendment. Also recall the female president of Radcliffe College who was frequently credited with having first suggested to Sargent Shriver the desirability of a preschool program for the poor. Enacting and influencing preschool policy, especially in the nineteenth century, but also more recently, could reasonably be claimed as an accomplishment by the sisterhood of well-to-do women.

Incorporation of the National Committee for the Day Care of Children did not occur, auspiciously enough, until two years before enactment of the 1962 Day Care Amendment. The feminine pioneers on the preschool frontier had seldom been formally organized as such. That condition often applied to women in general. Moreover, it also pertains to status circles, groupings of status equals who share life-styles and cultural perspectives. As with children, families, and proprietors, the lack of organization of such informal groupings, even in upper-class circles, might suggest a lack of influence on policy. The incidents recounted earlier refute that suggestion. Features of those incidents point out that formal organization is far from being the only basis for policy influence.

The two women mentioned earlier were not pursuing careers, income, prestige, or bureaucratic or professional jurisdiction through the initiatives they took. Either on a social level, both knew the political figures they were attempting to influence, or they had been brought together by social equals. Not to be overlooked is that one interaction took place at a luncheon, another at a cocktail party.

These features suggest several observations at a more abstract theoretical level. High status may compensate for lack of organized political pressure to influence national policy. Social prestige and political influence interact in several ways, because having high status—being socially well placed—means having readier access to the political arena. Commensalism—drinking or dining together—which Max Weber identified as an indicator of status equality, may provide natural opportunities for discourse on a wide range of matters. Informal or unorganized interests, such as friendships and status circles, may intersect with formal structures, such as governmental branches, political parties, and so on. Friends, social equals, who enter politics directly or indirectly through politically related professions (for example, the law), may be called on for advice or support in furthering one's ideal interests or the social policy objectives of one's affiliated group. Even if a friend's political jurisdiction or sphere of influence excludes the pertinent policy area, he probably can arrange contact with the pertinent colleague in the cabinet, officially or unofficially. (Thus, status equality served as an entering wedge, handled with social finesse, for the upper-class woman seeking support for day-care legislation from cabinet officers.) Obviously this requires a finely balanced delicacy to gain the desired influence while avoiding what may be construed as an abuse of genuine sociability for instrumental purposes.

Conversely, those with political influence may benefit from such interaction with their social peers, although it may not always be recognized as such. To hold political office, whether elected or appointed, usually means constant exposure to vested or self-seeking interests (material, professional, bureaucratic, programatic, and political). Yet those seeking to gain or hold high political office (senator, president) need the visibility gained from initiating programatic solutions addressed to broad social problems. This is not to deny the possibility of a genuine desire to serve the public interest. Getting fresh ideas to benefit the general interest from self-interested parties may appear as a contradiction in terms. Opinions, ideas, or an "appreciation" offered informally by or sought from materially disinterested social equals are more likely to be perceived as high-minded, sensible, and trustworthy. The presuppositions, associated world view, and implications for the social order of such views would probably be congenial to the listening peer. Suggestions to policy makers from status equals would appear to have a better than equal chance to affect policy. (Several other pertinent illustrations were mentioned earlier. One respondent involved in the preliminary planning on the Elementary and Secondary Education Act volunteered that having a friend in common with Commissioner Keppel had made his working relations with Keppel easier. Also, several respondents attributed the strong influence on Shriver exercised by the chairman of the Head Start Planning Committee to the personal friendship between that pediatrician and the Kennedys and Shrivers. Still another illustration, not previously mentioned, involved Harvard student volunteers engaged in antipoverty projects. They had been invited to make a presentation to President Kennedy's Cabinet Task Force on Poverty (chaired by Attorney General Robert Kennedy). An alumnus who had previously belonged to the same student group, then an aide to Senator Kennedy, had made the "cross-connection" between social circles and national policy. The presentation stimulated a legislative proposal for a National Service Corps.)

Because prestige attaches intrinsically to high political office, another relationship arises between political influence and status. Wives of high officeholders, by titular or actual participation, bestow prestige on official projects and programs. As Honorary Chairman of Project Head Start, Claudia (Ladybird) Johnson was seen as giving that program "a big boost" before it was launched by entertaining "a group of prominent women leaders, many of them presidents of national organizations, at a White House tea" (McLendon, 1965, p. 85). The involvement of a number of gubernatorial wives, Republican and Democratic, in Head Start presumably made a contribution within their home states (U.S., Congress, Senate, Subcommittee on Poverty of the Committee on Labor and Public Welfare, 1965, p. 73). A

president's or governor's wife, associated—even if only symbolically—with a program automatically furnishes an honorific testi-
monial and, if the enterprise is new, creates visibility, expands
familiarity, and enhances popular acceptance. Moreover, her
association encourages an inference of formal and informal support of the enterprise from on high. (To confuse an inferred
with an implied intention may produce disappointment. Patricia
Nixon's incumbency as Honorary Chairperson of the Day Care
and Child Development Council of America apparently was believed to signify or help gain her husband's support for preschool programs. His veto of day-care legislation in 1971 led to
a request to Mrs. Nixon to discuss the veto with the council's
executive committee. She responded by resigning ("Mrs. Nixon
Quits Day Care Unit," 1973).

To summarize, we suggest that within upper-class circles
status equality and unselfish goals in part may offset the absence of organized political influence on social policy making.
Women of high status and wives of prominent officials can participate in the policy process through a range of informal as well
as formal channels.

Although members of unorganized status circles may
have pursued ideal interests into the preschool policy arena,
most unorganized interests (mothers, children, and, before the
1970s, proprietors of small-scale enterprises) did not. With organized interest groups, the reverse applies: They may be legally
mandated to act, or it may be politic for them to be invited
and/or lobby in the arena.

In contrast to the nineteenth century, organized professional associations have come to constitute distinctive interest
groups and as such are active in social policy formation. We will
examine the functioning of professionals and their associations,
for the extent of their influence in shaping preschool policy in
the 1960s and two facets of professional involvement may not
be widely recognized. These facets are the criteria for selecting
professional advisors by political figures and professions as
interest groups in the policy arena.

Some highlights of the involvement of professionals in
the legislative enactments mentioned intermittently earlier can

be recapitulated. After the officer of the day-care association had lunched with the cabinet officers, an informal group of statesmen in the social work and child welfare professions was convened. They prepared a day-care proposal. That proposal was added to other documents prepared by consultants and ad hoc and advisory committees of nonfederal professional experts appointed to make a "thorough study" of the welfare system. A national association of welfare professionals, it may be recalled, had met with the Secretary of HEW to seek—successfully—appointment of its representatives to these study groups. President Kennedy's Welfare Message to the Congress, including the Day Care Amendment, grew out of the results of that review and study process.

Social welfare and day-care professionals were among the witnesses who testified and individuals who submitted letters to the legislative committees that conducted hearings on the amendment. The national day-care association, which includes members of several professions interested in day care, claimed credit for the unusual "volume of support" that measure received during the legislative hearings.

Professionals from a wide range of professions—child development, clinical psychology, developmental psychology, early childhood education, orthopsychiatry, pediatrics, social work, and sociology—played a larger part in the development of policy on Project Head Start. Professionals in psychology, child development, and early childhood education had carried out the foundation-funded early studies of "compensatory education" on which Head Start in part was modeled. Findings of one researcher's work in compensatory preschool education was widely disseminated by being mentioned in a presidential message to the Congress.

We should also call to mind the role played by professional associations. One senator, we recounted earlier, obtained technical aid on fiscal projections as supporting data for his legislative proposal from a national association of educators headquartered in Washington. That association also subsequently lent its support in legislative hearings to the aid to education bill.

Experts on early childhood had given impressive testimony at the hearings on the Economic Opportunity Act. Research evidence was reported on the "most debilitating" effects of cultural retardation on the later education of the child. Compensatory preschool programs were strongly urged; impressed legislators later cited the experts' views on the problem and the recommended solution.

Membership on advisory and planning committees on Head Start is as pertinent for us as the previous professional activities. Although those committees did not make such crucial decisions as whether to proceed with Project Head Start for the summer of 1965, it may be recalled that they essentially made policy on implementation of that program. The noneducator professional advisors viewed educators in the main as narrowly specialized and hidebound. Professional hostility as well as political considerations led to pervasive efforts to deemphasize the role of teachers and the education establishment in Head Start. Aside from the national reputations in their fields held by many of the members, the selection methods and criteria employed had quite apparently produced groups able to achieve a broad consensus on such professional and program issues.

The influence on preschool policy exercised by professionals varied to some considerable extent in relation to the level of prestige generally accorded their disciplines. The fields of medicine, pediatrics, orthopsychiatry, developmental psychology, and child development seemed more attractive to those holding high political office. (It may be recalled a physician was selected to direct Project Head Start to "lend it respectability." Professional prestige was at play, as well as a politically inspired interest in deemphasizing education.) The frequency with which representatives of professions are selected for presidential task forces, congressional commissions, and departmental advisory committees, or are invited to testify before legislative committees on issues pertaining to their expertise may be hypothesized as a rough index of professional prestige within the policy arena.

Intraprofessional criteria also were reported to have been employed in screening candidates for national policy advisory groups. Appointees often appeared to have been selected for the school of thought they represented within their discipline. Conversely, professionals reputed to have held rigidly traditional views, in education and social work, for example, were reportedly bypassed on several task forces dealing with the family, children, and preschool programs. In part, such screening eliminated potential sources of technical and theoretical incompatibility within the advisory groups, thereby enhancing the prospect for closure and consensus on policy recommendations. Thus, family-oriented social workers, educators placing priority on expansion of kindergartens or questioning the effectiveness of nursery school, or specialists preferring reform of the school system to compensatory education would have created conflict and possibly impeded preschool policy development. However, it may be conjectured that a more important determinant is the fit perceived between the intradisciplinary viewpoint and the range of anticipated policy directions consistent with the political outlook of the appointing authority. Of course, anticipations may turn out to be faulty.

Because the focus and emphasis of a task force's deliberations and recommendations reflect its composition, selection of the membership may decide in good measure the policy conclusion reached later (Cain, 1971). Several earlier reported instances indicate that high-level officials, such as White House staff and cabinet officers, showed by their selection of professional statesmen an appreciation of occupational prestige, competence, and compatibility between professional orientation and policy direction.

Professionals exercise influence, however, for reasons beyond the recognition accorded them by others as possessing specialized, valued knowledge and skill, as creators of normative slogans and images, or for their affinity with a proposed policy. Professional associations constitute organized groups sharing not only similar academic degrees, disciplinary perspectives, technical standards, and ethical codes, but also collective interests in regulating membership, widening career opportunities, protecting or expanding the specialized jurisdiction, and increasing the profession's status and income. In short, professional associations represent vested interests combining ideal, ideational, and "material" components (psychic income—status and power—as well as monetary income).

The larger the membership and better organized to defend those interests, the less likely is the association to be ignored in the policy process. A president or a senator planning education legislation will not lightly bypass the "blackboard power" of a teacher's union with nearly one million members. Aside from the potential voting power inherent in such a membership, the large, well-organized association will not usually be ignored on an issue within its jurisdiction for another reason. If its "interests and ideologies" are overlooked or slighted, it may have the power to block passage of the legislative policy proposal or create subsequent conflict (Bensman and Lilienfeld, 1973, p. 301). (Thus one federal official reported repeated efforts to get a message to the head of OEO that if the "interests and views of the educational community in a preschool program were not considered, they might later be critical and Head Start might become caught up in controversies." It may be recalled that controversy did erupt later regarding parental versus educational influence over Head Start programs.) Some of the ways in which relevant interests are discerned and taken into account in policy formation will be identified later in the discussion of the policy process. But the major professional organizations do not passively wait for an invitation to participate in that process. They employ paid lobbyists in the policy capitol to stimulate pertinent legislative proposals, give their point of view on other legislation, provide technical information and advice to legislators, and generally seek to educate politicians regarding the profession's specialized interests and perspectives.

Competition between professions also reveals the vested interest aspect of such corporate associations. Most often professionals treat interprofessional rivalry as clashes of their specialized perspectives on contiguous or overlapping facets of reality. That clearly is the sense, judging from the context, in which Anna Freud (1963, pp. 95-96) remarked, "psychoanalysis, whenever it has come into contact with pedagogy, has always expressed the wish to limit education." But in the usual meaning of "interest groups," interprofessional competition can be considered jurisdictional disputes. Thus, organizations and associations in the preschool field were cautioned, just after passage of ESEA made millions available for Head Start, that "there will be great competition for the dollar" (Niemeyer, 1966, p. 150).

Sometimes the conceptual and jurisdictional aspects cannot be separated. They seem interlocked in the remark by a respondent (a pediatrician influential in shaping Head Start program policy) that "the philosophy of OEO was to break down professional barriers, to start anew, to leave the professional establishments behind."

Several points highlight the place and functions of professions in relation to social policy making at the national level. To varying degrees, professionals in the natural and social sciences performed research, developed theories, and applied both to a range of preschool activities. Members of these professions were accorded the status of scientific experts in the social policy process. As such, their evidence, theories, and recommendations did carry influence. However, we conclude that the prestige differentially accorded the several professions and the individual professional's affinity with the direction of policy under development were preconditions to the exercise of substantial influence on policy. Professional associations represented another mode of policy influence, as organized special interest groups.

In part for these reasons, and in part because of the ineffectiveness of other groups related to preschool policy (beneficiaries, and federal child welfare and education officials), professionals wielded great influence on preschool policy. In the present study, we judge professionals as the group that had the second most active supportive influence in general on the preschool policies enacted. (The earlier observation of overlap between membership in some professions and status circles deserves reiteration.)

Although the two processes of professionalization and bureaucratization at times diverge and conflict, for the most part they reinforce each other. The professions, however, appear to have been more influential in the preschool policy enactments described previously than were long-established federal agencies. The pertinent agencies, the Children's Bureau (CB) and Office of Education (OE) played somewhat anomalous parts in the preschool enactments of the 1960s. Both had been bypassed in varying, but considerable ways. By contrast, a new competitor, the Office of Economic Opportunity (OEO) had been formed before Project Head Start policy even had been formulated or the program planned. Our review and analysis of the parts played by these organizations, as previously mentioned in passing, focuses on two questions thus implied: What explains the differing detours taken around the preexisting federal agencies in the 1960s? To what can we attribute the distinctive styles of bureaucratic performance between the old and the new agencies?

The Children's Bureau, in the Department of Health, Education, and Welfare, may be remembered from previous chapters as the agency established in 1912 that was assigned limited responsibility for day care within the World War II Lanham programs. Reflecting its social work origins, it had absorbed the child welfare conception of day care, and had further articulated and disseminated that view. That conception deemphasized the educational content of the program and stressed the social purposes of strengthening the family and preventing child neglect. In 1960, the CB and National Committee for the Day Care of Children had cosponsored a national conference on day care. It was a year later, at the luncheon attended by the official of that association and the Secretary of HEW, that the official was advised to proceed toward developing a day-care proposal independent of the CB.

The proposal submitted to and passed by Congress did *not* bypass the CB in its provision for program implementation. By attaching the 1962 Amendment to the child welfare portion of the Social Security Act, over which the CB had long had jurisdiction, the 1962 Amendment assigned the day-care program to the CB. Without having participated in the origination of the day-care program, the bureau received an initial appropriation of $5,000,000 and sole jurisdiction. Unlike the arrangements under the Lanham program, the amendment did not require the bureau to coordinate the day-care program with its older sister agency in HEW and long-term competitor, the Office of Education.

From the data collected, the OE was aware of the less-than-universal coverage of kindergarten programs in various parts of the country. No later than the 1960s, OE was advancing the aim, shared with the education establishment in general, to provide that type of "preschool" program to all children of eligible age. That office played no part of note in developing the Economic Opportunity Act and, so far as our data indicate, had no role whatsoever in the initiation of Head Start. (Officials in the Office of Education, however, did perform important technical and political service in developing the ESEA—a measure that barely referred to preschool programs.) We must again note the extensive, persistent hostility towards educators on the part of the top officials and advisors in the Office of Economic Opportunity. As a result, the newcomer OEO, not OE, had been given jurisdiction over Head Start. In addition, OE involvement in Head Start program planning was restricted to participation on a Joint Education Staff committee, which OEO had agreed to establish as an effort to convince Congress that Head Start would coordinate with, not overlap with, the Office of Education.

Head Start's initial funding of $150,000,000 for the summer of 1965 may have been doubly irksome to OE. By presidential approval, that sum derived from funds authorized under the Elementary and Secondary Education Act for education programs otherwise assigned to OE to administer. Perhaps that seemed an ungrateful arrangement to the Commissioner of Education, Francis Keppel, who had worked arduously and diligently to fashion an agreeable ESEA bill with the interested groups (National Catholic Welfare Conference, National Education Association, and so on).

To conclude this recapitulation, several points about OEO are pertinent. A new agency, it was deliberately staffed by a small number of full-time employees and a large number of part-time "advisors." Two full-time staff and numerous advisors feverishly administered the new Head Start program and its funds. According to some of the staff, Shriver had mastered the skill of evoking enthusiasm and stimulating high productivity from aides.

We will now extend and analyze this account with the aim of reaching answers to the two questions posed earlier. The account, as well as the narrative in previous chapters, clearly shows that preschool policy in the 1960s was impelled directly by executive pressure and indirectly from groups outside the federal bureaucracy. The situations described earlier are accurately subsumed under the concept of "suprabureaucratic policy formation" (Bensman and Lilienfeld, 1973, pp. 297-298). The concept points the direction in which the explanations for the policy detours in 1962 are to be found. What were the suprabureaucratic rationales for the roles in policy initiation and program implementation arranged for the preexisting federal bureaus?

The Children's Bureau's ambivalence toward day care, we believe, had made it hesitant to forcefully take the initiative in day-care policy. Perhaps the long-standing, unresolved competition over preschool programs with the Office of Education may have led to further bureaucratic hesitation within HEW. Reportedly, the ambivalence heightened by peer and superordinate assessments of the CB administration had led to the advice that the 1962 day-care proposal be prepared without guidance from the CB.

That bypass, however, only makes apparently more puzzling the award of the jurisdiction over day care to the CB in 1962. Several points appear pertinent. The conception and presuppositions about day care held by the CB were shared for the most part by the National Committee for the Day Care of Children and probably by the social work statesmen as well as the top administrators in HEW. Formulation of the 1962 day-care policy proposal as an amendment to the child welfare statute, therefore, made for consistency with professional viewpoints and consonance with the previous legislation. There was little reason for the politicians and professionals who formulated the amendment to fear the bureau's implementation would be at variance with their own program conception and intent. Stated

differently, in the absence of countervailing professional ideals
and ideas, authoritative action in initiating the day-care amendment and in passing the legislation would assumedly temper ambivalence and elicit bureaucratic compliance. Finally, we believe
that although unfavorable superordinate evaluation of an
agency might have given pause to assigning it responsibility for
developing a large day-care program, administering a program
modest in funding would not have appeared unduly risky.

The initiation as well as implementation of Head Start
were detoured around the Office of Education. Instead, responsibility was given to the new agency. Obviously other suprabureaucratic dynamics were at play. The educators in OE were
committed to other preschool priorities. Also, from the perspective of the top administration officers and policy advisors involved in planning Project Head Start, the educators were otherwise evaluated as suffering from professional and bureaucratic
trained incapacities. In that perspective, the federal education
bureaucracy would be resistant and could not be expected to
faithfully implement a program to which it was not committed.
Experienced politicos realize that policy implementation may
be as important as origination. In addition, officials perceived as
stodgy and rigid bureaucrats would hardly be considered able to
quickly launch and carry out a new program, especially one on
which the only guidance from the enabling statute was contained in the hitherto unheard-of phrase, "special remedial and
other noncurricular educational assistance." Undoubtedly the
old-line professional educators would have raised "technical"
and other embarrassing questions.

Flexibility and freedom of administrative movement were
especially desirable in the autumn of 1964. Running an effective presidential election campaign has its own urgent requirements, the pressures of which would have been increased greatly
by the necessity to coordinate policy, plans, and schedules with
the typical turgid pace of bureaucratic action.

Still another major benefit was derived by the governing
administration in bypassing the preexisting agency. Establishing
a new agency gave direct and firm control of the new program
to the administration in office. Instead of having to face an estab-

lished bureaucratic agency, the administration could create an agency in its image by the authority to appoint staff to the new organization. Rather than having to contend with preexisting bureaucratic regulations, precedent, and attitudes, the political chiefs could maneuver the program according to higher reasons of state. And, as we have seen, suprabureaucratic considerations won out. They led, in midwinter of 1964, to the decision, despite strong misgivings from professional advisors, to proceed to develop a brand-new, $150,000,000 program for the summer of 1965.

The suggested explanation of the policy detours around the existing federal agencies can now be summarized. Suprabureaucratic preschool policy initiation in the 1960s may be attributable to a combination of factors: bureaucratic timidity; professional and bureaucratic commitments to older program priorities; above all, the need during a presidential election period for flexibility in planning policy and campaign appeals. (Other political factors will be dealt with in the discussion of politicians as preschool policy makers.) Whether or not to bypass an established agency in arranging policy implementation depended on suprabureaucratic considerations of agency competence, compatibility of agency program ideals and ideas with the policy, and coordination of the projected timetable and scale of program development with political requirements.

Two styles of bureaucratic performance have been implicated in the foregoing account and analysis. The style of the old established agencies was widely seen, by political chiefs and by professionals inside and outside, as timid, routine, and rigid. Descriptions in the literature on bureaucracy reveal these traits as so widespread that some theoretical discussions of bureaucracy treat them as typically characteristic. Yet the achievement of the new agency in rapidly creating a large-scale Head Start program suggested flexibility and innovativeness. On the basis of the situations portrayed earlier, what factors can be said to have apparently contributed to innovational rather than traditionalistic practice?

One factor is suggested by an earlier example of other than rigid, banal, or uninspired bureaucratic behavior in the history of preschool policy and administration. Records and interview reports of preschool policy and program development under the WPA indicate federal officials then avoided outmoded program conceptions and applied progressive standards. Programs devised in national emergencies may well reflect a bureaucratic attitude other than "business as usual." A national crisis, however, did not surround the WPA counterparts in OEO, who also shunned encrusted conceptions, embraced forward-looking requirements, and displayed to the observer refreshing flexibility, openness, and enthusiasm.

Several other factors seem to have had bearing on the style of Head Start performance: an invigorating effect on bureaucratic behavior from expanding career opportunities in a new agency; staff, young and old, selected for enthusiasm, conviction, and perhaps ambition;[2] an administrator skilled in effectively exploiting professional enthusiasm as a personnel policy, which apparently sustained morale as problems arose and burdens of work increased; an administrator reputed to enjoy the confidence and support of and access to the president; a popular program resting on scientific claims; and the heady effect on employees of close support for the program from the highest political office.

All these appear to have constituted ideal preconditions to a flexible, creative, and inspired bureaucratic organization. Although some of these conditions are atypical and may not prove durable, they serve to illustrate dynamics often overlooked in static generalizations on bureaucracy.[3]

The various types of participants heretofore examined include interest and "disinterested" groups often not recognized as active in legislative policy formation. As members of functional groups or influential social circles, such individuals substantively participated in making legislative policy. In a meaningful sense, by participating in the making of preschool policy, they were legislating. The participants not in public bureaucracies performed that function despite being " 'outside of the pale and oversight of the state' " (H. E. Barnes, cited in Lasswell and Kaplan, 1950, p. 195). Now attention will focus on participants in the central governmental structures legally responsible for legislative policy making, those elected to national political office. The political figures central to the making of national preschool policy consisted of the president, senators, and members of Congress. Those appointed to high political posts, such as cabinet officers, top staff, and technical aides, served essentially as agents of their elected superiors. Some of them participated actively in fashioning policy. For the most part, they will be treated here as political and technical extensions of the elected officials. As an important illustration, we cite the "seminars" and other activities conducted by Commissioner Keppel "under Executive discipline" (Bailey, 1966).

We will discuss several dimensions of political behavior by national officeholders that have been somewhat neglected as exemplified by illustrations from the making of preschool policy. This will include several facets of the politician as self-interested person holding office. Then the suggested answer to the question, "Who plans the policy planning?" will be presented in a discussion of the national politician as manager of the machinery and operator of the dynamo of politics.

Politicians are not always recognized as having personal histories of potential relevance to policy. Personal, familial, or professional experiences prior to entering politics may, by welding personal and social concerns, forge strong interest in (or antipathy toward) a particular policy or program area. In this regard, the pro-day-care attitude of then Secretary of HEW Ribicoff may be mentioned; one informant ascribed Ribicoff's support of day care to his boyhood as an orphan. Of special pertinence here is the crucial political influence in the passage of the Elementary and Secondary Education Act of 1965 exercised by a former public school teacher, Lyndon B. Johnson, and a former law school teacher and dean, Wayne Morse.

Strong advocacy of such personally derived issues may serve a role task of national officeholders—achieving national rather than merely local repute. Some United States senators and members of the House of Representatives of the United States, taking their titles seriously, seek to establish a national as well as local constituency and reputation by defining issues in the national interest. (Of course, such issues need not have a past personal connection to the politician.) Morse's vigorous advocacy of national education programs, his service as Chairman of the Senate Education Subcommittee, his pride in showing visitors the presidential pen used for signing the ESEA, given him by President Johnson, may be seen in that light.

Presidents face an analogous challenge of historical rather than geographic scope—laying a basis for historical distinctiveness. We have previously cited Johnson's desire to be known as the "Education President."

This concern with reputation has competitive effects on national policy makers. One authority on the presidency reports great competition in claiming credit for a policy achievement: "Most men who share in governing have interests of their own beyond the realm of policy *objectives*. The sponsorship of policy, the form it takes, the conduct of it, and the credit for it separate their interest from the President's despite agreement on the end in view" (Neustadt, cited in Mayo and Jones, 1964, p. 367, note 157). Modern presidents and legislators compete strenuously for public notability in policy formation. This contest may occur between figures in the same party and sharing the policy objectives, which we believe to have been the case with Morse and Johnson. The outcome favored the holder of the highest office in the land. The Senator's pride in the administration's having done its "homework" by adopting his legislative formula may have provided some consolation.

These considerations of the professional politicians's personal background, of role aspects of elected national office, and of career planning for their own lifetime and thereafter by the highest elected officials reveal important, but sometimes overlooked dimensions of political behavior. That widespread human factor, self-interest, carries several meanings in relation to this "inside" perspective on the politician's subjective motives. (A federal administrator, referring to the education enactment in 1965, spoke of that factor in its usual meaning: "The legislator's influence is a function of intensity of interest, especially self-interest." But the self-interest of national policy makers, he added, "is not the same as for other people—the game they play in has much bigger stakes.") These may be influenced by, but are distinctly separable from objective interests and pressures affecting policy.

A less neglected aspect of presidential policy making, a situational factor that increased presidential policy leadership, has particular bearing here. It concerns one type of outcome of the election process. In 1968, a landslide victory significantly increased the weight, scope, and domain of power available to the victorious president. Such an election result, construed as an overwhelming mandate from the people, expanded the victor's self-confidence and also served to legitimate an enlarged exercise of power. Because power is relational rather than a "simple property" (Lasswell and Kaplan, 1950, p. 75), others holding political and other forms of power tacitly or explicitly acknowledged the enlargement. Thus powerful pressure groups, such as the United States Chamber of Commerce, decided to withhold objections to the education legislation, for the landslide victory made opposition seem futile. Some congressmen also acquiesced more readily to the superpowerful president (Meranto, 1967, pp. 80-81, 105). Those who drafted the ESEA are authoritatively reported as having believed President Johnson's landslide election " 'assured passage of any kind of education bill the President requested' " (cited in Broder, 1965).

Another landslide effect pertains to the form of policy established. Landslide victories create one of the political contexts in which policy makers can effectively establish policy without explicit legislative authorization. Creation of Project Head Start without any explicit mention in the Economic Opportunity Act and with only the barest of reference to preschool programs in the ESEA illustrates policy establishment by fiat. One Congressman, a respondent, explained why an executive would establish policy in such a form. He pointed out that legislation providing "broad and loose authority" would enable the administration in office to better "wheel and deal." The avoidance of specificity that later developments may prove embarrassing or onerous simplifies life for those implementing the legislation. It also protects them from being accountable.

Incidentally, national emergencies in the past created a context in which policy also was made by fiat. The WPA preschool program during the Great Depression and the preschool Lanham program during World War II were both created without benefit of explicit legislative authority. Not an electoral sweep, but public realization that an attitude of business as usual could not deal effectively with the common danger legitimatized the increase of executive and bureaucratic latitude. Thus, except for the authorization of day care in 1962, all the federal preschool programs examined in this study were developed without specific legislative approval.

A somewhat neglected dimension of political behavior in a society that is "complex, multidimensional, multiissued, and pluralistic" pertains to the function of overseeing the political machinery. Bensman and Lilienfeld (1973, p. 271) have described the "mechanics of politics" thus: "The politician . . . must deal with others who do not share . . . goals. Within the framework of these and other goals . . . he must attempt to work out agreements which allow for either the assembling of majorities or the creation of blocs large enough to achieve some degree of political effectiveness." A cabinet officer advising an advocate of day care on the allies to work with and those to exclude in drafting of a day-care bill may be recalled in this regard. Senator Morse's efforts to have the National Education Association and other potential allies "unite on legislation which would approach what we wanted" (Morse, 1965, p. 2) also illustrates this political function of aligning interest groups to work out a policy formulation. The stellar example in our study is Commissioner Keppel's "brokerage role" in forging a "consensus of the various interests" and in selling the resulting policy proposal to a broad coalition of forces (Meranto, 1967, p. 70; Bailey, 1966, pp. 5-9). These examples support the characterization of the politician as the political mechanic who attempts to build alliances, coalesce coalitions, organize interest groups, and create a politically effective consensus.

Several risks and consequences may be associated with creating or participating in a policy alignment. By oversight, the politician may neglect the interests or views of a pertinent group. An offended interest group, as we mentioned previously, may have sufficient influence to block enactment of the policy proposal. A salient illustration was cited earlier in this study. The policy planners who prepared the initial day-care proposal in 1962 apparently had failed to consider the strong Catholic interest in purchase of care. When a Catholic spokesman referred to the proposal as " 'un-American,' " (in U.S., Congress, House, Committee on Ways and Means, 1962, p. 578), experienced politicians realized the proposal was in jeopardy of creating an open ideological conflict. The more experienced "mechanics" effectively cleaned up the offensive policy formulation.

Another risk arises in bringing an alliance into being or in joining it. From the perspective of the policy maker (as articulated by a Congressional committee staff member), arriving at a "good bargain . . . or a conscionable compromise" is a principle of the legislative process. "It gets something done [whereas] the ideological approach to legislation often results in fruitless debate." However, because of the requirements of constructing a winning majority or effective plurality the participant may be labeled "compromiser or sell-out." "The very fact of working out a political majority or an effective political bloc requires the 'betrayal' of the absolute interests or demands of any one group. . . . The 'logic' that . . . operates . . . is minimization of conflict rather than the construction of a logical scheme" (Bensman and Lilienfeld, 1973, p. 271). The day-care policy situation in 1962 supplies a muted example of "selling out." The Catholic lay spokesman refrained from joining the prelate who had accepted the compromise day-care measure permitting purchase of care from private agencies. Instead, the layman held to the principled objection to funds for day-care services that the prelate and he had voiced earlier.

The major illustration of conflict avoidance as a political attitude in the policy arena concerns development of the Elementary and Secondary Education Act. The policy mechanics had drafted the bill so as to minimize sectarian conflict. An aide to Keppel (Halperin, cited in Broder, 1965, p. 23) later explained: "The particular provisions were negotiated among the interest groups involved . . . with concern over avoiding bitter controversy." By adopting this stance and successfully aligning a coalition around an acceptable policy formulation, stalemate was avoided and the first general aid to education measure in decades was achieved.

A related hazard in building alliances has been described by an experienced hand (Cohen, 1966) as the "most ungentlemanly or unladylike aspect of the political process," for he who coalesces or enters into an alliance "has a price to pay." Not only may cherished values become compromised, but allies may make strange bedfellows. This permits opponents who wish to smear the alliance to take tactical advantage by insinuations of a misalliance. For example, a member of Congress ascribed responsibility for devising the Elementary and Secondary Education Act to a melange consisting of the National Catholic Welfare Conference, Christopher Jencks (a declared socialist), Paul Goodman (a libertarian anarchist), and the Institute of Policy Studies.

A possible consequence of entering a coalition arranged by a national political figure flows from the leadership such figures may provide. Political management of the alliance may subject the various issues to simplified articulation in public speeches by professional politicians attuned more to the imagery than the subtlety of program and policy. President Johnson's statements gave pause to at least one academic ally. In his education message to Congress in 1965 ("Johnson's Message," 1965), one rationale for a preschool program, as part of the earlier announced "unconditional war on poverty," was given in reference to research on compensatory education that had "demonstrated marked success." The next day, Deutsch, whose research had been referred to, cautioned that such educational programs would not prevent civil violence and that preschool programs should not be set up without adequately trained teachers and a well-based curriculum (Terte, 1965). It may be assumed the cautious remarks of the researcher were less widely seen than the expansive claims of the president.

Our discussion of politics as the management of coalitions and the illustrations provided form the basis for concluding that national political figures aligned the diverse groups that effected preschool policy in the 1960s. Perhaps those who suffer consequences of values deflated, standards compromised, and so on would charge the political mechanics as having maligned their policy interests. However, to reduce the role of the highest elected officials in the nation to the mechanics of politics would distort such political roles. It would be naive to overlook the aspect of the politician as the wielder of political power. To neglect this aspect with regard to a presidency that has in recent decades increased its power considerably would be a particularly egregious oversight. We will briefly look at this dimension in order to highlight the nature of national policy as administered policy.

Viewed in terms of the whole social order, the state may be considered a political machine that "transforms economic, ideological, and other nonpolitical interests . . . into political, legal, and policy terms" (Bensman and Lilienfeld, 1973, p. 272). If the pertinent interest groups were considered a set of vector forces operating in a social field, policy could be viewed as the net outcome of the contending social forces. In that view, the policy outcome would resemble the "once spontaneous consensus" (Mannheim) characteristic of the liberal social order of an earlier century. But in a complex society, bureaucratically organized and highly centralized politically, spontaneous resolution is not likely to occur. Instead, professional politicians in the executive and legislative business typically make the arrangements. Holders of high political office may be regarded as transformers of power into policy. In making transformations the politician "adjusts and balances the ideological and interest demands upon him, upon his party, and upon the government, in terms of the relative strengths and pressures which these external groups make upon the political machinery of the state" (Bensman and Lilienfeld, 1973, p. 272). In short, the policy outcome largely reflects the existing balance of power held by the relevant parties.

The politician as political mechanic and as operator of the dynamo of politics constitute role demands attuned to objective conditions in mass society. Policies resulting from the transformations of interests in the political arena of modern mass society have a special quality. Theorists have pointed out that the arena represents the political analog of the market-

place, the alignment of parties to a policy agreement corre-
sponds to price in the market (Lasswell and Kaplan, 1950, pp.
78-81; Mannheim, 1940, pp. 333-334; Schorr, 1968, p. 147). It
is widely understood that price in a highly developed industrial
society does not represent the simple equilibrium point balancing demand and supply; rather, the arrangements made between
prevailing and countervailing economic forces, increasingly including the state, result in administered prices. Compared to
policy made earlier in this century, the outcome of the political
dynamics of policy making in a mass society with a highly centralized state results in administered policy. The preschool
enactments examined in this study all exemplify this modern
form of social policy.

Policy Processes

Our discussion of the political aspect of policy formation
dealt with the organized and unorganized interests and associated perspectives that the political machinery transforms into
an alignment. Here we dissect and examine phases or procedural
stages of the transformation.

The primary interest here is not in the phases per se, but
in their usefulness for ordering and highlighting the meaning of
salient features of the preschool policy process in the 1960s.
Specifically, we will explicate the utility of several phases for the
critical tasks of identifying interests relevant to the particular
policy issue, discerning their views, and translating the interests
and perspectives into a viable policy formulation.

The phases, processes, or functions taken together constitute an ideal typical sequence of the completed act of legislative
policy making. Four phases make up the sequence: the origina-
tive, intelligence, advisory, and decisive. (The terminology and
analysis here have been adapted from the discussion of political
functions in Lasswell and Kaplan, 1950, pp. 192-199.) Although analytically discriminable, in reality they may occur
concurrently, overlap, or not proceed in ideal typical order.

Origination or initiation of federal preschool policies, as
far as we were able to learn, primarily involved upper-class

women and professional politicians. Ideal interests of the former and a combination of ideal and practical interests of the latter converged. From time to time, even presumably hardheaded politicians seek to serve broad public interests. "Disinterest" groups of high-minded women may well have served as a balance wheel intermittently offsetting the pressures exerted on professional politicians by narrow interest groups.

The two types of policy initiators suggest a prerequisite to policy origination. It takes ready access to the political arena. Holding political office assures entree, while social intimacy with politicians makes it possible. Holding or representing economic and other forms of social influence, as exemplified by a large professional association, also heighten the chances of access.

The composition of the groups represented in initiating a policy proposal may essentially shape its content. If the initiators are so minded, intentionally they may incorporate their interests and ideals and be unmindful of others, or the concerns of other relevant groups may be mindlessly neglected. In either case, omitting the views of significant groups will lead to later difficulties in the advisory phase, unless the oversight is corrected in the intelligence stage of the process. The initial daycare proposal in 1962, which had been informally prepared by a day-care official and professionals outside the government, illustrates an omission that later jeopardized a legislative proposal.

The intelligence function means at the very least the provision to the decision maker of facts, estimates, and analyses. It may also include the description of goals and alternatives for purposes of consideration by the policy maker. Professionals of various disciplines inside and outside of government performed this function in regard to preschool policy.

The historical analysis of federal aid to education prepared by a staff member of the Library of Congress (U.S. Library of Congress, 1961) provides the outstanding illustration in this study of the contribution that data and analysis may make in the formulation of policy. We may recall the conclusion reached in that analysis that much of the federal role in education before 1960 had been justified in terms of the national defense provisions of the Constitution, as, for example, in the program of educational aid to defense-impacted areas. This provided the critical clue for which Senator Morse and his aides had been searching. Creatively building on that conclusion, they proceeded to forge a justification for federal aid to "lower" education in terms of the impact of other federal activity (AFDC and unemployment insurance). This federal connection was then employed by other policy makers in constructing the Economic Opportunity Act and the Elementary and Secondary Education Act.

The illustration also points to the significance of the availability of intelligence resources. The Senator, seeking information, analyses, and so on, had available to him the staff of the Library of Congress, of the General Accounting Office, and staff in his own office or committee. Otherwise the legislator is dependent on others for such technical help: federal specialists —if he is on good terms with the administration and the particular department, outside experts volunteering their skill, or paid lobbyists. Morse, it may also be recalled, had to turn to the NEA for technical aid in drafting his aid to education bill in 1964.

By comparison to the squad or platoon of specialists available to the legislator, the executive can muster regiments and whole divisions of experts. Furthermore, the bureaucracy possesses all sorts of data that the executive can more readily obtain. As a result, the executive has a distinct edge in the amount and kind of intelligence he or his aides can obtain in preparation for a policy proposal or for challenging a competing piece of legislation. As an example, we may cite the administrative and fiscal reservations expressed by Commissioner Keppel in his testimony opposing Morse's 1964 bill.

The advisory function means recommending policy alternatives, not just presenting options for consideration by the policy makers. The distinction is normatively and politically important. Presenting possibilities for consideration means merely to state expectations, "to characterize the state of affairs" in the past, present, or future (Lasswell and Kaplan, 1950, pp. 21, 193). Recommendations include not only expectations, but also "demands," statements of preference or volition. To be in a position to express desired goals implies the legitimacy of participation in selecting and shaping objectives. This represents a phase of the act of policy making one step closer to the actual decision of choosing the objective. It is closer to actual participation in the policy decision than simply describing past or present occurrences or future indications (that is, providing data and estimates). Possibly for this reason, it is suggested that higher status attaches to the advisory than to the intelligence role (Merton, 1949, pp. 168-169; Shils, 1949).

The advisory role takes on greater significance in certain policy contexts. Lasswell and Kaplan (1950, p. 193) explain that "The advisory function is especially important where . . . power . . . is concentrated in the hands of a few individuals, or where the specialists in various skills do not themselves exercise power of corresponding scope." Policy making at the Congressional and presidential levels exemplifies that context. The difference between types of decisions made by a presidential aide, Sargent Shriver, and those by the Head Start planning advisors illustrates the differential in influence. The decision to hastily proceed with a large-scale preschool program was taken by political figures. The professional advisors made important decisions on program policy—the overall program conception, its components (education, health, and so on), participants (parents and children), standards, and so forth—and on minor issues (to use the term *group leader* instead of *teacher*).

Consideration of differentials in influence suggests a distinction between formally appointed, formally invited, and informally consulted advisors. (An individual may fit into more than one category.) Individuals in all three categories appeared throughout the legislative histories recounted earlier. Appointment as an advisor on presidential, legislative, and departmental committees, commissions, and task forces carries great civic and professional prestige. Membership may provide extended opportunities to gain professionally valuable and sensitive information and a potential that the advice given may influence policy at a high level. Because membership is public information, care must be taken to avoid politically embarrassing appointments. For all these reasons, nominees for such appointment are carefully screened in terms of professional and political criteria. Earlier we indicated that expertise, affiliation with influential interest groups, programatic affinity, and ideological compatibility were the criteria reported to have been employed by the appointing authorities.

Informal advisors often are not publicly identified as such. They may be trusted and influential insiders or status elites.[4] On the other hand, high status or ideological compatibility is not required to be informally consulted by a politico or his agent. Thus, to avoid repetition of the 1961 stalemate over aid to education, Keppel informally sounded out a wide range of interests and viewpoints. Past opponents were quietly approached to ascertain with great specificity their bargaining position—the negotiable and nonnegotiable demands. By entering into informal discussions with interested groups, the political mechanic also learned whether past antagonists, such as the National Catholic Welfare Conference and the National Education Association, were willing to negotiate. Then by bringing together such opponents who, Meranto (1967, p. 81) reports, previously "had not even communicated with each other," the mechanic was able to determine the nature of a measure to aid education that both sides could support.

This case illustrates that the intelligence and advisory phases may overlap. It also indicates that informal consultation may advance to become a negotiating procedure, whereby the goals of the interest groups are adjusted and fitted into an overall policy formulation. When the process has advanced to the point of informal agreement on a specific legislative proposal, the consultees thereby join the alignment of interests supporting the devised policy. For these reasons, informal consultation can be a versatile mode of the policy process.

Formally inviting experts and interest groups to express their views on a legislative proposal serves as another means of carrying out the advisory function. Specifically, it provides formal opportunities for a wide range of groups to state their views and make their recommendations in public. Announcement of a hearing on a legislative bill or policy matter leads to requests of and offers to testify that then may be formalized by invitation. Ordinarily a broad spectrum of ideological and interest positions is encouraged to appear. Differences between the majority and minority parties on the committee result in invitations to witnesses who may present divergent views. As we mentioned earlier, a Republican Congressman had invited Bronfenbrenner to testify regarding the importance of preschool programs at the hearings on the Economic Opportunity Act proposed by President Johnson. Pressure groups interested in the measure under legislative consideration may stimulate requests to testify in person and submission of written statements or letters. As an example, we may think back to 1962, when the national day-care association apparently organized a large volume of support. In these ways formal hearings permit the legislators to identify a wide range of interest groups relevant to the policy matter at hand.

Had the political mechanics who managed the alignment in support of a bill under consideration initially neglected to sound out an important interest group, it would surely seek to be heard. For example, we may recall the Catholic groups that obviously had not been consulted in the preparation of the initial day-care bill presented their opposing views in strong terms at the hearings. In this way politicians can overcome limitations of their knowledge about the multiplicity of groups defining the proposal or policy. Public hearings therefore tend to assure that the legislators will not overlook the policy preferences of groups with interests pertinent to the policy matter being heard. Not only are additional relevant interest groups thereby identified, but their views can be then taken into account. If backed by sufficient influence in terms of votes on the committee, as in the case of the day-care bill, the heretofore neglected aims would be accommodated by one of several legislative tactics. This will be dealt with later in our discussion of the decisive stage.

Legislative committee hearings also allow witnesses to describe their own or constituencies' policy position with as much exposition, precision, and clarity as they are able or wish to achieve. If the witness is not sufficiently clear or is overly ambiguous, the opportunity to pose questions permits legislators to carefully gauge the position of the witness. In the hearing reports, one may on occasion discover the delicate interrogatory skill with which a solon subtly leads a witness to delineate the points of high and low principles his group holds and expediencies it accepts. As a limpid illustration, we can point to the question from a legislator to a prelate that produced an agonized admission that it seemed " 'churches [were] indeed selling their services' " (cited in U.S., Congress, House, Committee on Ways and Means, 1962, p. 591). By such colloquies, the interests and bargaining position of the pertinent groups can be discerned with pinpoint accuracy. The full range of testimony presented and interrogatory exchanges thus provides the legislators a panoramic view of the material and ideal interests aligned along the gradient from full support to bitter opposition to the specific proposal. Moreover, since witnesses indicate particular points found offensive and may offer suggestions for remedy, the legislators may thereby receive additional advice of potential practical use. The suggestions made by Arthur Flemming during the House hearings on the Elementary and Secondary Education bill (Meranto, 1967, p. 75) may be cited as an illustration.

We have said that witnesses can express their position at hearings. More precisely, witnesses typically provide two critical types of information. As indicated earlier, they state their views on the policy question at issue. In addition, usually at the outset the witness more or less explicitly refers to his or her group's base of influence. An individual officially representing only himself may allude to the expertness or type of authority he claims by explicit mention of academic degrees, legal certification, length of experience, titles, or positions held. A witness representing a constituency at the very least will identify (or be asked to identify) the organization he is testifying for. If the group is well-known, that identification may be translated easily by legislators into potential political influence. Every politician could make that translation, perhaps in national terms and very likely for his own district or state, if the witness is a spokesman for a national professional association, such as the National

Education Association, or major church group, such as the National Catholic Welfare Conference or the National Council of the Churches of Christ. Spokesmen of a less well-known group may state its size of membership, geographic base, or other implied indicator of its influence. (The hearing reports examined for this study did not contain any overt, public claim of political influence.)

On a relatively controversial measure, such as the education bill in 1965, announcement of the hearings attracted various organized interests eager to express their position and hopeful of influencing the final legislation. Organizations like the national Catholic organization and the national teachers association were bound to be invited because of their influence. Testimony at hearings by such organizations, that had been informally consulted in the negotiation process orchestrated by Keppel, constitutes a reaffirmation in public of agreements reached earlier in private. In this way, public hearings may have the quality of a ritual. In this vein, open hearings serve another vital legislative function. The various viewpoints presented provide legislators with a "cover," rationalizations available for supporters or opponents of a measure who may later be questioned about the "reasons" for their stand, that conceals the conflict of tangible interests at play (Edelman, 1970, pp. 134-135). When these "reasons" appear in the committee report and in the debates on the floor of the legislature, they then become part of the legislative history, in the technical sense, and have meaning in any subsequent judicial effort to establish the legislative intent of the statute.

To summarize the pertinent points, formal committee hearings on a proposed piece of legislation serve as an institutionalized arrangement for (1) assessing the strength of an alignment and of the opposition on the policy proposal, and (2) auditioning the policy formulation around which the proponents and opponents are initially aligned. Public hearings may also be a means by which the issues involved in a policy matter can gain exposure and be communicated to the general public. For all these reasons, advisory hearings in public are vital preliminaries to the decisive stage of legislative policy formation.

In terms of legislated policy, the term *decisive stage* refers to that part of the process resulting in the termination of the course of legislative action. The decisive stage begins at the committee level. Based on the hearings the legislative managers of the bill may conclude that the differences among the interest groups are still too wide to produce an alignment that could gain the votes necessary to enact the bill. The decisive phase would terminate at that point. In the case of the day-care and education bills more optimistic judgments were reached. In both cases, objectionable features identified and remedies suggested by witnesses at the hearings pointed to promising revisions. Managers of the day-care bill proceeded to prepare a "clean" version while the education bill was amended. Tactical considerations are believed to have guided choice of the methods of revision.

A "clean bill" means a legislative proposal revised to remove previously unreconciled differences, producing a compromise acceptable to the major interests involved and, therefore, possibly passable as legislation. By reviewing the testimony at the day-care hearings, omission of a provision or arrangement permitting purchase of day care from church groups was clearly visible as a defect objectionable to the Catholic spokesman. Cleaning eliminated the offensive omission and added attractive "language" in order to accommodate the expressed preferences of the influential objector.

Amending a bill accomplishes the same end of producing a formulation judged to be acceptable to an effective alignment of outside interests and legislative votes. The specific amendments of the education bill were also identified from testimony at hearings. In this case, the revisions followed along the lines of suggestions from a leading Protestant layman (making loans rather than grants to parochial schools, stipulating public ownership of materials to be made available to such schools, and so forth). By amending or cleaning the original measure, the managers thus gain an opportunity to rectify objectionable omissions or commissions in the original bill. This provides a second chance to achieve an effective compromise.

In contrast to the hearings in public, when committees revise or launder legislation they do so in executive session.

Edelman (1970, p. 147) points out that political and bureaucratic "Bargaining is private by its very nature and the actual language of the negotiations never publicized." No doubt this enables the professional politicians to talk in frank or un-Aesopian language. Most interests and bargaining points can be discussed openly by the politicos and their staff, who may appreciate lofty ideals but who have a vocational orientation to the mechanics and dynamics of arranging alignments of interests and votes. This pragmatic orientation[5] is inherent in the legislative function of reconciling conflicts between influential groups by securing a compromise.

By approving an amended or clean bill, the committee indicates an acceptable legislative bargain has been reached. The revision symbolizes a reconstructed alignment of interests and viewpoints. Its approval by the committee serves as a rough initial gauge of its later chances within the legislative mill. Eventually, directly or through an intervening structure, such as the Rules Committee or the Ways and Means Committee, it may reach the floor of a house. As a result of the committee system, action taken by the initial committee is endorsed often enough for us to consider it a precursory decision. Action on the floor may be considered a sequential decision. By the pragmatic test, endorsement by the full chamber confirms the effectiveness of the alignment of political and nonpolitical interests and perspectives, symbolized in the policy formulation, as organized by the political managers and shepherded through the legislative process. In a mass society, that process also reflects planfulness, as exemplified in the prearranged events described earlier.

The foregoing account of policy procedure somewhat merges the processes by which the preschool legislative enactments in the 1960s moved along from origination to legislative decision. (This account does not present a complete assessment of the legislative policy process but highlights pertinent events in the preschool policy enactments of the 1960s. For a fuller description and assessment of the legislative process in 1965, see Meranto [1967, Chap. 5].) However, when policy is established by fiat of a powerful president, the typical sequence becomes circular, with origination and decision largely coinciding.

"All" that remains after the decisive stage is administrative implementation. Policy making in that field then shifts to a large extent into the bureaucratic world, with intermittent return visits to the legislative arena.

Policy Dilemmas

At the outset of this study, several dilemmas that confronted preschool policy makers were noted. Four predicaments were listed: (1) the obstacle to a federal role in education created by the constitutional reservation to the states of powers not delegated to the federal government; (2) the difficulty in the postwar years of gaining passage of federal aid to education in face of (a) a constitutional prohibition against the establishment of religion, and (b) the balance of political influence on this issue between Protestants and Catholics; (3) the inconsistency between the democratic value of formal equality and enactment of preschool programs not for all children of a given age, but for those who meet other selective criteria, such as impoverishment; and (4) the tension between familial and social parenthood, between the high normative value ascribed to the familial rearing of very young children and governmental support of nonfamilial child care programs.

The preschool legislation, we said, may be viewed as attempts to resolve these dilemmas. In this concluding section, an answer will be given to the question of the extent to which the legislation overcame the hindrances or relieved the tensions. We have concluded that essentially the preschool enactment deepened the major dilemma, tension between familial and social parenthood, but had only a slight or ephemeral effect on the other predicaments. Those conclusions will now be developed, starting with the more peripheral matters.

Justifying a federal role in elementary and secondary education occupied Senator Morse and his aides and, as we have seen, a solution was created by drawing a connection between aid to education and the impact of federal programs related to poverty. The evidence overwhelmingly indicates Morse's solution "worked" in the sense it contributed significantly to gaining approval of an act authorizing extensive federal aid to "lower" education.

Claims by proeducation supporters that ESEA approximated a program of general federal aid to education was refuted, however, by later pertinent developments. Categorical provisions in that law, such as the allocation of funds to impacted school districts and to parochial schools, required detailed federal rules and regulations. Those soon gave rise to complaints of red tape and federal control by state and local officials. Accordingly, such officials, as well as officers of the National Education Association, were sympathetic to Republican proposals in 1967 to drop the poverty impact focus of ESEA in favor of a general "block grant" to the states (Grant, 1967; Herbers, 1967a; Farber, 1967). These criticisms apparently later led President Nixon to propose replacing Title I of the ESEA with revenue sharing funds by a budgetary shift (Rosenbaum, 1973).

These events so soon after passage of the ESEA indicate the relations between the federal and state governments regarding aid to education were caught up in broader political and economic issues. Perhaps even in 1964-1965 the weak opposition to ESEA on the part of the states reflected the attraction of federal funds to hard-pressed state governments. At this point in time we believe the nature of federal-state relations is due as much or more to consideration of fiscal shares as to provisions of the Constitution.

The church-state problem also was addressed in the ESEA. As we have seen, the various provisions pertaining to this issue succeeded as a compromise necessary to gain Protestant and Catholic support. However, earlier mention was made of the difficulties that soon arose, such as parochial schools doing the hiring of school personnel to be on the public payroll.

Also pointed out were fragmentary indications of another possible consequence that civil liberties lawyers had anticipated. Attempts in some Southern states to circumvent prointegration court rulings by allocating public funds to each parent for purchase of education in private—presumably segregated—schools add racial impetus to the political and fiscal pressure for nonpublic schooling. If funds allocated under such policies were to derive from the federal treasury, it would mean the realization of fears about potential uses of the church-state provisions of the ESEA. It appears too early to tell whether proposals to give parents public funds or vouchers to purchase schooling will lead to an educational system with a diminished public but expanded private sector, parochial and proprietary.

In the main, however, we do not view the ESEA as having had a clear, telling, or lasting effect on the continuing dilemma of public aid to church schools.

The choice between universal versus selective provision was said earlier, in Chapter Three, to pose a basic normative choice for social policy. It has obvious far-reaching ideological ramifications. Rather than being available for children in the various social classes, all the preschool programs examined here established selective criteria, such as welfare or poverty status. These criteria follow necessarily from the major rationales for enacting the day-care and Head Start programs, relief from relief and combating poverty. That is, the criteria of selectivity were explicitly linked to the benefit to the national interest presumably provided by these programs. This linkage connects criteria of eligibility to a potent social value, to aims that ostensibly serve the nation as a whole.

On the normative level, programs based on selective criteria can only serve as negative examples to those who advocate universalism. In this sense, perhaps the day-care and Head Start legislation contributed to stimulating a proposal based on the opposing potent norm of democratic equality. In 1971 the House and Senate passed a "revolutionary" measure "extending day-care services to children of the wealthy as well as the poor" (Hunter, 1971d, p. 35; see also Hicks, 1971). President Nixon vetoed the measure, questioning its need and desirability, and fearing it would destroy the fabric of family life.[6] Other critics were opposed because of a belief it would eventually cost $20,000,000,000 a year (Hunter, 1971c). (Nixon's fear did not induce a veto of liberalized tax deduction subsidy of child care for working mothers, enacted that same year. We will take up this subsidy issue later.) Since then, the earlier hope of egalitarian-minded parents, professionals and legislators, of civil-rights, church, labor, and women's liberation groups, for universally available public programs have been all but extinguished in the national policy arena.

One structural effect of universal programs has been noted before. They would benefit the middle and upper classes as well. On the normative level, this indicates that no one program can resolve the inherent American dilemma of egalitarian ideals in a stratified society. Principled and consistent advocacy of democratic equality calls for a "radical critique" of the existing social order as a barrier to such equality (Bensman and Lilienfeld, 1973, p. 240). Finally, in regard to the universal-selective dichotomy, we must again remark on another dimension to which it has been applied.

On the programatic level, the selective orientation is said to affect program quality. Programs for the poor are said to become poor programs. Again, the evidence presented regarding the nonuniversalistic WPA-Lanham and Head Start programs does not support that contention. These programs adopted progressive conceptions of preschool programs and model program standards. This points to the relevance of programatic factors, such as the level of funding, adequacy of standards and of their implementation, quality of the curriculum, and, not least, experience and training of the staff, as significant policy considerations in addition to universality-selectivity.

We come now to the last dilemma, familial versus social parenthood. Given a focus on preschool programs, it has been for us the central and perhaps more convoluted of the predicaments. One complexity became clear in the course of the study. Social parenthood of preschool children, the exercise of heretofore parental obligations and duties of child rearing by people who are not kin, involves more than governmental surrogates. As has been shown, philanthropic and proprietary caretakers have played significant parts in the history of preschool programs, parts that intertwine with those of public preschool programs. This suggests an important correction of the historian Duby's (cited in Aries, 1962, p. 355) or the philosopher Russell's view of the simple institutional juxtaposition of family and state. Other organizations interpose between those two institutions (Greenblatt, 1975). Therefore, before proceeding to the central conclusion regarding government preschool policy and the family, we will touch briefly on prospects for the nongovernmental sector in the preschool field.

Industrial day care continues as a diminutive facet of day care. Some business and service organizations have recently established essentially subsidized day-care programs for their employees or clients. The industrial day-care centers of World War I and II have been emulated by a small but not unimpressive number of hospitals (U.S. Department of Labor, 1970), unions, federal agencies, and private organizations, for example, the Ford Foundation. Not surprisingly, in light of the heavy involvement of women in the textile industry, the Amalgamated Clothing Workers of America has been at the forefront of union interest in day care. Still other firms operate a day-care locator service for interested employees, enter into contracts with a day-care center to reserve a specified number of places for employees' children, or may participate in joint labor-management trust funds for the establishment of child-care centers for the member employees' children (U.S. Department of Labor, 1971). In the late 1960s, an estimated ninety colleges and universities in the nation had day-care centers on their campuses; for the most part, they cater to children of students, but attendance by faculty and staff children is not unknown (Greenblatt and Eberhard, 1973, p. 12).

The conduct of or direct payment by corporations for day care of their employees' children, however, remains for the most part an exception in peacetime business practice. An expansion of this form of day care does not appear likely. This prediction rests on the historic policy of the business firm, as of the state, to generally place on working parents fiscal responsibility for child care to the extent the market and polity permit. More recent developments serve to reinforce this forecast. Provisions for federal tax deductions for child care of working mothers have been liberalized, as we shall see below; this can only tend to obviate employer operation of day-care programs. Also, if a movement in the proprietary sector were to advance, the overall volume of available day care could increase measurably. We will turn to a discussion of that movement, the formation of franchised day-care centers and of a change in government policy on proprietary day care.

The explosive growth of nursery schools following Proj-

ect Head Start, from 1965 to 1970, and progress in the rationalization of managerial techniques attracted corporate capital to
the preschool field. Several local proprietary chains were established. Conglomerate planning began on networks of commer-
cially franchised day-care programs. Most well publicized, perhaps for a matronymic incongruity, was the plan for a chain of
"preschool educational play centers" by Performance Systems,
Inc., formerly known as Minnie Pearl's Chicken System, Inc.
(Morton, 1969). How the subsidiary firm, American Child Care
Centers, Inc., was conceived, for whom, by whom, and other
elements of the plans warrant a brief glance.

A former governor of Kentucky, Edward T. Breathitt,
had recognized a marketplace potential: "He became aware,
when he was chairman of the President's Commission on Rural
Poverty, of a need for nursery programs for families too pros-
perous to place their children in Head Start or in programs run
by philanthropies but not wealthy enough to afford the traditional high-quality private schools" (Morton, 1969, p. 20).

The head of the parent company, John Jay Hooker, Jr., a
Tennessee gubernatorial candidate in 1966, labeled the central
technique "systems management." " 'Our idea was that once we
had mastered the chicken business, we were really in the systems business. What we are doing is selling a system of running a
small business. We have centralized accounting . . . various techniques . . . a method of reducing it to a system.' . . . As for nursery schools, the same technique can be applied. . . . [They]
will conform to one architectural design; equipment, food, staff
training and curriculum will also conform to company-wide
standards" (Morton, 1969, p. 20).

A chain of 1,000 centers, with from 125 to 150 children
in each was projected. Fees were tentatively set at $20, $25,
and $30 for all-day, five days a week, day care of a child. Pur-
chasing a franchise called for a sizable investment: $44,500, of
which the company would loan $15,000, and about $144,000
for building and land. (The last point raises a tangential, but important issue. Costs of construction and land for day-care centers was a matter almost entirely not addressed in policy deliberation on public day care. Astronomical sums would be

required, and, for day-care proponents, just getting public funds for operating programs was enough of a challenge. For the most part, day-care center buildings from the mid-nineteenth century on probably consisted of large homes bequeathed to philanthropic organizations, private homes [not infrequently the proprietor's residence] and small commercial-type structures, facilities or buildings leased or loaned by public authorities [such as schools], a small number of fortunate places newly constructed for day-care use, and apartments in federally-funded public housing projects. If federal policy changes, to be discussed shortly, presage major reliance on the proprietary sector, that possibility would avoid the problem of considering a multibillion capital expenditure for a large public day care system.)

Although the corporate planners hoped their day-care system would be the wave of the future, American Child Care Centers folded in 1971. Reports are not clear whether the franchisers learned that measuring up to high standards of child care is not child's play,[7] the required investment proved excessive, or if other complications of high corporate finance led to the disenfranchisement (Lublin, 1972).

In spite of this failure, we believe it would be premature to reject any prospect of the bureaucratization of familial functions. Barrington Moore, Jr. (1962, pp. 399, 401), speculated on the subject more than a decade ago, musing that the large, formal organizations that accompanied industrialization might develop "from such contemporary forms as the creche, play school and boarding school [and] assume a much larger share of the burden of child rearing . . . . Though a considerable part of the task of raising children is not routine, a very great portion is repetitive. For these reasons one may expect that semibureaucratic arrangements will continue to encroach on the traditional structure of the family. No doubt many individual variations, combinations, and compromises will remain for some time to come. Yet, one fine day human society may realize that the part-time family, already a prominent part of our social landscape, had undergone a qualitative transformation into a system of mechanized and bureaucratized child rearing, cleansed of the standardized overtone these words now imply." Although the fine day of bureaucratized residential facilities with mechanized feeding and waste disposal has not yet arrived, corporate finance has, along with a managerial orientation much more sophisticated than that of a Mom and Pop program in a family home—in short, the means of modern, large-scale business management has reached the doorstep of preschool programs. In addition, involvement of political figures at the gubernatorial level gave clear indication that the proprietary sector would no longer neglect the national policy arena. A noteworthy change in federal policy occurred at this time.

In 1971, the year the broad child-care act was vetoed, a plan to reform the AFDC system, the Family Assistance Plan (FAP) had been proposed. The plan explicitly provided for purchase of day care from profit-making enterprises. The House Ways and Means Committee (U.S., Congress, House, Committee on Ways and Means, 1971, p. 167), which supported the plan, stated its views on child care forcefully: "[the Committee] does not intend that the lack of child care . . . be cited as an impediment to the success of the [FAP] program . . . [the government] may purchase child care directly through contracts with public or nonprofit agencies. . . . [It] may buy child care from private, profit-making enterprises." Profit-making centers were to be contracted with, for day care of children on welfare, when child care was not available through HEW.

For the preschool field, that legislative proposal is a landmark aside from its controversial guaranteed income provision. The evidence examined in this study indicates this was the first time the profit-making sector of child care was explicitly acknowledged and sanctioned in federal legislation.[8] It marked the end of the century of proprietary invisibility in day-care policy. (Symbolic invisibility of proprietary preschool affairs also ended at about this period. Articles appeared in commercial publications [for example, in that of the Bank of America National Trust and Savings Association, 1969] and a journal oriented to the proprietary day-care market was in the planning stage in 1973.) That the provision for profit-making enterprises signaled an era of support for that sector of child care is shown by the fact that *it* was retained although the plan itself was not enacted. Currently, proprietary programs are providing child care funded under the child welfare section of the Social Security Act passed in 1962, as well as under other sections of the act. That is, child care largely supported by federal funds is purchased from proprietary vendors. The magnitude of such purchases is not known.

For the various reasons indicated—corporate financial interest, managerial skills, political influence, favorable federal policy, and presumably unsatisfied market demand—short of an economic catastrophe, we believe expansion of the proprietary sector can be safely predicted. Increased influence in shaping federal preschool policy also appears most likely. What remains unclear is the caliber of child care such surrogates provide.

The federal legislation of focal interest in this study obviously has played, in general, an important part in the advance of social parenthood. At this point, we will assess more specifically the relationship of government policy and the family as an institution and offer our prognostication.

The highlights of federal policy need to be summarized. We have seen that the earliest approximation to a federal policy on the family had been enunciated by the first White House Conference on Children, in 1909, to the effect that "home life is the highest and finest product of civilization. . . . Except in unusual circumstances, the home should not be broken up for reasons of poverty" (cited in Bremner, 1971, p. 365). Before 1933, although the federal government had no program to aid families, federal activity was not at variance with those high ideals.

In 1933, the goal of strengthening family life was explicitly incorporated into federal policy. The ADC program of federal support of dependent children in their own homes was established; the exceptional circumstances of mass unemployment justified employment of mothers in the WPA program. Manpower shortages during World War II also justified federal efforts to facilitate maternal employment (Lanham Act; subsidies for industrial day care). After the wartime crisis, federal policy returned to the traditional norm of protecting and safeguarding family life. Thus, until 1962 tension between the ideal of familial rearing of young children and federal policy had arisen only during national emergencies.

In 1962, political concern over burgeoning welfare costs constituted the "exceptional circumstances" that justified en-actment of federal aid for day care. The aid represented an attempt to cut welfare expenditures by facilitating employment of mothers with young children on the ADC rolls. And in 1964-1965, when an internal threat to the social order was per-ceived, the Head Start program was established to interrupt the cycle of poverty at an early age. Thus, after 1962, federal poli-cies conflicted with the ideal of familial parenthood without a justification of national emergency.

Subsequent welfare laws and rules since the mid-1960s have intensified those strains. For example, in 1967 day-care services and funds were extended, but also, "a large measure of choice about working was removed from [AFDC] mothers" (Schorr, 1968, p. 11). Physically well mothers were declared eligible to mandatory registration for work or work training in 1972.[9] Data on day-care expenditures for children of mothers on welfare provide a gauge of the extent to which welfare moth-ers are required, encouraged, or "volunteer" to work; the data also reveal the extent to which the 1962 policy of seeking "relief from relief" has advanced. In fiscal 1962, $5,000,000 were appropriated for day care; in 1970, $109,000,000 were ex-pended for day care of AFDC children; by 1974, day care for AFDC children cost $695,000,000.[10] These data clearly suggest the extent to which the aim of getting mothers off the welfare rolls and onto payrolls has become the dominant federal policy pertaining to the family.

Summarizing to this point, increasingly since the mid-1960s, and especially now in the 1970s, the former reasons of state have been declared inoperative and new priorities have been established. Policies promulgated in the higher interest of family welfare now diverge markedly from the apotheosized resolution of the White House Conference on Children in 1909. That doctrine smacks of apostasy from the standpoint of the current policy for families on welfare. Compelling the AFDC mother to get work training and to work is in the interest of a higher morality. For the state and its allies, work is now the higher ethic, in contrast to which poverty is both cost-ineffective and immoral, and family unity dispensible.

Furthermore, federal tax policy in 1971 extended that ethic and the dispensibility of family unity to nonwelfare mothers. Assistance was provided to nonpoor working mothers in the form of liberalized income tax deductions for child care expenses. Its major provisions are as follows: If family income falls under $18,000 a year, the working wife can declare up to $400 a month for such expenses as a deduction in computing federal income tax. The deduction is prorated downward for higher family incomes, reaching zero when combined husband-wife income rises to $27,600. This provision does not cover "women whose family income is too low to benefit from a tax deduction" (*Economic Report of the President*, 1973, p. 110). In short, the federal government now shares to a much larger extent than ever before the cost of child care for children of working mothers in the independent lower and middle classes.

At present, then, the federal government can be said to have two major programs pertaining to child care: one for children of dependent families (impoverished and/or on welfare), and another for children of independent families. There are similarities and differences between the two programs. Both conflict with the older, normative conception of the family and with the associated goal of public policy, protecting and safeguarding family unity. Also, both programs involve vast amounts of federal support.[11] However, in contrast to direct governmental payments for day care of poor children, such as those in the AFDC program, a tax subsidy appears less visible or comprehensible and receives less publicity as a form of federal support.

Perhaps the greatest difference between the two programs concerns freedom. Freedom, the opportunity to make effective choices among open alternatives, is much less available to dependent mothers and their children. We refer not only to the older compulsion to work stemming from destitution. Now federal requirements and related pressures also compel mothers on welfare to accept work training and employment. In addition, if such a mother can find only one source of child care and she deems it unacceptable, the rules mandate the child-care arrangements be accepted unless the mother can prove its unsuitability (*Federal Register*, 1972).[12] To state this issue squarely, the two major federal child care provisions reflect and reinforce a number of inequities across social class lines.

In concluding this study, we will restate the central problem, summarize what has been learned, and state our major conclusions. At the outset, we assumed the widespread prevalence of a strong value commitment to the rearing of very young children in the home and suspected the preschool enactments of the 1960s formed a major watershed in the shift from parental to federal responsibility for such child rearing. The presenting problem was the reasons for the shift in federal policy in the 1960s. This shift pointed to the central problem: to unravel the dynamics of the tension between familial and social parenthood. Our central aims were to identify the conditions under which intervention into early child care by surrogate agencies occurred and to explain the forms of such intervention.

The early history showed that surrogates for home rearing occurred before the 1960s for reasons of economic hardship associated with industrialization and economic and military emergencies of national scope. Such intervention into familial child rearing violated social norms pertaining to family functioning, but the surrogate provisions arose as a result of higher reasons of governmental or economic necessity. These pressures overcame the resistance of basic institutions (such as the state and church) and of tradition to programs of social parenthood.

Prior to the 1960s, the varied forms of intervention became differentiated as to purpose, sponsorship, clientele, program content, and repute. Only a few highlights need to be recapitulated here. Philanthropic auspices primarily were associated with programs aimed at relieving the familial effects of economic hardship and acculturating immigrants. The need to stimulate maternal employment during national emergencies resulted in public sponsorship of day care and nursery schools. From 1860 to 1960, profit-seeking proprietors and proprietresses responded to the demand for preschool programs that philanthropic largesse or public expenditures did not supply. The proprietary sector, although ignored by philanthropy and the government, increased during periods of a vacuum in social preschool policy.

Day-care programs, which in general apparently were custodial in orientation from their inception until the 1930s, became stigmatized as a form of relief during the 1920s. Nursery schools, on the other hand, were defined as educational enterprises. These distinctions in content and repute did not apply to the large-scale federal preschool programs of the Great Depression and World War II. Nevertheless, the distinctions persisted in the postwar period.

Just as depression and world war overcame earlier pressures against federal intervention into early child care, the recognition of poverty provided the parallel macrocondition for federal involvement in the 1960s. More specifically, federal preschool policy at that time sought to reduce both relief rolls and the danger of civil disorder in the slums. A number of legislative solutions were employed to overcome obstacles to federal support of preschool programs, such as a rationale for federal aid to education that satisfied objections relating to states' rights and a breakthrough that defused the church-state controversy regarding aid to education.

Since the 1960s, preschool programs have advanced and federal provisions for care of children of dependent and independent families have broadened. The extensive federal provisions for and the various forms of surrogate child care[13] represent a marked deepening of the tension between the nineteenth-century normative conception of the family and federal policy. Regardless of which form of preschool education comes to dominate in the future, it is evident that now, for the first time in the nation's history, social parenthood competes effectively with families on a mass basis for influence over the preschool-age child.

Federal policy, since its decisive turn in the mid-1960s, has been a significant influence in the transformation of familial rearing of preschool-age children. The preschool policies examined in this study thus fit closely the evaluation of the familial effects of state policy in Europe by Bertrand Russell (1959, p. 138): "Although the law means to uphold the family, it has in modern times increasingly intervened between parents and children, and it is gradually becoming, against the will and intention of lawmakers, one of the chief engines for the breakup of the family system." (The atheist Russell thus agreed with the Bishops of the United States [1949, p. 1] who earlier had seen a similar disparity between declaration and consequence of family policy: "An unbelieving world professing recognition of the essential value of family life, actually discounts that value and moves to destroy what it claims to cherish." Obviously Russell and the clerics imply a specific concept of the family system.) Since the 1960s, that engine has increasingly driven welfare mothers to arrange for surrogate child care. However, non-governmental forces also have been at work. What economic dependency makes necessary for working mothers in the poorer classes—transfer of some child-rearing responsibilities out of the home—the desire for careers, independence, and affluence has made increasingly attractive to middle-class mothers. The outpouring of mothers of preschool-age children into the labor force since the 1960s suggests those attractions as well as a flight from exclusively full-time maternal rearing of very young children.

Thus the nineteenth-century normative conception of the family, with its emphasis on the full-time child-rearing role of the mother, has become attenuated. Perhaps a new, twentieth-century "liberated" conception will be articulated and become accepted. If so, preschool programs, many of which were justified as bolstering the older family conception, will have played an important part in its replacement.

Finally, we must note one last aspect of the preschool policies examined in this study. Although the various preschool policies projected ideals such as overcoming dependency and cultural deprivation, the programs did not posit educational or familial goals as their ultimate objective. The present study, therefore, largely supports the conclusion that "nursery education in the United States has had as its primary objective the welfare of persons other than the children" (Sears and Dowley,

cited in Leeper, Dales, Skipper, and Witherspoon, 1968, p. 47).
To recognize these disparities, of course, does not challenge the
importance the programs may have had for the children and
their parents. "Higher" national interests were to be served,
such as cutting relief costs and preventing riots. We see here the
unavoidable intermingling and clashing of high ideal and potent
material interests implicated in these as in most social policies.
As we remarked in the discussion of the rationales held by a
number of the policy makers who were interviewed or whose
testimony was cited, inconsistencies, contradictions, and ironies
were plentiful. We conclude this policy analysis, therefore, with
Chesterton's sketch of the sentimentalist (cited in Cremin,
1964, p. 377), who looks familiar: " 'the man who wants to eat
his cake and have it . . . he will not see that one must pay for an
idea as for anything else. . . . He will have them all at once in
one wild intellectual harem, no matter how much they quarrel
and contradict each other.' "

Notes

[1] In nineteenth-century Europe, socially well-placed women also
were in the avant-garde of preschool education. The Baroness Berta von
Marenholtz-Bulow, "the great propagandist of Froebelism," first attracted
French interest to kindergartens. In Italy, Madame Salis-Schwabe brought
forth that type of program, Countess Maria Montessori the nursery school
("Kindergarten," p. 802). In England two ladies, Margaret McMillan and
Grace Owens, initiated the nursery schools (Forest, 1930, p. 322).

[2] Staff conviction has been suggested as an important component in
the life cycle of social experiments or demonstration projects. Fred Hechinger (1966a) explained the demise of New York City's Higher Horizon
program (of educational and cultural enrichment for elementary and
junior high school children from the slums) in part as related to the rou-
tinization of professional commitment: "In fact, once a pilot project is
translated into large-scale, routine operation, the number of staff needed
to retain the momentum gets even larger. The founding cadre almost inevi-
tably consists of enthusiastic, single-minded and devoted experimenters,
ready to work overtime to prove their point. As the personal, emotional
involvement is replaced by routine professional action, the extraordinary,
self-propelling impact declines" (p. E7).
    Powledge attributed the achievements of Deutsch's Institute for
Developmental Studies largely to the " 'dedication and savvy' " of the
staff (cited in Buder, 1968).

[3] It is necessary to add an historical footnote in order to avoid leaving related issues untouched and giving an inaccurate impression. To form a new agency obviously meant cost inefficiencies; it resulted in duplicating overhead services and adjunct programs (for example, school lunch) found in preexisting competitors. Legislators concerned with organizational esthetics, opponents of the new program, or others concerned with the costs and growing pains of a rapidly expanding program attacked the new agency. These objections or fears were voiced during Head Start's infancy. That the benefit of an agency beholden to an incumbent administration may be a detriment to its successor was soon evident when Lyndon B. Johnson was succeeded by Richard M. Nixon. The earlier Republican and Chamber of Commerce suggestions to divide OEO up and distribute its programs to older, "more established" federal agencies were then pursued in earnest. Head Start was one of the first parts proposed to be carved out (Loftus, 1968b; Farber, 1969a). By 1969-1970, the day-care component of Head Start, retaining the Head Start name, was transferred to the Office of Child Development, successor to the old Children's Bureau. In 1974, the remainder of Head Start also was shifted to an even older established agency, the Office of Education.

To those who authorized the changes in the name of administrative orderliness, the results may seem ironic. Other subsequent reorganizations in HEW resulted in the splitting up of responsibility for day care between the Office of Child Development and the Social and Rehabilitation Service. For a current report on the resulting administrative inefficiencies, see U.S. Department of Health, Education, and Welfare (1974).

[4] An illustration was reported by a respondent in a position to have such information. According to the anecdote, in the summer of 1966 President Johnson was searching for a social policy concerning children in the aftermath of the controversy that had erupted over the Moynihan Report. He sent aides around the country to search for pertinent ideas. A meeting with Natalie Heineman, wife of a high Democratic Party supporter (Benjamin W. Heineman), educated in social work and a child welfare advocate, was said to have stimulated eventual formation of the President's Task Force on Early Childhood.

[5] Pragmatism was revealed by the Democratic caucus, extending for ten days, on the antipoverty bill. With one party enjoying a wide margin over its opponents, the majority contingent in the committee found it tempting to ask, Why waste time debating the issues with an opposition deficient in votes to affect the outcome? The caucus of a majority became a committee meeting of the majority without the minority members. (The latter, it may be remembered, charged "lock out.") This reveals the legislative function of securing a compromise itself may be subject to the pragmatic approach: Compromise is called for in the political arena when practicality requires it. It also suggests that partisanship may take precedence in policy making over presumably serving the general interest.

[6] The veto message drew a retort from child psychologists Bronfenbrenner and Bruner, who criticized the alternative legislation proposed by

the President. The President's proposal amended the AFDC program and related day-care provisions. His proposal, the psychologists asserted, would not give mothers freedom of choice, but would break up families by forcing welfare mothers to work. Furthermore, they pointed out, it went counter to the "first and principal recommendation of the President's own White House Conference on Children, [which] recommended that 'the Federal Government fund comprehensive child-care programs . . . universally available, with initial priority to those whose needs are the greatest' " (Bronfenbrenner and Bruner, 1972, p. 41).

[7] American Child Care apparently understood that professional educators and most nonprofit day-care personnel question whether quality and profit would be compatible in their franchised centers. They had planned to closely supervise franchised units and provide them with consultation. The sophistication and interest in measures to achieve the "quality program" of the stated intent was shown by their having hired consultants in several pertinent disciplines from nationally prestigious, academic institutions. Such advice may have been reflected in their promotional literature, which cited studies "showing that a child's experiences in his first six years may determine his character and mental capacity for the rest of his life" (Morton, 1969, p. 20).

[8] A diminutive implicit exception should be mentioned. The Small Business Act authorizes the government to make and/or insure loans to small businesses unable to obtain credit elsewhere. Profit-making day-care centers may qualify. In 1965, fifteen loans were made involving $264,432 in federal loans; in 1968, thirty-two loans involved $763,895, of which the government loaned 92 percent and insured the remainder (see Malone, 1969, pp. 20-21).

[9] More than 1,200,000 mothers were estimated as affected. Mothers of children under six years of age are *not* required to sign up. " 'But even some who are not required to sign up under the new law will do so anyhow,' Secretary Richardson said, 'because they want to go to work.' An estimated 300,000 mothers with children under six will make up the bulk of these 'volunteers,' he said" (U.S. Department of Health, Education, and Welfare, 1972, pp. 1-2). (The basis for predicting that 300,000 mothers of preschool children "will make up the bulk of these 'volunteers' " was not provided.)

[10] The 1970 figure appears in Appendix Table 9, the 1974 figure appears in U.S. Department of Health, Education, and Welfare (1974, p. 37). Two important qualifications attach to the 1974 figure. First, it includes expenditures for day care of AFDC children in their own homes, in family day-care homes, as well as in day-care centers. (The breakdown of expenditures in these various types of day-care arrangements is not available.) Thus it would be an overstatement of expenditures for day-care centers alone. Second, the figure includes only federal expenditures; it excludes state matching expenditures, which range between 10 and 50 percent of

federal outlays (depending on differences in authorizations for the various subprograms involved). To this extent, the 1974 figure understates governmental day-care expenditures.

Several additional points are required to round out the fiscal picture. Excluded from these figures are *day-care* expenditures under the Head Start authorization; in 1970, $99,500,000 were spent; in 1972 we estimate Head Start spent approximately $350,000,000 (see U.S. Department of Health, Education, and Welfare, 1974, p. 1). In 1970, federal day-care expenditures in all programs amounted to $222,000,000 (see Table 9); in 1972, over $700,000,000. Again, these figures exclude state and local matching funds. We estimate at present annual government expenditures for day care have approached the one-billion-dollar mark.

This fiscal note would be incomplete if we did not point out the magnitude of expenditures for day care under the original child welfare day-care amendment passed in 1962. Again, in fiscal 1962, $5,000,000 had been appropriated; by 1970, that figure dropped to $1,500,000; and in 1974 it was $1,800,000. In other words, the 1962 statute justifying day care as relief for relief became the leading edge of a wedge that, twelve years later, amounted to almost $700,000,000 (day care for AFDC children). Meanwhile the original authorization has shrunk, remaining an ironic memento to a child welfare conception of day care now surpassed by the more dominant conception (stimulating employment of mothers on welfare).

[11]We can only partially gauge the comparability of federal funds involved. The federal expenditure for "dependency" day care in 1970 amounted to $222,000,000; in the same year, tax deductions for child-care expenses claimed for income tax purposes by working mothers amounted to an almost identical sum, $221,000,000 (U.S. Internal Revenue Service, 1973, Table 8.6, p. 332). To be sure, the amount itemized for such a deduction represents only the allowable portion of expenses that may be deducted. Furthermore, an allowable deduction of, let us say, $1,000 reduces taxable income by that amount; it does not save the working mother $1,000 in the amount of taxes she has to pay.

However, we must recall that in 1971 the tax provisions for child-care deductions were made substantially more generous. It is not inconceivable, then, that the total *deductions* for child-care expenses for tax purposes may approximate federal *expenditures* for "dependency" day care; *tax benefits* realized by the nonpoor working mothers probably would be much less than such expenditures.

[12]Developments regarding federal child-care standards are pertinent in regard to these rules. First, serious and potentially dangerous deviations from federal and state day-care standards have been reported by HEW in the programs receiving federal welfare funds. In a sample survey in nine states, 80 percent of the day-care centers serving welfare cases did not meet the pertinent health and safety standards; 41 percent failed to meet standards relating to number of children per staff member. Federal auditors concluded, "the lives of the children receiving the care may be endan-

gered" (see U.S. Department of Health, Education, and Welfare, 1974, pp. 20, 23, 25).

Second, HEW has been equivocal about maintaining the 1968 Federal Interagency Day Care Requirements. It proposed in 1972 to revise those standards; Congress then stipulated that the standards not be diluted. The present status of HEW policy on this issue had best be left to description by HEW auditors: "Although considerable effort has been devoted to revision of the Federal standards, the [HEW] officials were unable to tell us when, if ever, they will be officially published" (U.S. Department of Health, Education, and Welfare, 1974, p. 17).

What constitutes appropriate standards is not as self-evident as many professionals believe. Several reports acknowledge that model standards "are rarely met" (Lansburgh, 1971, p. 118; Prescott, 1965, p. 39). Controversy arose over the charge, by the House Ways and Means Committee, among others, that restrictively high standards impede growth of badly needed day-care services. The controversy has also stimulated planning and experimental work unfettered by the unquestioned acceptance of conventional wisdom. The "unreality" of previous standards is seen more clearly as simply having assumed a day-care marketplace of unlimited resources. "The economics of the marketplace," it is noted, "must define the relevant range of types of child care in which we define quality" (State of Vermont Family Assistance Planning Unit *and* Mathematica, Inc., 1971, p. 15). Answers to the question as to which marketplace federal day-care standards will aim at apparently remain unsettled.

[13]A newer preschool program mainly involving nongovernmental surrogates must be noted. In 1969, nursery school and day-care programs lost the monopoly in preschool education. That year a compensatory preschool program was launched on educational (nonprofit) television, namely Sesame Street. It had been planned by organized twentieth-century philanthropy—the Carnegie Corporation and Ford Foundation, and by the federal government—the United States Office of Education. Its popularity, effectiveness as established by research, and lower cost to parents may make it a strong competitor, especially to nursery schools (see Gould, 1968).

Appendix:
Statistics on
Child Care Programs

Table 1. Estimated Number of Day-Care Centers and Children,
United States, 1892-1969

Year	Centers	Children[a]
1892 (1)	90[b]	N.A.[e]
1897 (1)	175[b]	N.A.
1900 (2)	175[b]	N.A.
1923 (2)	613[b]	22,822
1929 (3)	516	27,147
1930 (2)	700	N.A.
1931 (4)	800	N.A.
1934 (4)	650	N.A.
1936 (5)	684	N.A.
1937 (4)	N.A.	40,000[c]
1944 (4)	3,102[d]	129,357
1951 (6)	1,500[b]	N.A.
1960 (7)	4,426	141,138
1962 (8)	N.A.	185,000
1964 (9)	6,308	213,000
1965 (10)	7,334	252,000
1969 (10)	13,600	518,000

[a]Enrollment figures prior to 1960, capacity for 1960 and later.

[b]Exclusively or primarily under charitable auspices.

[c]WPA program only.

[d]Lanham program only.

[e]N.A. means data not available.

Sources: (1) Whipple (1929); (2) White House Conference (1930a); (3) White House Conference (1930b), Table I, p. 154; (4) Kadushin (1967); (5) Beer (1938); (6) Moustakas and Berson (1955); (7) Low (1962); (8) Lansburgh (1971); (9) Kearns (1966); (10) U.S. Department of Health, Education, and Welfare (1966a, 1969).

Table 2. Number of Licensed Day-Care Centers and Aggregate Capacity, by Auspices,
United States, 1960, 1965, and 1969

Auspices	Number of Centers			Aggregate Capacity		
	1960 (1)	1965 (2)	1969 (2)	1960	1965	1969[a]
All	4,426[b]	7,334	13,600[b]	141,138[b]	252,000	518,000[b]
Public	276	347	730	15,561	20,000	34,700
Voluntary	1,109	2,234	4,100	49,160	92,000	178,000
Proprietary	2,497	4,753	7,600	66,714	140,000	266,000

[a]Excludes Head Start and Title I (ESEA) Centers.

[b]Includes centers not reporting auspices.

Sources: (1) Low (1962); (2) U.S. Department of Health, Education, and Welfare (1966a and 1969).

Table 3. Estimated Number of Nursery Schools and Children
Enrolled, United States, 1920-1970

Year	Nursery Schools	Children Enrolled
1920 (1)	3	N.A.[d]
1924 (1)	25	N.A.
1928 (1)	89	2,000
1929 (2)	229[a]	4,890[a]
1930 (3)	203	N.A.
1932 (4)	300	N.A.
1934-35 (1)	1,900[b]	75,000[b]
1936 (1)	2,185	N.A.
1937 (4)	1,900	40,000[b]
1942 (1)	1,909	39,000[b]
1943 (1)	1,180	32,000[b]
1945 (1)	1,481	51,000
1951 (5)	2,039	N.A.
1964 (6)	N.A.	471,000
1965 (7)	N.A.	890,000
1970 (7)	N.A.	1,500,000[c]

[a]Combines "Relief Nursery Schools" and "Nursery Schools"; excludes Kindergarten.

[b]WPA or Lanham program only.

[c]Includes three- and four-year-olds only.

[d]N.A. means data not available.

Sources: (1) Goodykoontz, Davis, and Gabbard (1947), Almy and Snyder (1947); (2) White House Conference (1930b), Table I, p. 154; (3) Forest (1930); (4) Campbell, Bair, and Harvey (1939); (5) Moustakas and Berson (1955), Tables I, pp. 48-49, 65-66, 83, 93, 113-114, 142, 150; (6) Schloss (1965); (7) Rosenthal (1971).

Table 4. Estimated Number of Nursery Schools by Auspices, United States, 1924-1951

Year	All Auspices	Public	Non-Public				
			Total	Proprietary	Lab	Philanthropic	Other
1924 (1)	25	1	24	N.A.[d]	N.A.	N.A.	N.A.
1928 (1)	89	17	72	N.A.	N.A.	N.A.	N.A.
1929 (2)	229[a]	5	224	100	56	66[b]	2
1930 (3)	203	13	190	73	74	43	N.A.
1932 (4)	300	N.A.	300	N.A.	N.A.	N.A.	N.A.
1934-36 (1)	2,185	1,900[c]	285	285	N.A.	N.A.	N.A.
1937 (4)	1,900	1,500[c]	400	N.A.	N.A.	N.A.	N.A.
1942 (1)	1,909	974[c]	935	622	122	156	35
1951 (5)	2,039	47	1,992	1,310	224	124[b]	334

[a]Combines "Relief Nursery School" and "Nursery School"; excludes kindergartens, whether separate or combined with nursery schools.

[b]Includes parochial programs.

[c]Virtually all WPA programs.

[d]N.A. means data not available.

Sources: (1) Goodykoontz, Davis, and Gabbard (1947), and Almy and Snyder (1947); (2) White House Conference (1930b), Table V, p. 158; (3) Forest (1930); (4) Campbell, Bair, and Harvey (1939); (5) Moustakas and Berson (1955), Tables I, pp. 48-49, 65-66, 83, 93, 113-114, 142, 150.

Table 5. Estimated Number of Kindergartens and Children
Enrolled, United States, 1856-1965

Year	Number of Kindergartens	Children Enrolled[a]
1856 (1)	1	N.A.
1873 (2)	42	1,252
1888 (1)	N.A.[c]	31,227
1898 (2)	2,884	143,720
1900 (3)	N.A.	225,394
1904-05 (2)	3,176[b]	205,118[b]
1910 (3)	N.A.	346,189
1920 (3)	N.A.	510,949
1930 (3)	N.A.	777,899
1934 (1)	N.A.	639,281
1940 (3)	N.A.	660,909
1950 (3)	N.A.	1,167,203
1960 (3)	N.A.	2,276,712
1962 (3)	N.A.	2,437,852
1964 (4)	N.A.	2,716,000
1965 (5)	N.A.	2,887,000

[a]Excludes subcollegiate departments of institutions of higher education, residential schools for exceptional children and federal schools (for Indians or on federal Installations).

[b]Public programs only.

[c]N.A. means data not available.

Sources: (1) Goodykoontz, Davis, and Gabbard (1947), and Almy and Snyder (1947); (2) "Infant Schools" (1910); (3) U.S. Department of Health, Education, and Welfare (1967); (4) Schloss (1965); (5) Schloss (1966).

Table 6. Estimated Kindergarten Enrollment by Auspices, United States, 1888-1965

Year	Total	Public	Private[a]
1888 (1)	31,277	15,145	16,082
1898 (2)	143,720	70,000[b]	73,720[b]
1900 (3)	225,394	131,657	93,737
1904-05 (2)	N.A.[c]	205,118	N.A.
1910 (3)	346,189	293,970	52,219
1920 (3)	510,949	481,226	29,683
1930 (3)	777,899	723,443	54,456
1934 (1)	639,281	601,775	37,506
1940 (3)	660,909	594,647	57,341
1944 (1)	N.A.	700,877	N.A.
1950 (3)	1,167,203	1,034,203	133,000
1960 (3)	2,276,712	1,922,712	354,000
1962 (3)	2,437,852	2,064,852	373,000
1964 (4)	2,716,000	2,254,000	462,000
1965 (5)	2,887,000	2,291,000	596,000

[a] Charitable, sectarian and proprietary programs.

[b] Estimated ("more than half were private" in 1898).

[c] N.A. means data not available.

Sources: (1) Goodykoontz, Davis, and Gabbard (1947), and Almy and Snyder (1947); (2) "Infant Schools" (1910); (3) U.S. Department of Health, Education, and Welfare (1967); (4) Schloss (1965); (5) Schloss (1966).

Table 7. Estimates of Children Under Six Years of Age in Various Child-Care Arrangements,
United States, Mid-1960s (in Thousands)

		Not Exclusive Maternal Care					
		Children of Working Mothers Only					
Child Population	Exclusive Maternal Care[a]	Self-Care	Home Care by Father	Home Care by Surrogate	Care in Surrogate Home	Day Care	Nursery School[b]	Kindergarten[b]
		1965 (2)	1965 (2)	1965 (2)	1965 (2)	1965 (2)	1965[c] (3)	1965 (3)
1966 (1)								
24,150	17,191	21	558	1,218	1,179	206	890	2,887

[a]This figure is the remainder after subtracting the number of children reported in the various child-care arrangements from the total number of children, United States, under six years old. (Detail figures do not always add to total due to rounding.)

[b]The number of children of working mothers is not known.

[c]Excludes 573,000 enrolled in summer Head Start programs.

Sources: (1) U.S. Bureau of the Census (1966); (2) Low and Spindler (1968); (3) Schloss (1966).

Table 8. Estimates of Children Under Six Years of Age in Various Child-Care Arrangements, United States, Mid-1960s (in Percent)

Child Population	Exclusive Maternal Care	Not Exclusive Maternal Care						
		Children of Working Mothers Only						
		Self-Care	Home Care by Father	Home Care by Surrogate	Care in Surrogate Home	Day Care	Nursery School	Kindergarten
1966 (1)		1965 (2)	1965 (2)	1965 (2)	1965 (2)	1965 (2)	1965 (3)	1965 (3)
100.0[a]	71.20	.09	2.30	5.00	4.90	.90	3.70	12.00

[a]N = 24,150,000.

Sources: (1) U.S. Bureau of the Census (1966); (2) Low and Spindler (1968); (3) Schloss (1966).

Table 9. Federal Funds for Day-Care Programs,[a]
by Administering Federal Organization and Program,
Fiscal 1967, 1968, and 1970 (in Millions)

	Fiscal Year		
Organization and Program	*1967 (1)*	*1968 (2)*	*1970 (3)*
All Programs	$ 85.1	$ 80.2	$222.2
Department of HEW			
AFDC	—[b]	N.A.[c]	94.0
AFDC-Work Incentive	—	1.0	15.5
Child Welfare Services	5.6 (2)	6.2	1.5
Work Experience and Training[d]	4.3	2.3	—
Department of Labor			
Concentrated Employment	—	N.A.	7.5
Office of Economic Opportunity			
Children of Migrant Workers	4.0	0.7	1.2
Community Action	1.2	—	—
Head Start	70.0	70.0	99.5
Parent and Child Centers	—	N.A.	3.0

[a]Excludes federal expenditures for research, small business loans, and staff training; and excludes expenditures by state, local, and private organizations.

[b]— means authority or policy for day-care expenditures not yet established or terminated.

[c]N.A. means data not available.

[d]Funds authorized under the Economic Opportunity Act; program phased out in 1969 and superseded by AFDC, Work Incentive Program.

Sources: (1) U.S. Department of Labor (1967); (2) Malone (1969); (3) Boyer (1971).

References

Allen, W. Y., and Campbell, D. *The Creative Nursery Center.* New York: Family Service Association of America, 1948.

Almy, M. C., and Snyder, A. "The Staff and Its Preparation." In N. B. Henry (Ed.), *The Forty-Sixth Yearbook of the National Society for the Study of Education.* Part 2: *Early Childhood Education.* Chicago: University of Chicago Press, 1947.

Alschuler, R. H. (Ed.) *Children's Centers.* Issued by the National Commission for Young Children. New York: Morrow, 1942.

Anderson, J. E. "The Theory of Early Childhood Education." In N. B. Henry (Ed.), *The Forty-Sixth Yearbook of the*

National Society for the Study of Education. Part 2: *Early Childhood Education.* Chicago: University of Chicago Press, 1947.

Arden House Conference. "Proceedings of the Arden House Conference—A Conference on 'Pre-School' Enrichment of Socially Disadvantaged Children,' December, 1962." *Merrill Palmer Quarterly,* 1964, *10,* 207-309.

Aries, P. *Centuries of Childhood: A Social History of Family Life.* New York: Knopf, 1962.

"Baby-Farming." *Encyclopedia Britannica.* (11th ed.), vol. 3, pp. 97-98.

Bailey, S. K. *The Office of Education and the Education Act of 1965.* ICP Case Series No. 100. Syracuse, N.Y.: The Inter-University Case Program, 1966.

Bank of America National Trust and Savings Association. "Day Nurseries for Preschoolers." *Small Business Reporter,* 1969, *8,* 1-8.

Becker, D. G. "Exit Lady Bountiful: The Volunteer and the Professional Social Worker." *Social Service Review,* 1964, *38,* 57-72.

Beer, E. S. *The Day Nursery.* New York: Dutton, 1938.

Beer, E. S. *Working Mothers and the Day Nursery.* New York: Whiteside, 1957.

Bell, W. "The Practical Value of Social Work Services: Preliminary Report on 10 Demonstration Projects in Public Assistance." In U.S., Congress, House, Committee on Ways and Means, *Hearings on H.R. 10032,* 87th Cong., 2nd sess., February 7, 9, and 13, 1962, 371-376.

Bensman, J., and Lilienfeld, R. *Craft and Consciousness: Occupational Technique and the Development of World Images.* New York: Wiley, 1973.

Bensman, J., and Vidich, A. J. *The New American Society: The Revolution of the Middle Class.* Chicago: Quadrangle, 1971.

Bertolaet, F. "The Education of Disadvantaged Youth." In U.S., Congress, Senate, Subcommittee on Education, Committee on Labor and Public Welfare, *Hearings, Elementary and Secondary Education Act of 1965,* 89th

Cong., 1st sess., January 26, 29; February 1, 2, 4, 8, and 11, 1965, pt. 1, pp. 501-510.

Bishops of the United States. "The Christian Family." Leaflet. Washington, D.C.: National Catholic Welfare Conference, 1949.

Bishops of the United States. "The Child: Citizen of Two Worlds." Leaflet. Washington, D.C.: National Catholic Welfare Conference, 1950.

Bishops of the United States. "The Place of the Private and Church-Related Schools in American Education." Mimeographed. Washington, D.C.: National Catholic Welfare Conference, November 20, 1955.

Boyer, S. "The Day Care Jungle." *Saturday Review,* February 20, 1971, pp. 50-51.

Bremner, R. H. (Ed.) *Children and Youth in America: A Documentary History.* Vol. 2: *1866-1932.* Cambridge, Mass.: Harvard University Press, 1971.

Broder, D. S. "President Johnson's Stand Called Factor in Eventual School Aid Passage." *New York Times,* September 9, 1965, p. 23.

Bronfenbrenner, U., and Bruner, J. "The President and the Children." *New York Times,* January 31, 1972, p. 41.

Brozan, N. "Day Care In Crisis: Without the Money, Ideals Are In Peril." *New York Times,* November 17, 1972, p. 54.

Buder, L. "Report Card On the Aid Bill." *New York Times,* May 7, 1967a, p. E9.

Buder, L. "School Board Urged To Reduce Role in Pre-Kindergarten Setup." *New York Times,* May 17, 1967b, p. 39.

Buder, L. "Success of a Test." *New York Times,* January 14, 1968, p. E13.

Burgess, E. W. "The Effect of War on the American Family." *American Journal of Sociology,* 1942, *48,* 343-352.

Cain, H. P., Jr. "Confidential Presidential Task Forces: A Case Study in National Policy Making." Unpublished doctoral dissertation, Brandeis University, 1971.

Calhoun, A. W. *A Social History of the American Family.* New York: Barnes and Noble (University Paperback ed.), 1960. (Originally published 1919.)

Campbell, D. S., Bair, F. H., and Harvey, O. L. *Educational Activities of the Works Progress Administration.* Washington, D.C.: U.S. Government Printing Office, 1939.

Chamber of Commerce of the United States of America, Task Force on Economic Growth and Opportunity. *The Disadvantaged Poor: Education and Employment.* Washington, D.C.: Chamber of Commerce of the United States of America, 1966.

Chandler, C. A., Lourie, R. S., and Peters, A. D. Dittman, L. L. (Ed.), *Early Child Care: The New Perspectives.* New York: Atherton Press, 1968.

"Charity and Charities." *Encyclopedia Britannica.* (11th ed.), vol. 5, pp. 860-891.

"Children Under Six." Report of a multiprofessional conference cosponsored by the National Child Research Center and the Washington School of Psychiatry, Washington, D.C., May 14 and 15, 1964.

"Church and State In the Schools." Editorial. *New York Times,* November 18, 1966, p. 40.

Cohen, W. J. "The Political Process—The Social Worker and His Professional Association." Address presented at the National Seminar on Social Action Strategy and Future Income Maintenance, National Association of Social Workers, Chicago, May 29, 1966.

Cohen, W. J., and Ball, R. M. "Public Welfare Amendments of 1962 and Proposals for Health Insurance for the Aged." *Social Security Bulletin,* 1962, *25,* 3-22.

Cremin, L. A. *The Transformation of the School: Progressivism in American Education, 1876-1957.* New York: Vintage, 1964.

Cuban, L. "The Cardozo Peace Corps Project, Experiment in Urban Education." In U.S., Congress, Senate, Subcommittee on Education, Committee on Labor and Public Welfare, *Hearings, Elementary and Secondary Education Act of 1965,* 89th Cong., 1st sess., January 26, 29; February 1, 2, 4, 8, and 11, 1965, Part 6, 2973-2979.

Deardorff, N. R. "Child: Child Welfare." *Encyclopedia of Social Sciences.* Vol. 2, 1930, pp. 373-380.

Deutsch, M. "The Influence of Early School Environment on School Adaptation." Paper presented at Symposium on School Dropouts, Washington, D.C., December 2-4, 1962. Cited in J. W. Getzels, "Pre-School Education," in *Contemporary Issues In American Education*. Consultants' papers prepared for use at The White House Conference on Education, July 20-21, 1965, Washington, D.C. U.S. Department of Health, Education, and Welfare. OE Bulletin No. 3, 1965. Washington, D.C.: U.S. Government Printing Office, 1965.

Dewey, J. *The Child and the Curriculum.* Chicago: University of Chicago Press, 1956a. (Originally published 1902.)

Dewey, J. *The School and Society.* Chicago: University of Chicago Press, 1956b. (Originally published 1900.)

Economic Report of the President, Together with The Annual Report of the Council of Economic Advisers. Washington, D.C.: U.S. Government Printing Office, 1973.

Edelman, M. *The Symbolic Uses of Politics.* Urbana: University of Illinois Press, 1970.

"Education I." *New Catholic Encyclopedia.* Vol. 5, 1967, pp. 111-162.

Ervin, S. J., Jr. "Letter to the Editor." *New York Times,* August 26, 1966, p. 30.

"Excerpts from President's Special Message to Congress on Health and Education." *New York Times,* March 1, 1967, p. 26.

Falconer, M. P. "Child: Institutions for the Care of Children." *Encyclopedia of Social Sciences.* Vol. 2, 1930, pp. 410-412.

Farber, M. A. "Parochial Schools Warn City to Expedite Aid." *New York Times,* August 18, 1966a, p. 29.

Farber, M. A. "Private Schools Ask Share In Aid." *New York Times,* November 15, 1966b, p. 61.

Farber, M. A. "Educators Bid U.S. Drop Reins On Aid." *New York Times,* July 6, 1967, 1, p. 27.

Farber, M. A. "Nixon Weighs New Agency For Childhood Services." *New York Times,* March 2, 1969a, p. 24.

Farber, M. A. "Head Start Report Held 'Full of Holes.'" *New York Times,* April 18, 1969b, pp. 1, 18.

Federal Register, August 10, 1972. *37,* Title 45, chap. 2, pt. A, sec. 220.18, p. 1358.

Fishman, K. D. "Matriculating . . . At 3?" *New York Times Magazine,* February 26, 1967, pp. 72, 74.

Fleiss, B. H. "The Relationship of the Mayor's Committee on Wartime Care of Children to Day Care in New York City." Unpublished doctoral dissertation, New York University, 1962. Cited in A. B. Mayer and A. J. Kahn, *Day Care As a Social Instrument: A Policy Paper* (New York: Columbia University School of Social Work, 1965).

Forest, I. "Preschool Education." *Encyclopedia of Social Sciences.* Vol. 12, 1930, pp. 320-324.

Freud, A. *Psychoanalysis for Teachers and Parents.* Boston: Beacon Press, 1963.

Gans, R. "Young Children At the Turn of This Era." In N. B. Henry (Ed.), *The Forty-Sixth Yearbook of the National Society for the Study of Education.* Part 2: *Early Childhood Education.* Chicago: University of Chicago Press, 1947.

Getzels, J. W. "Pre-School Education." In *Contemporary Issues In American Education.* Consultants' papers prepared for use at The White House Conference on Education, July 20-21, 1965, Washington, D.C. U.S. Department of Health, Education, and Welfare, Office of Education, Bulletin No. 3, 1966. Washington, D.C.: U.S. Government Printing Office, 1965.

Goldstein, J., and Katz, J. *The Family and the Law.* New York: Free Press, 1965.

Goodykoontz, B., Davis, M. D., and Gabbard, H. F. "Recent History and Present Status of Education for Young Children." In N. B. Henry (Ed.), *The Forty-Sixth Yearbook of the Society for the Study of Education.* Part 2: *Early Childhood Education.* Chicago: University of Chicago Press, 1947.

Gore, L. L., and Koury, R. E. *A Survey of Early Elementary Education in Public Schools, 1960-61.* Washington, D.C.: U.S. Government Printing Office, 1965.

Gould, J. "Educational TV Network To Teach Preschool Child." *New York Times,* March 21, 1968, pp. 1, 94.

Graham, F. P. "High Court Restricts State Aid to Church Schools." *New York Times,* June 29, 1971, pp. 1, 18.

Grant, G. "School Aid, GOP Style, Is Gaining." *Washington Post,* April 23, 1967, pp. A1, A6.

Greenblatt, B. "The Family and the Social Structure." In J. Bensman and B. Rosenberg (Ed.), *Sociology: Introductory Readings in Mass, Class, and Bureaucracy.* New York: Praeger, 1975.

Greenblatt, B., and Eberhard, L. *Children On Campus: A Survey of Pre-kindergarten Programs at Institutions of Higher Education in the United States.* Washington, D.C.: Day Care Council of America, 1973.

Greenblatt, B., and Katkin, D. "Prolegomenon to a Curriculum for Some Occasions." *Social Work Education Reporter,* 1972, *20,* 54-61.

Greenleigh, A. *Facts, Fallacies, and Future: A Study of the Aid to Dependent Children Program of Cook County, Illinois.* New York: Greenleigh Associates, 1960. Excerpted in U.S., Congress, Senate, Committee on Finance, *Hearings on the Public Assistance Act of 1962 (H.R. 10606),* 87th Cong., 2nd sess., May 14, 15, 16, and 17, 1962, pp. 313-314.

Gurin, A., Guberman, M., Greenblatt, B., and Thompson, G. *Cost Analysis in Day-Care Centers for Children.* Waltham, Mass.: Brandeis University, 1966.

Harrington, M. *The Other America: Poverty in the United States.* Baltimore: Penguin, 1963. (Originally published 1962).

Hechinger, F. M. "Education: Reaching For the Deprived." *New York Times,* July 11, 1965a, p. 8.

Hechinger, F. M. "White House Conference Points Up New U.S. Role." *New York Times,* July 25, 1965b, p. E9.

Hechinger, F. M. "Head Start Falls Behind." *New York Times,* December 5, 1965c, p. E9.

Hechinger, F. M. "Education Curtain For Higher Horizons." *New York Times,* July 10, 1966a, p. E7.

Hechinger, F. M. "N.E.A. Asks Start of Schooling at 4." *New York Times,* July 1, 1966b, pp. 1, 32.

Hechinger, F. M. (Ed.) *Pre-School Education Today.* New York: Doubleday, 1966c.

Hechinger, F. M. "Expansion of Preschool Program Proposed by State Regents." *New York Times,* December 22, 1967a, p. 20.

Hechinger, F. M. "Schools vs. Riots." *New York Times,* July 30, 1967b, p. E7.

Henry, N. B. (Ed.) *The Forty-Sixth Yearbook of the National Society For the Study of Education.* Part 2: *Early Childhood Education.* Chicago: University of Chicago Press, 1947.

Herbers, J. "House Blocks G.O.P. Plan on Control of School Aid." *New York Times,* May 25, 1967a, pp. 1, 33.

Herbers, J. "M'Cone Says U.S. Could Be Ruined By Racial Strife." *New York Times,* August 23, 1967b, pp. 1, 30.

Herzog, E. *Children of Working Mothers.* Department of Health, Education, and Welfare, Children's Bureau, Publication No. 382. Washington, D.C.: U.S. Government Printing Office, 1960.

Hicks, N. "Specialists Hail Child-Care Bill." *New York Times,* September 12, 1971, p. 74.

Hobbs, M. A. "War Time Employment of Women." In E. D. Bullock (Compiler), J. E. Johnsen (Ed.), *Selected Articles on the Employment of Women.* New York: Wilson, 1920.

Hoffman, E. "Head Start Rules Scored By Educators." *Washington Post,* December 11, 1966, pp. A1, A16.

Hunter, M. "Myrdal Says Special Treatment For Negroes Would Stir Hatred." *New York Times,* January 24, 1964, p. 16.

Hunter, M. "Johnson Presses For Greater Aid." *New York Times,* January 13, 1965, p. 75.

Hunter, M. "Panel On Schools Wants U.S. Funds Focused on Poor." *New York Times,* August 21, 1967a, pp. 1, 21.

Hunter, M. "Poor Schools Called a Cause of Riots." *New York Times,* July 25, 1967b, p. 14.

Hunter, M. "Day Care Aid Plan Set By Conferees." *New York Times,* November 11, 1971a, p. 1.

Hunter, M. "House Backs Day Care Program Covering All Economic Levels." *New York Times,* October 1, 1971b, p. 35.

Hunter, M. "Nixon Veto Seen On Day-Care Bill." *New York Times,* November 21, 1971c, p. 95.

Hunter, M. "Senate Approves a Broad System of Child Service." *New York Times,* September 10, 1971d, pp. 1, 21.

"Infant Schools." *Encyclopedia Britannica.* (11th ed.), vol. 14, pp. 533-534.

"Johnson's Message to Congress Outlining Broad Program of Educational Gains." *New York Times,* January 13, 1965, p. 20.

Kadushin, A. *Child Welfare Services.* New York: Macmillan, 1967.

Kahn, A. J. "The Function of Social Work in the Modern World." In A. J. Kahn (Ed.), *Issues in American Social Work.* New York: Columbia University Press, 1959.

Kearns, D. "Day Care." Draft submitted to HEW Task Force on Handicapped Child and Child Development, n.d. (around 1966).

Kihss, P. "Schools Plan Cuts to Raise Funds to Aid Early Grades." *New York Times,* June 5, 1967, pp. 1, 33.

"Kindergarten." *Encyclopedia Britannica.* (11th ed.), vol. 15, p. 802.

Kreisberg, M. "Food Service in Private Elementary and Secondary Schools." U.S. Department of Agriculture, Marketing Research Report No. 678, n.d. In U.S., Congress, Senate, Subcommittee on Education, Committee on Labor and Public Welfare, *Hearings, Elementary and Secondary Education Act of 1965,* 89th Cong., 1st sess., January 26, 29; February 1, 2, 4, 8, and 11, 1965, pt. 1, pp. 419-444.

Lajewski, H. C. *Child Care Arrangements of Full-Time Working Mothers.* Children's Bureau Publication No. 378. Washington, D.C.: U.S. Government Printing Office, 1959.

LaNoue, G. R. Letter to the Editor. *New York Times,* August 21, 1967, p. 28.

Lansburgh, T. W. "Child Welfare: Day Care of Children." *Encyclopedia of Social Work.* Vol. 1, 1971, pp. 114-120.

Larson, R. G., and Olson, J. L. *Final Report: A Pilot Project for Culturally Deprived Kindergarten Children* (tentative draft), Unified School District No. 1, Racine, Wisconsin,

April 1965. Cited in J. W. Getzels, "Pre-School Educa-
tion." In *Contemporary Issues in American Education.*
Consultants' papers prepared for use at The White House
Conference on Education, July 20-21, 1965, Washington,
D.C. U.S. Department of Health, Education, and Welfare,
Office of Education Bulletin No. 3, 1966. Washington,
D.C.: U.S. Government Printing Office, 1965.

Lasch, C. *The New Radicalism in America 1889-1963: The Intellectual As a Social Type.* New York: Vintage, 1967.

Lasswell, H. D., and Kaplan, A. *Power and Society.* New Haven:
Yale University Press, 1950.

Leeper, S. H., Dales, R. J., Skipper, D., and Witherspoon, R. L.
Good Schools For Young Children. New York: Macmillan, 1968.

Leiby, J. "Social Welfare: History of Basic Ideas." *Encyclopedia
of Social Work.* Vol. 2, 1971, pp. 1461-1476.

Lenroot, K. F. Foreword. In E. O. Lundberg, *Unto the Least of
These.* New York: Appleton-Century, 1947.

Lewis, V. S. "Charity Organization Society." *Encyclopedia of
Social Work.* Vol. 1, 1971, pp. 94-98.

Lippmann, W. *Public Opinion.* New York: Penguin, 1946.

Loftus, J. A. "School Districts Shun Head Start." *New York
Times,* January 21, 1968a, p. 55.

Loftus, J. A. "Head Start Shift Voted By Senate." *New York
Times,* July 18, 1968b, p. 37.

Low, S. *Licensed Day Care Facilities for Children.* Washington,
D.C.: U.S. Government Printing Office, 1962.

Low, S., and Spindler, P. G. *Child Care Arrangements of Working Mothers in the United States.* Children's Bureau Publication No. 461. Washington, D.C.: U.S. Government
Printing Office, 1968.

Lublin, J. S. "Day Care Franchises Beset With Problems, Find
Allure Is Fading." *Wall Street Journal,* November 11,
1972, p. 1.

Lundberg, E. O. "Aid to Mothers With Dependent Children."
The Annals, 1921, *98,* 97-105.

Lundberg, E. O. "Factors in Planning Community Day-Care
Programs." Reprinted from *The Child,* 1942, *6,* 281-285.

Washington, D.C.: U.S. Government Printing Office, U.S. Department of Labor, Children's Bureau, 1942.

Lundberg, E. O. *Unto the Least of These.* New York: Appleton-Century, 1947.

MacDonald, D. "Our Invisible Poor." Sidney Hillman Reprint Series No. 23. New York: Sidney Hillman Foundation, n.d. (Originally published, *The New Yorker,* January 19, 1963, pp. 82-132.)

Malone, M. "Federal Involvement in Day Care." Washington, D.C.: Library of Congress, Legislative Reference Service, March 3, 1969.

Mannheim, K. *Man and Society in an Age of Reconstruction.* London: Kegan Paul, Trench, and Trubner, 1940.

Marris, P., and Rein, M. *Dilemmas of Social Reform.* New York: Atherton Press, 1969.

Mayer, A. B., and Kahn, A. J. "Day Care As a Social Instrument: A Policy Paper." New York: Columbia University School of Social Work, January 1965.

Mayo, L. H., and Jones, E. M. "Legal Policy Decision Process: Alternative Thinking and the Predictive Function." *The George Washington Law Review,* 1964, *33,* 318-456.

McLendon, W. "Project Headstart Gets Going." *Washington Post,* February 15, 1965, p. B5.

Mead, M. "The Contemporary Family As an Anthropologist Sees It." *American Journal of Sociology,* 1948, *13,* 453-459.

Meranto, P. *The Politics of Federal Aid to Education in 1965: A Study in Political Innovation.* Syracuse, N.Y.: Syracuse University Press, 1967.

Merton, R. K. *Social Theory and Social Structure.* New York: Free Press, 1949.

Moore, B., Jr. "Thoughts on the Future of the Family." In M. Stein, A. J. Vidich, and D. M. White (Eds.), *Identity and Anxiety.* New York: Free Press, 1962.

Morse, W. "The Administration, the Congress, and the Schools." Mimeographed. Address to the American Association of School Administrators, Washington, D.C., May 13, 1965.

Morton, J. "Nursery Schools Will Be Opened By Chicken Chain." *The National Observer,* February 17, 1969, pp. 1, 20.

Moustakas, C. E., and Berson, M. P. *The Nursery School and Child Care Center.* New York: Whiteside, 1955.

Moustakas, C. E., and Berson, M. P. *The Young Child In School.* New York: Whiteside *and* Morrow, 1956.

"Mrs. Nixon Quits Day Care Unit." *New York Times,* February 9, 1973, p. 41.

National Catholic Welfare Conference. "Synopsis of NCWC Legal Department Study, 'The Constitutionality of the Inclusion of Church-related Schools in Federal Aid to Education.' " Mimeographed. National Catholic Welfare Conference, Washington, D.C., December 14, 1961.

National Committee for the Day Care of Children. *Day Care— Where the Action Is.* Pamphlet. Washington, D.C.: Day Care and Child Development Council of America, n.d.

National Education Association. "School Programs for the Disadvantaged." Circular No. 2, February, 1963. Cited in U.S., Congress, Senate, Subcommittee on Education, Committee on Labor and Public Welfare, *Hearings, Elementary and Secondary Education Act of 1965,* 89th Cong., 1st sess., January 26, 29; February 1, 2, 4, 8, and 11, 1965, pt. 2, pp. 752-813.

National Industrial Conference Board. *Wartime Employment of Women in the Metal Trades.* Boston: National Industrial Conference Board, 1918.

Niemeyer, J. "Organization Problems in Expanding Day Care Services." In U.S. Department of Health, Education, and Welfare, *Spotlight On Day Care.* Washington, D.C.: U.S. Government Printing Office, 1966.

"Nursery School Enrollment Rose as Population Dropped." *New York Times,* August 18, 1974, p. 12.

Oettinger, K. B. "A Half Century of Progress for All Children." *Children,* 1962, *9,* 43-51.

Parsons, T. *Essays in Sociological Theory: Pure and Applied.* New York: Free Press, 1949.

Parsons, T. "The Stability of the American Family System." In

N. B. Bell and E. F. Vogel (Eds.), *The Family*. New York: Free Press, 1960.

Passow, A. H. "Education in Depressed Areas." In A. H. Passow (Ed.), *Education in Depressed Areas*. New York: Teachers College Press, 1963.

Perkins, C. D. Letter to the Editor. *New York Times,* August 26, 1966, p. 30.

Perlis, L. "Day Care." Mimeographed. Address before the National Conference on Day Care, Washington, D.C., May 14, 1965.

Prescott, E. *A Pilot Study of Day-Care Centers and Their Clientele*. Department of Health, Education, and Welfare, Children's Bureau Publication No. 428. Washington, D.C.: U.S. Government Printing Office, 1965.

"Project Headstart." *New York Times,* May 24, 1965, p. 30.

"Project Head Start Revises Guidelines On Role of Parents." *New York Times,* January 10, 1967, p. 31.

Pumphrey, R. "Social Welfare: History." *Encyclopedia of Social Work.* Vol. 2, 1971, pp. 1446-1459.

Radin, N. "Child Welfare: Preschool Programs." *Encyclopedia of Social Work.* Vol. 1, 1971, pp. 128-139.

Reissman, F. *The Culturally Deprived Child*. New York: Harper & Row, 1962.

Reston, J. "Washington: President Johnson and Education." *New York Times,* November 8, 1967, p. 46.

Richmond, J. B. "Communities In Action: A Report On Project Head Start." *Pediatrics,* 1966, *37,* 905-911.

Richmond, J. B. "How Long, Oh Lord, How Long? A Proposal For the Extension of Day-Care Programs." Editorial. *American Journal of Orthopsychiatry,* 1967, *37,* 4-7.

Rosenbaum, D. E. "Dismantling of a Landmark Act As Federal Program Proposed." *New York Times,* January 30, 1973, p. 20.

Rosenthal, J. "Enrollment in Nursery Schools Found Soaring in Last 5 Years." *New York Times,* March 10, 1971, pp. 1, 26.

Ross, L. Memorandum on Summary Findings of Preschool Experts in consultation with the Office of Economic

Opportunity, to R. Boone, J. Sugarman, and S. Kravitz. Washington, D.C., December 1, 1964, pp. 1-5.

Rowe, R. "The Care and Education of Young Children." *Child Care In Massachusetts, The Public Responsibility.* Washington, D.C.: The Day Care and Child Development Council of America, 1972.

Ruderman, F. *Child Care and Working Mothers.* New York: Child Welfare League of America, 1968.

Russell, B. *The Autobiography of Bertrand Russell 1914-1944.* New York: Little Brown, 1951.

Russell, B. *Marriage and Morals.* New York: Bantam, 1959.

Schloss, S. "Enrollment of 3-, 4-, and 5-Year-Olds in Nursery Schools and Kindergartens: October 1964." Washington, D.C.: U.S., Department of Health, Education, and Welfare, Office of Education, Release OE-20079, June 1965.

Schloss, S. *Nursery-Kindergarten Enrollment of Children Under Six: October, 1965.* Washington, D.C.: U.S. Government Printing Office, 1966.

Schloss, S. *Nursery-Kindergarten Enrollment of Children Under Six: October, 1966.* Washington, D.C.: U.S. Government Printing Office, 1967.

Schorr, A. L. *Explorations in Social Policy.* New York: Basic Books, 1968.

Schorr, A. L. *Children and Other Decent People.* New York: Basic Books, 1974.

Sears, P. S., and Dowley, E. M. "Research On Teaching In the Nursery School." In N. L. Gage (Ed.), *Handbook of Research On Teaching.* Chicago: Rand McNally, 1963. Cited in S. H. Leeper, R. J. Dales, D. Skipper, and R. L. Witherspoon, *Good Schools For Young Children.* New York: Macmillan, 1968.

Selover, W. C. "The View From Capitol Hill: Harassment and Survival." In J. L. Sundquist (Ed.), *On Fighting Poverty: Perspectives From Experience.* New York: Basic Books, 1969.

Semmel, B. *Imperialism and Social Reform: English Social Thought, 1895-1914.* New York: Doubleday, 1968.

Semple, R. B., Jr. "Head Start Value Found Temporary." *New York Times,* October 23, 1966, pp. 1, 70.

Shils, E. A. "Social Science and Social Policy." *Philosophy of Science*, 1949, *16*, pp. 219-242.

State of Vermont Family Assistance Planning Unit *and* Mathematica, Inc. *Family Assistance Planning Papers.* Vol. 6: *Evaluation and Experimentation in Child Care.* March 1971.

Steinhilber, A. W., Will, R. F., Sokolowski, C. J., and Murray, J. B. "State Law Relating to Transportation and Textbooks for Parochial School Students, and Constitutional Protection of Religious Freedom." Cited in U.S., Congress, Senate, Subcommittee on Education, Committee on Labor and Public Welfare, *Hearings, Elementary and Secondary Education Act of 1965,* 89th Cong., 1st sess., January 26, 29; February 1, 2, 4, 8, and 11, 1965, pt. 1, pp. 185-230.

Stretch, J. J. "The Rights of Children Emerge: Historical Notes On the First White House Conference On Children." *Child Welfare*, 1970, *49*, 365-372.

Sundquist, J. L. "Origins of the War on Poverty." In J. L. Sundquist (Ed.), *On Fighting Poverty: Perspectives From Experience.* New York: Basic Books, 1969.

Swift, J. W. "Effects of Early Group Experience: The Nursery School and Day Nursery." In M. L. Hoffman and L. W. Hoffman (Eds.), *Review of Child Development Research.* Vol. 1. New York: Russell Sage Foundation, 1964.

Terte, R. H. "Pre-School Drive Growing By Leaps." *New York Times,* January 13, 1965, pp. 75, 94.

Tyson, H. G. "Day Nursery." *Encyclopedia of Social Sciences.* Vols. 5, 6, pp. 13-16.

U.S., Bureau of the Census. *Current Population Reports: Population Estimates.* Series P-25, No. 352. Washington, D.C.: U.S. Government Printing Office, November 11, 1966.

U.S., Congress, Senate. *Congressional Record,* 88th Cong., 2nd sess., July 22, 1964a, *110,* pp. 16055-16057, 16078, 16090-16091.

U.S., Congress, Senate. *Congressional Record,* 88th Cong., 2nd sess., July 23, 1964b, *110,* pp. 16142.

U.S., Congress, House. *Congressional Record,* 88th Cong., 2nd sess., August 5, 1964c, *110,* pp. 17616, 17623-17624.

U.S., Congress, House. *Congressional Record,* 88th Cong., 2nd sess., August 6, 1964d, *110,* pp. 17706-17708, 17674-17675, 17679.

U.S., Congress, Senate. *Congressional Record,* 88th Cong., 2nd sess., August 11, 1964e, *110,* 18420.

U.S., Congress, House. *Congressional Record,* 89th Cong., 1st sess., March 24, 1965a, *111,* pt. 5, 5734, 5739, 5755, 5758, 5770.

U.S., Congress, House. *Congressional Record,* 89th Cong., 1st sess., March 25, 1965b, *111,* pt. 5, 6018.

U.S., Congress, House. *Congressional Record,* 89th Cong., 1st sess., March 26, 1965c, *111,* pt. 5, 6146-6149.

U.S., Congress, House. *Poverty Message From the President of the United States,* 88th Cong., 2nd sess., March 16, 1964, Document No. 243.

U.S., Congress, House, Committee on Education and Labor. *House Report No. 1458: Report to Accompany H.R. 11377,* 88th Cong., 2nd sess., June 3, 1964.

U.S., Congress, House, Committee on Ways and Means. *Hearings on H.R. 10032,* 87th Cong., 2nd sess., February 7, 9, and 13, 1962.

U.S., Congress, House, Committee on Ways and Means. *Report on H.R. 1.,* 92nd Cong., 1st sess., 1971, H.R. 92-231.

U.S., Congress, Senate, Committee on Finance. *Hearings on the Public Assistance Act of 1962 (H.R. 10606),* 87th Cong., 2nd sess., May 14, 15, 16, and 17, 1962.

U.S., Congress, Senate, Committee on Labor and Public Welfare. *Enactments By the 88th Congress Concerning Education and Training, 1963-64.* A Committee Print Prepared in the Legislative Reference Service, Library of Congress, October 1964.

U.S., Congress, Senate, Committee on Labor and Public Welfare. *Report on Elementary and Secondary Education Act of 1965.* 89th Cong., 1st sess., Calendar No. 137, Report No. 146, April 6, 1965.

U.S., Congress, Senate, Select Committee on Poverty of Committee on Labor and Public Welfare. *Hearings, Economic Opportunity Act of 1964.* 88th Cong., 2nd sess., June 17, 18, 23, and 25, 1964.

U.S., Congress, Senate, Subcommittee on Education of the Committee on Labor and Public Welfare. *Hearings, Expansion of Public Laws 815 and 874 (S. 2528 and S. 2725),* 88th Cong., 2nd sess., July 29 and 30, 1964.

U.S., Congress, Senate, Subcommittee on Education of the Committee on Labor and Public Welfare. *Hearings, Elementary and Secondary Education Act of 1965 (S. 370).* 89th Cong., 1st sess., pts. 1, 2, 3, 4, 5, and 6, January 26, 29 and February 1, 2, 4, 8, and 11, 1965.

U.S., Congress, Senate, Subcommittee on Poverty of the Committee on Labor and Public Welfare. *Hearings, Expand the War on Poverty,* 89th Cong., 1st sess., June 28 and 29, 1965.

U.S., Department of Health, Education, and Welfare. *Day Care Services: Form and Substance.* Report of a Conference, November 17-18, 1960. Children's Bureau Publication No. 393. Washington, D.C.: U.S. Government Printing Office, 1961.

U.S., Department of Health, Education, and Welfare. *Programs for the Educationally Disadvantaged.* Washington, D.C.: U.S. Government Printing Office, 1963b. Cited in U.S., Congress, Senate, Subcommittee on Education, Committee on Labor and Public Welfare, *Hearings, Elementary and Secondary Education Act of 1965,* 89th Cong., 1st sess., January 26, 29; February 1, 2, 4, 8, and 11, 1965, pt. 2, pp. 641-751.

U.S., Department of Health, Education, and Welfare. *Child Welfare Statistics, 1965.* Washington, D.C.: U.S. Government Printing Office, 1966a.

U.S., Department of Health, Education, and Welfare. *Spotlight on Day Care: Proceedings of the National Conference on Day Care Services, May 13-15, 1965.* Children's Bureau Publication No. 438. Washington, D.C.: U.S. Government Printing Office, 1966b.

U.S., Department of Health, Education, and Welfare. *Digest of Educational Statistics, 1967.* Washington, D.C.: U.S. Government Printing Office, 1967.

U.S., Department of Health, Education, and Welfare. *Child Wel-*

fare Statistics, 1969. Washington, D.C.: U.S. Government Printing Office, 1969.

U.S., Department of Health, Education, and Welfare. *H.E.W. News.* Press release for A.M. papers, June 20, 1972.

U.S., Department of Health, Education, and Welfare. HEW Audit Agency. "Child Care Services Provided Under Title IV, Social Security Act." Mimeographed. Washington, D.C.: U.S. Department of Health, Education, and Welfare, Audit Agency, 1974.

U.S., Department of Health, Education, and Welfare, Children's Bureau. *Licensing of Child Care Facilities by State Welfare Departments.* Washington, D.C.: U.S. Government Printing Office, 1968a.

U.S., Department of Health, Education, and Welfare, Children's Bureau, Social Security Administration. "Legislative History." 87th Cong., 2nd sess., January 1962-October 13, 1962. Amendments to Title V, Public Welfare Amendments of 1962, P.L. 87-543, November 1962.

U.S., Department of Health, Education, and Welfare, U.S. Office of Economic Opportunity, and U.S. Department of Labor. *Federal Interagency Day Care Requirements.* Washington, D.C.: U.S. Government Printing Office, 1968.

U.S., Department of Labor. *Employed Mothers and Child Care.* Washington, D.C.: U.S. Government Printing Office, 1953.

U.S., Department of Labor. *Federal Funds for Day Care Projects.* Washington, D.C.: U.S. Government Printing Office, 1967.

U.S., Department of Labor. *Child Care Services Provided by Hospitals.* Women's Bureau Bulletin No. 295. Washington, D.C.: U.S. Government Printing Office, 1970.

U.S., Department of Labor. *Day Care Services: Industry's Involvement.* Women's Bureau Bulletin No. 296. Washington, D.C.: U.S. Government Printing Office, 1971.

U.S., Internal Revenue Service. *Statistics of Income—1971, Individual Income Tax Returns.* Washington, D.C.: U.S. Government Printing Office, 1973.

U.S., Library of Congress. *The Historic and Current Federal*

Role in Education. A Report to the Subcommittee on Education of the Committee on Labor and Public Welfare, U.S. Senate. Prepared at the request of Senator Wayne Morse of Oregon by the Legislative Reference Service, Committee Print. 87th Cong., 1st sess. Washington, D.C.: U.S. Government Printing Office, 1961.

U.S., Office of Economic Opportunity. *Concept of a Child Development Center: Relationship To Preschool and Day Care.* Pamphlet. Washington, D.C.: U.S. Office of Economic Opportunity, 1965a.

U.S., Office of Economic Opportunity. "Improving the Opportunities and Achievements of the Children of the Poor." Report of the Planning Committee on Project Head Start, and accompanying memorandum. Mimeographed. Washington, D.C.: U.S. Office of Economic Opportunity, 1965b.

U.S., Public Law 87-543, 76 Stat. 172 (Public Welfare Amendments of 1962) 1962.

U.S. Public Law 88-452, 78 Stat. 508. Economic Opportunity Act of 1964. 1964.

U.S. Public Law 89-10, 79 Stat. 27. Elementary and Secondary Education Act of 1965. 1965.

Van Kleeck, M. "Women Workers During Reconstruction." In E. D. Bullock (Compiler), J. E. Johnsen (Ed.), *Selected Articles on the Employment of Women.* New York: Wilson, 1920.

Veblen, T. B. *The Theory of the Leisure Class.* New York: Random House, 1931. (Originally published 1899.)

Weber, M. *General Economic History.* New York: Free Press, 1950.

Whipple, G. M. (Ed.) *The Twenty-Eighth Yearbook of the National Society for the Study of Education: Preschool and Parental Education.* Bloomington: Public School Publishing, 1929.

White House Conference on Child Health and Protection. "Day Nurseries." Section 4: "The Handicapped Child (Prevention-Maintenance-Protection)." Mimeographed; available in files of Children's Bureau of HEW. [Around] 1930a.

White House Conference on Child Health and Protection. "Sur-

vey of Institutions for the Education and Training of
Young Children." *Preliminary Committee Reports.* New
York: Century, 1930b.

"Who Should Teach Young Children?" Report of the Second
Multiprofessional Conference on Children Under Six, cosponsored by the National Child Research Center and the
Washington School of Psychiatry, Washington, D.C., May
6 and 7, 1965.

Wiener, J. *Survey Methods For Determining the Need For Services To Children of Working Mothers.* Washington, D.C.:
U.S. Government Printing Office, 1956.

Wishy, B. *The Child and the Republic: The Dawn of Modern
American Child Nurture.* Philadelphia: University of
Pennsylvania Press, 1968.

Wrong, D. H. "The 'Break-up' of the American Family." *Com-
mentary,* 1950, *9,* 374-380.

Wyman, G. *Report for the Secretary of Health, Education and
Welfare.* In U.S., Congress, House, Committee on Ways
and Means, *Hearings on H.R. 10032,* 87th Cong., 2nd
sess., February 7, 9, and 13, 1962, pp. 65-106.

Yarmolinsky, A. "The Beginnings of OEO." In J. L. Sundquist
(Ed.), *On Fighting Poverty: Perspectives From Experience.* New York: Basic Books, 1969.

Zeitz, D. *Child Welfare.* New York: Wiley, 1959.

Index

307